THE END OF
BUSINESS-AS-USUAL

WEB 3

How the Next
Generation of the
Internet Will Reshape
Business and Society

GC Cooke

First published in 2022 by Graham Cooke,
in partnership with whitefox publishing

Copyright © Graham Cooke, 2022

ISBN 978-1-915036-86-5
Also available as an ebook
ISBN 978-1-915036-87-2

Edited by Karen McCreadie, wordarchitect
Cover design by Couper Street
Author photography by Phil Adams
Typeset by seagulls.net
Project management by whitefox
Printed and bound by CPI

CONTENTS

DISCLAIMER

This book is designed to provide helpful information on web3 and its implications for business. Nothing in this book constitutes financial or legal advice; the views expressed are those of GC Cooke and do not necessarily reflect the views of any organization he is connected to. GC Cooke may hold some positions in the projects mentioned as part of a crypto portfolio. Please note, any mention of a project or platform should not be viewed as an endorsement of that project or platform in any way; it is simply a demonstration of a particular web3 capability and use. Readers should also be aware that some of the projects or platforms mentioned may disappear or morph into something else – again the focus is and should remain on the capability that the project or platform demonstrates.

Although the publisher and the author have made every effort to ensure that the information in this book was correct at press time and while this publication is designed to provide accurate information in regard to the subject matter covered, the publisher and the author assume no responsibility for errors, inaccuracies, omissions, or any other inconsistencies herein and hereby disclaim any liability to any party for any loss, damage, or disruption caused by errors or omissions, whether such errors or omissions result from negligence, accident, or any other cause.

Unless otherwise indicated, all the names, characters, businesses, places, events and incidents in this book are either the product of the author's imagination or used in a fictitious manner. Any resemblance to actual persons, living or dead, or actual events is purely coincidental. Neither the publisher nor the author shall be held liable or responsible for any loss or damage allegedly arising from any suggestion or information contained in this book.

ABOUT THE AUTHOR

GC Cooke has been developing internet-based products for the last 20 years. After studying Politics and Economics at Newcastle University, he joined Google in 2005 as one of the earliest European employees working on the Google Ad Platform and Google Analytics. After Google, he founded Qubit, a leading SaaS company in the e-commerce space, providing AI personalized shopping recommendations to over one billion users per month across more than 300 leading brands such as Louis Vuitton, Estée Lauder and TK Maxx. He sold Qubit to Coveo Solutions in 2021 shortly before going public on the Toronto Stock Exchange (TSX) and remains a strategic advisor at Coveo. He is also a non-executive director of ITV plc where he supports ITV with their digital strategy. GC Cooke is currently focused on a number of web3 projects in music publishing, real-time blockchain data mining and crypto asset management.

To continue the conversation, you can contact the author on web3@ grahamcooke.xyz

Prologue

As I will explain in detail throughout this book, web3 is much more than just cryptocurrency, yet crypto is still synonymous with web3, so when crypto becomes especially volatile everyone's interested in the story. What I have come to realize over the years is that the price volatility acts as an incredible marketing tool for this new technology movement.

As I was wrapping up this book and preparing to deliver it to the publishers, some big web3 stories broke and collectively triggered the equivalent of the global financial crisis (GFC) of 2007 in web3 … again.

One of the biggest stories at the time was TerraUSD or UST, a once celebrated algorithmic stablecoin, that plummeted in value from its $1 peg in May 2022 causing a tremor across the whole web3 ecosystem. Terra lost 90 per cent of its value in one day and nearly $50 billion was stripped from the crypto markets in one week![1] What followed was a systemic set of events that resulted in another of the largest crypto ecosystems, Celsius, locking its clients from withdrawals while it attempted to address its treasury. More casualties followed, with even more almost certainly in the pipeline.

Two things surprised me. First, although there was plenty of commentary about how these problems heralded the end of web3, informed journalism took a different tack. For example, *The Economist* stated, 'Crypto's detractors have long argued that it is useless – unless you are a money-launderer or con-artist – and predicted its demise. The crash [Terra] will convince many that they are right. In fact, the picture is rather different: a sorting process is underway, as the dodgiest parts of the crypto world are exposed, while the other bits prove more resilient.'[2]

This is progress. Following previous crypto-winters (and there have been a few), crypto and all things web3 have been summarily dismissed as nonsense or declared dead by the media. But not this time.

The second thing that surprised me was that the common denominator between many of these casualties was not some sort of inherent problem with the technology or some sort of hack. In the quest for the best yields, these projects over-leveraged, or miscalculated risk, borrowing against their treasuries and making the same mistake that led to the GFC and countless other market or business collapses. First, they mis-assumed risk and applied models against prices that were deemed impossible to reach. It is the same central story of just about every financial crash since the beginning of time. This is not a web3 phenomenon; this is a business fundamentals phenomenon that could be applied to any industry.

In the GFC the mis-assumed risk was that the property market would continue to rise. Therefore, even if mortgages were given to people who could only pay for the interest (sub-prime), the bank was protected because they still owned the asset of the house. Of course, the market did drop, and we all know what happened. In this case Terra, Celsius and many of the hedge funds all made the same potential mis-assumed risk – that the price of crypto would continue to go up and they could continue to deliver excessive returns to users. The Terra ecosystem was promising 20 per cent APR. Celsius, 18 per cent APR. And the hedge funds, assuming that Bitcoin would never drop below $20,000, employed a highly leveraged strategy that failed when Bitcoin did drop below $20,000. In each case the mis-assumed risk created massive liquidations, with many selling and withdrawing their investment and a number of these platforms having to halt withdrawals due to their solvency, just like an old-fashioned 'run on the bank'. And the rest, as they say, is history. The story is as old as time; it's just that this time it's all been applied to web3 entities. Whenever there is innovation there is a speculative frenzy followed by a wanton misunderstanding of risk in the pursuit of massive returns. We assume we are rational actors, who weigh the data and proceed accordingly, but 'desire clouds the equation. If we want something enough, our tolerance for risk goes up fast.'[3] Then it all collapses. And what ends up happening is that the phoenix rises from the ashes and the good projects continue to prevail.

Besides, these so-called web3 failures are not true web3 where the trust was baked into the blockchain, but rather web2 capabilities and a maintained reliance on institutional trust dressed up in web3 'trustless' clothing. They failed because they all made the same faulty assumption of risk, not because web3 is dead. All the speculation about price movements of Bitcoin and Ethereum or the implosion of a particular platform is acting as a potent distraction from what the underlying technology is really capable of. What I hope you will learn from this book is how not to be distracted by this noise and focus on the bigger picture.

The web3 technology phenomenon is in fact designed so that these things should happen a lot less, because you – as the user or participant – will be the ultimate custodian.

True web3 is about the emergence of distributed trust over institutional trust (more on that in Chapter 3). As Thomas Stackpole of the *Harvard Business Review* puts it, every time there is a story like Terra or a drop in value of Bitcoin, 'skeptics rush to dismiss it as dead, railing that it was always a scam for nerds and crooks and was nothing more than a fringe curiosity pushed by techno-libertarians and people who hate banks'.[4] But in truth they are part of the sorting process mentioned by *The Economist*. Each failure accelerates the evolution; it doesn't repress it. If the platform is weak, it will fail. If the protocol is weak, it will fail. If the risk assessment is weak, it will fail. And the sooner web3 becomes less about making a ton of money for the get-rich-quick brigade and more about interweaving a completely new way for humanity to interact, come together and create products, services and a better world, the better.

It is almost unfair to call these companies out, simply because they are not the first to make the same mistake and they will not be the last. This holds true for all the companies, entities or platforms I refer to in this book. Some will survive; some will not. New versions will emerge from the chaos. The individual entities are not really that important. Just stay focused on the capability and how it might impact your business. Each failure becomes part of the sorting process, which will make the whole web3 ecosystem stronger.

I fully appreciate that it may be tempting to listen to stories about the end of web3 as a plausible reason not to read this book or to dismiss the growing pressure you may feel to better understand web3 and its implications on your life and business. I strongly recommend you don't.

As we thaw out from the 2022 'crypto-winter' we would do well to focus on more than just price speculation, and to explore what web3 can actually do for business and society more deeply. This book is going to illuminate the bigger narratives and the big forces at play that have already emerged and are already disrupting business and society in a positive way. These do not change, regardless of the near collapse of a few projects.

Introduction

History is littered with innovation that has disrupted the status quo. Some of those inventions have fundamentally changed the world, with their impact spreading far beyond the industry or sector from which they emerged. In all of these stellar innovations it's possible to trace each one's journey to some pivotal moment or tipping point that creates a rift between life before and life after that particular innovation.

The humble shipping container certainly falls into this category. Although the idea of some sort of transportation container has its origins in late-eighteenth-century English coal mines, and the first container ship was launched in 1931 by Southern Railway UK, the containers differed in size and structure. What we now refer to as a 'shipping container' is actually an 'intermodal container' – the simple but brilliant invention of trucking company owner Malcolm McLean. What McLean did was standardize the container. His 'containerization' changed shipping forever: a deceptively simple corrugated steel box with standardized dimensions that could be loaded and unloaded, stacked and transported between a truck, ship or railcar without being opened (hence 'intermodal'). Producers or manufacturers could load the container, and no one would touch the merchandise again until it reached its destination.

As an owner of a transportation business McLean was probably looking to solve the glaring inefficiencies and problems that had plagued his industry for centuries. For long enough certain consumer goods like fresh fruit, vegetables and meat could not be transported more than a hundred miles from their point of production because any further and the goods would spoil and be worthless. The whole process just took too long. It took too long because everything was loaded from one method of transport to another by hand.

1

FIGURE 0.1: BREAK BULK CARGO

The technique was known as break bulk cargo because bulk cargo was broken up into smaller containers such as sacks, boxes, crates, drums or barrels (see Figure 0.1).

This method dates back to the Phoenicians, but it's easy to see from Figure 0.1 the other serious problem … it's very hard to maximize the use of space when packing barrels or to safely pack fresh fish, leather shoes and bottles of vodka together without creating damage to some of the cargo. And, finally, 'shrinkage' (theft) was rife. Often dock worker wages were as low as $20 a day and all the whisky they could carry home.

The intermodal container changed all that. On 26 April 1956, a converted Second World War tanker, the SS *Ideal X*, left Newark port in New Jersey (see Figure 0.2).

This was the pivot point. This simple innovation transformed business. Our economy and our lives would not be the same without the intermodal

FIGURE 0.2: THE SS *IDEAL X*

container. And its impact is more evident than almost any other invention of the twentieth century.

And what made it so powerful was the standardization. In a world with countless currencies, different languages, countless plug sockets and different sides of the road to drive on, we universally agreed on the dimensions of a shipping container. This meant that something loaded in Kentucky could be offloaded onto a truck in Japan or a train in Paris or a cargo plane in Nigeria. It always fitted; the system was always seamless. What used to take a week could be done in a matter of hours. It cut shipping times from Europe to Australia from 70 days to 34 days without increasing the speed of travel! Shipping costs plummeted.[1]

This simple standardized metal box became the greatest driver in the development of the global economy and trade networks. It transformed efficiency, reduced costs and massively increased productivity and profit. Almost overnight everyone in the transportation network could grasp the huge commercial incentive and benefit of using the intermodal container. The shipping companies could standardize their ships around the container, making them even more efficient. Ports around the world exploded in growth and shipping capability. Transportation links improved dramatically across road and rail networks as the shipping container traveled from the point of origin to its final destination. The businesses filling the containers benefited because they were able to reduce waste, theft and shipping time, therefore increasing profit. *And* the consumers benefited through access to a greater array of products, often at reduced prices. Essentially, the standardized shipping container triggered a virtuous capitalist cycle of unprecedented global productivity and exponential growth.

Standardization transformed efficiency, reduced costs and massively increased productivity and profit.

It was the shipping container that transformed the Chinese economy, lifting billions out of extreme poverty. It also facilitated the American Dream and the expansion of the American middle class. It was the shipping container that kickstarted globalization and an era of explosive productivity. It was the shipping container that allowed orchards in Spain to sell their produce on UK supermarket shelves. Its impact has spread far beyond the transportation industry to genuinely improve people's lives.

> **STANDARDIZATION TRANSFORMED EFFICIENCY, REDUCED COSTS AND MASSIVELY INCREASED PRODUCTIVITY AND PROFIT.**

Even earlier than the shipping container, the English philosopher Sir Francis Bacon was credited with coining the phrase 'knowledge is power'. In the early fifteenth century, the power of knowledge belonged to the Church and the Crown. They decided what information was produced and distributed. Books or manuscripts were handwritten and copied by scribes. The truth was, therefore, whatever was in those manuscripts. Needless to say, the Church and the Crown tried to control that information; but another game-changing innovation, the Gutenberg printing press, changed all that. By the end of the fifteenth century, a single print shop in Germany had expanded to around 270 printers across Europe. That was the pivot point. The printing press had a profound religious, social and educational impact far beyond the simple printing of documents or books. It triggered the very beginning of the Information Age and was instrumental in the dissemination of knowledge. The Renaissance and the Scientific Revolution would not have been possible without the printing press because it democratized information and allowed knowledge to spread regardless of whether that knowledge was approved by the Church.

These two innovations alone changed the world in ways that are hard to even fathom. I deliberately chose these examples not just because they demonstrate that disruptive innovation never ends (so we need to get used to it), but also because they highlight two critical themes in our evolution as a species *and* in the evolution of the internet. First, the insane power and potency of standardization as a mechanism for increased productivity and explosive growth. And second, the human flourishing that can occur when the control and distribution of anything is decentralized. In the case of the printing press, it was the control and distribution of information that was decentralized, but standardization and changes to control and distribution *always* herald disruption.

What is web3?

Web3 aims to apply decentralization and game theory to all of our digital life via two main concepts.

First, decentralized storage, computation and communication, which is largely an extension of web1. The database has been fundamental to all iterations of the internet. At its simplest it's just a ledger or record-keeping system and web3 offers a distributed ledger. There is significant value to be gained from decentralized storage, computation and communication, and this may or may not happen on the blockchain.

Blockchain, the term most commonly associated with web3, along with cryptocurrencies and smart contracts, makes up the second concept. These capabilities facilitate new economic models. They may also use a lot of energy and take up a lot of computational space. It may be, therefore, that viable decentralized web3 architecture uses blockchain for payments and important information that needs to be verified and everything else is held in decentralized, secure storage capabilities or use less energy intensive proof-of-stake systems.[2]

In the play *Arcadia*, playwright Tom Stoppard states, 'The future is disorder. A door like this has cracked open five or six times since we got up on our hind legs.' The shipping container and the printing press represent two of those doors that have opened up new worlds and new possibilities. Web3 is another. I will argue in this book that the impact of web3 is set to be even more far reaching and profound than both the shipping container and the printing press combined.

Stoppard goes on to say, 'It is the best possible time to be alive, when almost everything you thought you knew is wrong.' That is certainly true of web3, which will bring new possibilities and new opportunities for growth and profitability – if we pay attention now!

The End of Business-as-Usual

According to the Innosight 2021 Corporate Longevity Forecast, 'creative destruction continues apace – and at a high level … tracking of corporate longevity of S&P 500 firms [Standard & Poor's 500 stock market index] shows a steady churn rate of companies dropping off the index as new entrants join the list and corporate lifespans continue their downward trajectory'.

Innosight's analysis shows that the average tenure of companies on the S&P 500 peaked at 35 years in the late 1970s and again in the mid-1980s. By the late 1980s it had dropped below 20 years and was forecast to drop even further (see Figure 0.3).

About 50 per cent of the S&P 500 will be replaced over the next ten years if those forecasts are accurate.[3] One-third of the firms in the Fortune 500 in

FIGURE 0.3: AVERAGE LIFESPAN FOR COMPANY ON THE S&P 500 INDEX

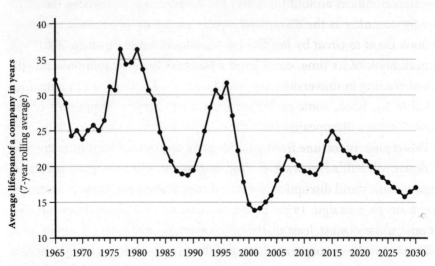

Adapted from original source: Statista.com 2022

1970 no longer existed by 1983 – killed by merger, acquisition, bankruptcy or break-up.[4] Using Standard & Poor's Compustat database information on about 30,000 companies that traded publicly in US markets between 1950 to 2009, researchers found that the average life span is about ten years, taking acquisitions, mergers and bankruptcy into account. And this mortality rate held true regardless of how established the companies are or what they do.[5]

The digital revolution has already reshaped the S&P 500. In 1969 industrial companies represented a third of the index; 50 years later, only 68 firms are industrials. Over the same time span, info-tech companies went from 16 to 68, and it was these kinds of companies that were tied for the top spot.

In the past few years alone, many renowned and once-successful corporate giants have been jettisoned from the S&P 500: Eastman Kodak, National Semiconductor, Sprint, US Steel, Dell and the *New York Times*. New additions to the list include Facebook, PayPal, Level 3 Communications, Under Armour, Seagate Technology and Netflix.

Tracking the comings and goings of the S&P 500 for the last 50 years, the Innosight study shows that the duration companies spend on the list fluctuates in cycles mirroring the overall state of the economy and the *disruption from new technologies*.[6]

In truth, companies have been playing musical chairs in various share-market indices around the world for decades. But the time in the chair is rapidly declining as the disruption rapidly increases. Just look at the business book *Good to Great* by Jim Collins (Random House Business, 2001) – a landmark book of its time, considered a business bible by millions and still required reading in universities the world over. And yet of the 11 companies detailed in the book, some no longer even exist. Almost 90 per cent of the Fortune 500 have disappeared since the original list was created in 1955.[7]

This change of fortune from good to great to gone will not miraculously slow down. We will never wake up one morning to discover that accelerated change, volatility and disruption are now things of the past. There is no return to some sleepy nostalgic 1950s board meeting and two-hour lunch. Today, right now, is the slowest, least disrupted it's ever going to be.

These shrinking corporate longevity tenures are also mirrored by the shrinking tenures of the CEOs who run them.[8] Only those who are focused on the future and are paying attention to the next wave of innovation and disruption will survive.

To add to that fragility and complexity, web3 is already disrupting what a company even is. If Bitcoin was a company, its market capitalization would have ranked it anywhere from the sixth highest in the world to the thirteenth. But Bitcoin is not a company. It has no CEO, no board, no shareholders and no employees. This is an astonishing statistic. Despite the drop in the value of Bitcoin in Q2 of 2022 (caused mainly by a loss of confidence in web3 following various high-profile collapses), it would still have ranked in the top 20 companies in the world. And yet people are still worried about having Bitcoin in their portfolio!

No business, however successful right now, can endure over the long term without reinventing itself. But today those reinventions must go far beyond business models and strategy tweaks to developing proficiency in, and relaunching on, new platforms. Business leaders are already doing this to some extent. Just think of cloud computing as an example. When the cloud first emerged, no one wanted it. No one fully appreciated the point of difference and the advantages that cloud-based systems could provide. One of the biggest stumbling blocks to cloud adoption was the sense of ownership and control. It required a shift in mindset from data stored on a specific machine in a specific location to data being stored in the cloud. And yet it would be hard to find a single CEO or business leader who doesn't now fully understand the cost, accessibility and efficiency benefits of the cloud, having successfully reinvented their business onto that new platform. What cloud did for IT capabilities, web3 will do for all the other business processes.

Leaders must also be vigilant for what Innosight's report calls 'fault lines' – the weakening foundations in their business model or the shifting needs of their customer base. Web3 will cause havoc to existing business models and customer needs whether we are ready for them or not.

This is not always easy among present-day obligations. In a separate survey of executives from 91 companies with revenue greater than $1 billion across more than 20 industries, leaders were asked: 'What is your organization's biggest obstacle to transform in response to market change and disruption?' Forty per cent of survey respondents blamed 'day-to-day decisions' that paid the bills but also undermined their stated strategy to change. This challenge is even more acute around web3.

Web3 is everywhere. It's even made it out of the tech industry journals into the *Financial Times,* *The Economist,* the *New York Times* and beyond. The discussions may still vary from the inane to the complex and cover everything from web3 being nothing more than a storm in a crypto teacup to a rebranding exercise for capitalism to a vision of some utopian new world order.

> **WEB3 IS AN INTERMODAL CONTAINER, A GUTTENBERG PRESS, DISRUPTION ON STEROIDS.**

As a business leader or senior executive, it might be tempting to ignore web3 for a few more years. Most leaders are already struggling to keep up with their day-to-day decisions or the disruption that is knocking on their front door, never mind having time to consider the disruption that might be coming down the pipeline. And if this was business-as-usual disruption, they might be valid. But it is not business-as-usual disruption. Web3 is an intermodal container, a Guttenberg press, disruption on steroids. It is once-in-a-lifetime, game-changing disruption.

Besides, there is no ignoring it. Web3 is already here. The architecture, while not perfect, is functional … right now. The genie is out of the bottle and it's never going back in. We are already past the pivot point. For web3 that pivot point was 31 October 2008 when the Satoshi Nakamoto white paper was published (more on that in Chapter 3). Just as we will never go back to break-bulk cargo or writing out manuscripts by hand, we will never go back to a world without web3 capability. It will only accelerate.

We live in a highly disruptive world. Business leaders and senior executives are expected to stay across a vast array of political, economic, social, technical, legal and environmental (PESTLE) issues, changes or advances that are disrupting their industry or may impact their business at some point. In reality, it's an impossible task, which is why so many business leaders fail to engage with these trends until it's too late. It is incredibly challenging to break free of organizational inertia, where the existing mindsets and processes keep the cogs turning, but it must be done.

Businesses that understand the approaching tsunami can adapt and embrace the change to deliver even more value for greater profit and success. Those that ignore it or imagine they can fight their way out of it, litigate against it or somehow protect themselves from it will simply become less relevant in their market – and political economist Joseph Schumpeter's 'creative destruction' is all but assured.

My hope is that this book will inspire you to engage with web3, adapt where necessary and reap the considerable benefits of it, even in a hybrid capacity. Part I looks to the past. By taking a whistle-stop tour through the three iterations of the internet, web1, web2 and web3, we can better appreciate the patterns that created them, grew them and caused the next version to emerge. What we need, especially in business, is a way to recognize the trends and changes quickly so we can get ahead of the disruption that matters and ignore the rest. The way to do that is pattern recognition via developmental frameworks that act as a road map to change. If we can see the patterns in the disruption and understand how many of these patterns or threads of disruption build on top of each other, it is possible to arm ourselves with the insight that will allows us to navigate that new future.

One of the biggest barriers to understanding web3 is that it can appear crazy (more on this in Chapter 1). Why would anyone want digital real estate? What is an NFT? Is cryptocurrency just a fad? Many of the current web3 capabilities seem crazy. But once you fully appreciate the patterns you will see just how logical they really are. Web3 is a little like those Magic Eye puzzles where on first glance you can see nothing of relevance – it's just a mess of crazy color and swirls. But if you look at it in just the right way, an image of a butterfly suddenly pops into view. And, ironically, as soon as you see the butterfly you can't unsee it. Instead of fearing web3, or willfully ignoring it, you will understand its genesis and evolution as well as its inevitability and its significant opportunity. Web3, emerging from web2 – which itself emerged from web1 – is as inevitable as night following day. As well as the patterns of innovation, we'll also explore some frameworks and conceptual models that can help us recognize the innovations that will disrupt business, politics and society, and what we can do about it.

This book will explain these patterns so you can better understand web3 and its potential implications on your business and allow you to predict what's around the corner. The discussion will keep the technical side to an absolute minimum and instead focus on the application of the technology and how that is going to change business and society. Part I will also demonstrate how web1 and web2 disrupted the 'demand side' of supply and demand in business.

Part II explores the present. It unpacks how web3 is already disrupting the 'supply side' of business. This Supply-side Revolution is going to disrupt the supply of talent, capital and operations as well as further disrupt demand. Where web1 and web2 completely changed how businesses sold their products and services, web3 is putting the power in the hands of producers, creators, coders and collaborators who are coming together in new ways to completely change what and how products and services are created and offered to customers in the first place! This power shift is significant. Consumer spending is a $50-trillion-a-year industry and the value of all assets in the world is estimated to be $300 trillion. Web3 and beyond will impact both of these enormous markets – potentially having a dramatic effect on the distribution of that wealth in the process. Part II explores in detail how this redistribution and unbundling is already happening.

Part III looks to the future – what's coming for business and for us as 'prosumers' and how web3 has the capacity to change society and humanity for the better. The conclusion will also cover what can go wrong so we have a solid sense of the risks. Web3 heralds unprecedented interconnectivity and cooperation across a diverse and global ecosystem that will allow people from all types of background to come together in new ways to produce goods, services and solutions that are more innovative, efficient and equitable. More people benefiting from greater connection and productivity.

So, let's get to it.

PART 1

HISTORY OF THE WEB

Chapter I

Web1: The Emergence of an Information System

To fully understand and appreciate the ramifications of the disruption that is occurring today we must look to the past so we can appreciate and learn to recognize the constant and repeating patterns that drive this disruption. These patterns are as strong and irrefutable as gravity; they drove disruption 10,000 years ago and will still be driving it 10,000 years from now.

If we take a stroll back through the computing era, for example, long before web anything, computing power emerged as mainframe computing in the 1960s. They were huge, incredibly expensive machines that were housed in particular locations. A small number of people would travel to the computer, use it and leave. In an attempt to increase efficiency and squeeze more value from the hardware, time-sharing evolved in the 1970s to allow the mainframes to be used by multiple users at the same time, which dramatically reduced the cost of computing capability. In May 1974, the Institute of Electrical and Electronics Engineers (IEEE) published a paper entitled 'A Protocol for Packet Network Intercommunication'. The paper's authors, Vint Cerf and Bob Kahn, described an Internet Protocol (the same IP that is part of your IP address) for sharing resources that would become the foundation of the internet we still use today. But it was never going to take off because there was no way to access it unless you could get to a mainframe, which was still off-limits for most people, and they were still laborious to operate and prone to error. It was

What is a protocol?

Computer capability is rooted in a couple of principles. First of all, the computer itself always has a microprocessor, memory and a hard drive. Second, you need a keyboard, a mouse and a screen to successfully interface with the microprocessor, memory and hard drive. It's then possible to write code that directs this interface. The different hardware interfaces, internal systems of the computer and the screen all need to talk to each other. This is a protocol. Essentially a protocol is an information packet of agreed instructions around how a particular outcome is achieved that works alongside the code. For example, when you plug in your USB keyboard or use your wireless Bluetooth mouse, USB and Bluetooth are the respective protocols that have standardized and agreed how this information should travel. In effect they are 'shipping containers' for data.

this limitation that triggered the move to PCs, which started very tentatively in the 1970s and really took off in the 1980s.

These innovations, from the mainframe to time-sharing to the PC to the internet and beyond, are examples of the same pattern that has repeated endlessly throughout history where the technology is either too far ahead of the user or the ability to access it, or the technology is too far ahead of the market, or some other piece of the puzzle is just not in place yet to allow that technology to take root. The challenges that are encountered by the first people to use the new technology become opportunities for further innovation.

Hard Drives and the Innovator's Dilemma

Take the invention of the hard drive as an example. IBM invented the hard drive in 1953. Although revolutionary, it was very large; each 'disk' was 24 inches in diameter. And it couldn't actually hold very much information. The initial capacity was just 5 megabytes, about the size of a single photo your iPhone takes today (see Figure 1.1).

But even with its flaws, people were excited about hard drives because they could use them to store records on a computer. When we pull back the

FIGURE 1.1: A PARTIALLY DISMANTLED IBM 350

veil on web1 and look at the fundamentals, or the key innovation in that era, that innovation was a visualized database that connects to other computers over a distant local area network (LAN). This capability was made possible by the hard drive and the ability to interact with that data.

Of course, as soon as people realized that they could store records on a machine, they wanted to store more records and more data, which led to bigger hard drives being developed. IBM and others then put more things inside the same-sized device so they could double the storage capacity. In 1965 Gordon Moore, CEO of Fairchild Semiconductor and later co-founder of Intel, created Moore's law, which predicted that the number of transistors in an integrated circuit would double every two years as technological progress advances. He was right and storage capacity increased exponentially for several decades.

As a result of this exponential growth, new patterns emerged that led to two diverging paths of innovation. On one path were those who believed that the next advance would be around more storage on the large discs. On the new diverging path were those who believed the next advance would be to create smaller hard drives, but with less storage than the larger discs. Again, this always happens. It is always this divergence that creates what is known as the 'Innovator's Dilemma'. This is a theory put forward by the late Clayton Christensen to explain the evolution of innovation – any innovation.[1] You may be aware of the Innovator's Dilemma, but it's worth just recapping here.

There are two parts of the dilemma: S-curves, which we will cover shortly, and what might be described as the incumbent blind spot, which is crucial to the story of the hard drive or any innovation.

What happened is that the people who were using the massive hard drives were pretty happy. The drives were big and not very pretty, but they did what the customer wanted. They stored the data they wanted to store. The new hard drive players decided that smaller would be better even though smaller meant less storage capacity. Those who were already in the hard drive market were confused. 'Why would I want a hard drive that allows me to store less information?'

So, the customers of the incumbent companies did not switch to the new, smaller hard drive option. This created a 'Dilemma Zone' where the new product was worse at pretty much everything except for one specific dimension or characteristic[2] – in this case, the physical size of the hard drive. And while the smaller hard drive did not appeal to the incumbent audience, over time a new audience appeared who were attracted to the new product because of that single dimension. This was also coinciding with the advent of the PC, so smaller hard drives started to make sense because the market for them was very different to the market for mainframes.

There are always six stages to the Innovator's Dilemma:

» Stage 1: Disruptive technology is often developed by established companies.
» Stage 2: Existing customers undervalue the changes that do not address their specific needs.
» Stage 3: Established players renew their focus on 'sustaining' technology development.

» Stage 4: New entrants introduce the disruptive technology to small 'fringe' markets (attacker's advantage).
» Stage 5: Disruptive technology moves 'upmarket'.
» Stage 6: Established firms try to catch up.[3]

So, in this case, there are now two types of hard drive: the bigger hard drives with more storage capability but limited market, and the smaller hard drive with less memory but a potentially bigger market. A battleground emerges where it's unknown which type will win. And when it's a truly disruptive innovation, the new entrant that was originally mocked and ridiculed as having created something no one wants with less utility starts to win new customers. And that increased uptake creates the momentum to flip everyone over to the new entrant and the incumbent disappears or fades into the background.

French painter and sculptor George Braque said, 'Two ideas are always needed: one to kill the other.' This almost always happens with innovation. Think Betamax versus VHS, Netflix versus Blockbuster, CDs versus Napster or later Spotify or Nokia versus iPhone.

Two ideas, each with their own merits, where one will emerge triumphant. Even when the new solution has fewer features than the incumbent, its one differentiating feature becomes so important over time that it is the reason that the market flips over to it and the innovator wins the battle. This is the first aspect of the Innovator's Dilemma.

The second is the phases that this journey from innovation to acceptance takes. Each innovation will travel through four distinct innovation phases.

» Phase 1: Competition based on *Functionality*
» Phase 2: Competition based on *Reliability*
» Phase 3: Competition based on *Convenience*
» Phase 4: Competition based on *Price*

First, there is the functionality battle where the incumbent or currently accepted solution will add more and more features to maintain their appeal and stay ahead of the competition. However, those additional features far exceed what the market needs or wants. It is this disparity that excites the new entrant as they seek to meet a need the market does want. Once the functionality battle has been won, in our case with smaller hard drives, the competitive battleground shifts to reliability. Which of the options on the market are the most reliable? Next comes convenience. In the hard drive example this battleground was the domain of portable hard drives and tiny USB sticks that could hold a phenomenal amount of data – all very easily transported and accessed. Finally, the last phase of competition is on price. This is where hard drives are today. They have become a commodity. So much so, it is impossible to attend a corporate conference without getting a free branded USB stick! All the hard drive manufacturers produce very small, very reliable hard drives with massive storage capability. The only differentiator is price. There's literally nothing more to innovate on a hard drive, until we use DNA to store data.

We see this pattern in everything from the hard drive to PCs to the internet and more. And it is important to bear in mind as we travel through each of the explanatory chapters about web1, web2 and web3. But first, let's take a closer look at web1.

The Emergence of Web1

The easiest way to think about web1 is to think of it as the creation of an information exchange system.

Since the Internet Protocol, many more protocols have been created. Where Internet Protocol set up a standardization for how computers would communicate with other computers, new protocols were built on top of a File Transfer Protocol and a Simple Mail Transfer Protocol (SMTP). You might recognize SMTP as it's the protocol that allows us to send and receive emails. If you've ever set up an email account, you will have been asked to complete SMTP fields to make your email work – essentially telling your system where to deliver the emails to. A database was at the heart of all these systems. A database and the ability to search that database were therefore absolutely critical to web1. In its simplest form a database is just a ledger or a record-keeping system.

Ledger systems can be seen in antiquity. For example, 'khipus', or knotted string devices, were used by the Inca people to record information like censuses and tax records. The Babylonians kept ledgers using reeds and wood. A ledger is just a place to store know*ledge*, hence the term *ledger*. The same is still true today in company ledgers and databases.

The first computerized database, the Integrated Data Store or IDW, was invented by Charles Bachman in the early 1960s. This was followed by IBM's Information Management System, and both were forerunners of the 'navigational database'. In the 1970s progress jumped significantly with the development of the relational database – one that shows the relationship between different data records. This made the data searchable in a way that navigational databases were not and reduced data storage costs. IBM, working on prior innovations, created the first database using Structured Query Language (SQL), and in the 1980s SQL became the standard language for databases.

> "THE EASIEST WAY TO THINK ABOUT WEB1 IS TO THINK OF IT AS THE CREATION OF AN INFORMATION EXCHANGE SYSTEM."

The database is central to the digital revolution, from the mainframes, PCs and across all three iterations of the web. What they are, where they are stored, what is stored, who controls them and who has access to them are the perennial questions that in many ways drive these evolutions forward. The database is the common thread that runs through web1, web2 and web3.

The game-changing database protocol in web1 was MySQL, an open-source relational database management system, which provided an alternative to the proprietary database systems offered by IBM and Oracle. The 'My' part was the name of the co-founder's daughter. Almost the entire internet was at one point built on this database standard. And a huge part of the transition from web1 to web2 was the effort in web2 to take control of the data inside those open-source databases, to create control and ownership for profit. But we will cover that in more detail in the next chapter.

In each era, Stage 4 of the Innovator's Dilemma triggers an attacker's advantage where new entrants introduce the disruptive technology to small 'fringe' markets. This always creates some sort of innovation plot twist, which acts as an accelerator to the innovation and adoption in that era. This usually occurs somewhere in the middle of the S-curve. This innovation plot twist throws everyone off-kilter and almost always creates a significant business risk to those who ignore it. The innovation plot twist accelerator in web1 was HTML.

Prior to HTML, although there were many protocols, they all shared one key similarity – they were all text based. An email is text based; a file is sent and that file contains text-based metadata. A database is text or number based. A phone line could be connected to a computer, which would allow for the transfer of information via a variety of these protocols.

None of the protocols visualized these capabilities anywhere. They tended to live inside businesses or universities or were the domain of the geeks and nerds (techies and early users), including me as a ten-year-old kid messing about with computers in my bedroom.

> **THE INNOVATION PLOT TWIST ACTS AS AN ACCELERATOR TO THE ADOPTION IN THAT ERA.**

In 1980, physicist contractor at CERN Tim Berners-Lee changed all that when he proposed and prototyped a system for CERN researchers to use and share documents. Nine years later Berners-Lee wrote a memo proposing an internet-based hypertext system, writing the browser and server software for hypertext mark-up language, better known as HTML, in late 1990.

HTML was the protocol for visualizing information on a computer and it was a revelation. For the first time, it allowed people to create digital visualizations of information. It was possible to create a digital page where you could choose to add text, color, images and buttons. What used to be only possible via a full-color printing press could be represented digitally on a screen. That said, the early website pages were pretty hideous compared to what we are used to now, but at the time HTML was a game-changer.

The first publicly available description of HTML was published online by Berners-Lee in 1991. It described 18 elements comprising the initial, relatively simple design of HTML, 11 of which still exist today in HTML4.

HTML kicked off a period of intense collective development, where early users in bedrooms and universities were creating free open-source protocols that anyone could use. It was the new frontier, and would-be techies and programmers jumped in because it was exciting and fun. There was no intended commercial strategy when HTML was launched; the appeal was simply to see what was possible.

This early exuberance was part of what would become web1's Achilles heel – reach, density and accessibility. The expectation of those involved, certainly in the early years, was that everyone would run their own server. But those people were the pioneers, the programmers and the early users, and while *they* were happy to build their own website on their server, very few other people were.

This too was an example of the Innovator's Dilemma. When the internet first came on the scene no one except the early users were interested. It couldn't really do much and so people who were already pretty happy with their PC and the various software programs they could use on it couldn't see the attraction. Why use a bad web application when their PC already did everything they needed but so much better?

Web1 could easily have stalled at this point and been nothing more than a footnote in history, but a few companies became interested in finding ways to commercialize the various protocols and it was these interventions that brought web1 into the mainstream, because they increased what was possible on the internet.

Do you remember CompuServe? CompuServe was way ahead of the web1 movement, and in fact at one point it was the largest consumer information company in the world. They were perfectly placed to take advantage of HTML and the emerging visual online world. It is a classic example of a key input to the Innovator's Dilemma – S-curves. This is where waves of innovation feed into new waves that themselves feed into new waves of innovation. It is essentially the story of the evolution of anything – emergence, differentiation and finally integration.

CompuServe started life in 1969 as a subsidiary of a life insurance company, focused on business customers. Ironically, they emerged because they wanted to sell excess server capacity (which is how Amazon created their cloud business). The objective of the business was to provide in-house computer processing support to the insurance arm and to develop as an independent business in the computer time-sharing industry by renting time on its mainframes. By 1977 it was offering dial-up online information services to customers, so they really were at the forefront of technology that would later merge into web1. Over time, the CompuServe network evolved into a complicated multi-tiered network incorporating many of the emerging protocols of the time, including the Internet Protocol.

By 1981 CompuServe was offering email, real-time chat and a video-text-like service permitting personal computer users to retrieve software from the mainframe computer over telephone lines. They were also a world leader in other commercial services including the collection and consolidation of financial data from various data feeds. They were probably one of the first companies in the world to recognize the inherent power and potential wealth of data.[4]

Little wonder that CompuServe was also one of the first companies to recognize the potential of web1. What HTML did was allow them to make their information much more visually appealing and to reach beyond their typical business audience. CompuServe knew that people didn't want to build their own pages or work out how to manage a server but they did want the information, so they set out to create a sort of walled-garden information superhighway. At its peak in the early 1990s, CompuServe was known for its online chat system, message forums covering a variety of topics, extensive software libraries for most computer platforms, newsfeeds and a series of popular online games. It was CompuServe that introduced the world to the GIF format for pictures.

CompuServe, like many others, set out to commercialize the protocols and lock people into their controlled channel in what was very media-centric thinking. This maneuver also points to another very common theme or pattern that occurs over and over again where the old guard or existing businesses seek to shoehorn new technology into existing business models or accepted or known ways of operating. This is a natural instinct, but it is almost always implemented in the wrong way. We saw the exact same move when Time Warner merged with AOL in 2000. It was, and still is, the largest corporate merger in history at $165 billion. At the time, everyone thought it was game over. A media company and an online giant joining forces meant that the internet or web1 would effectively become a monopoly and everyone else would be pushed out. Of course, that didn't happen, and it is now also widely regarded as the most disastrous merger of all time.[5]

Essentially, this pattern is just the journey through the stages of the Innovator's Dilemma. More recently we saw it with Facebook when they bought up Instagram and WhatsApp – both Stage 6 maneuvers where the established firm tries to catch up. New entrants (Stage 4), in this case Instagram and WhatsApp, had introduced disruptive technology to small fringe markets and had grown exponentially because of some differentiating feature. For Instagram that differentiating feature was the focus on images and image sharing, and for WhatsApp the differentiating feature was the ease of use and connectivity to everyone else in a user's phonebook. Both eventually moved upmarket into the mass market and so Facebook bought them to catch up on these disruptive innovations. At the time, it was speculated that up to 85 per cent of what people did on Facebook was photo sharing, and 50 per cent of the photos being shared to someone's Facebook page were coming from Instagram, so they bought Instagram in 2012 for $1 billion.[6] Two years later Facebook bought WhatsApp for $19 billion because everyone was ditching Facebook Messenger for WhatsApp because it was so much better.[7]

Incumbents always start to get worried when disruptive innovation nips at their heels and they always start to spend enormous amounts of money to solve the problem. Such a tactic is a little like fighting gravity.

And yet it is almost always attempted. In January 2022, J. P. Morgan announced the same play: a $12 billion tech spend to beat financial technology companies (fintechs).[8] This is just Stage 6 – the established firms, in this case the banking giant J. P. Morgan, trying to catch up. But throwing lots of money at a problem and applying old-world thinking to new technology rarely works. To be fair to J. P. Morgan, they are attempting to embrace web3.

> "INCUMBENTS ALWAYS START TO GET WORRIED WHEN DISRUPTIVE INNOVATION NIPS AT THEIR HEELS."

A month after their big announcement, Onyx, the bank's blockchain unit, opened a 'lounge' in the Decentraland metaverse.[9] Decentraland is a virtual world that is owned by its users. But J.P. Morgan are still coming at it from a 'how can *we* own this, instead of the building a community of users' – which is the antithesis of web3.

FIGURE 1.2: INNOVATOR'S DILEMMA S-CURVE

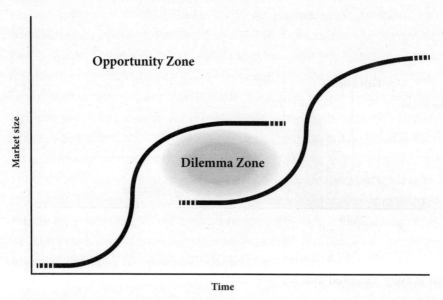

Source: *The Innovator's Dilemma*, Clayton Christensen, 1997

There is very little doubt that we will see more established companies playing catch-up by embarking on enormous mergers in the hope of staving off the inevitable as web2 peters out. This is always the pattern: the Innovator's Dilemma creating waves of innovation known as S-curves (see Figure 1.2).

All innovation, especially technology innovation, follows these overlapping waves or S-curves. Let's just take a quick march through web1 to demonstrate this. Whenever anything is invented it's usually a minimum viable product (MVP) that emerges from a university lab or research facility. As a result, it's pretty basic, so it's often ignored or dismissed by the market as a stupid or crazy idea. Every new product or service travels through what is known as an adoption lifecycle (see Figure 1.3).

This journey to acceptance, originally called the diffusion process, was first identified by agricultural researchers in the 1950s to help explain how different seed types were adopted by American farmers. One of those researchers, Everett Rogers, went on to describe how new ideas and innovations spread from those first people or 'innovators' to a product or service

26

FIGURE 1.3: INNOVATION ADOPTION LIFECYCLE

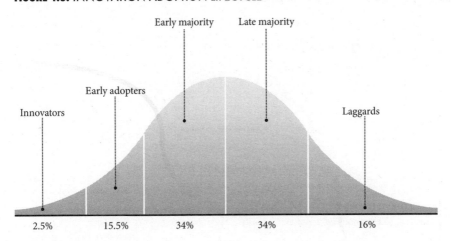

that is fully accepted and embraced by the mass market (the early and late majority).

According to Rogers, different types of people adopt new technology at varying rates. The 'innovators' are happy to be first and like to push and test the innovation. Once more improvements have been made, the 'early adopters' get on board, followed by the mass market. We can see this in everything from PCs to smartphones to Bitcoin. Initially the relative speed of adoption was plotted as a normal distribution (a bell curve) with the primary differentiator being an individual's psychological disposition to new ideas.[10]

It is this psychological disposition that also creates a sizeable chasm in the adoption lifecycle. And 'crossing the chasm', a phrase coined by organizational theorist and author Geoffrey A. Moore, is therefore imperative to widespread use and adoption of a product or service. Moore noticed that the march towards acceptance was not linear. It wasn't simply that a growing number of people started to use the innovation. In reality, there was a psychological difference between the innovators and the early adopters, who were willing to accept some level of poor functionality in order to be first in the market, as opposed to the rest of the market (see Figure 1.4).

The early majority, late majority and the laggards didn't care about being first or getting the latest tech; they cared about functionality and would not

FIGURE 1.4: MOORE'S ADAPTED ADOPTION LIFECYCLE

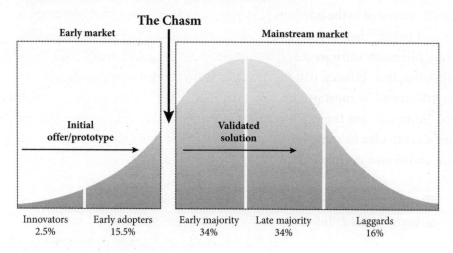

Source: Crossing the Chasm, Geoffrey A. Moore, 1991

get involved until those issues and bugs had been solved. Needless to say, many innovations never make it across that chasm. If they do, they move from being a crazy idea to something everyone is talking about. This, together with the late majority, is the bulge of the S. It is super-exciting, and the additional innovations tend to be more incremental and are harder for the user to recognize. This growth lasts for a couple of years and then things slow down again.

At this point the questions shift from, 'Will this work?' or 'Will anyone want it?' to 'How do we deal with a million users or 10 million users?' In technology this cycle tends to run on a 5-to-20-year cycle.

As I mentioned earlier, the PC emerged in the very early days of the 1970s, largely in response to the cumbersome and inaccessible mainframes. But they didn't cross the chasm from early adopters to the majority market until the 1980s with the IBM PC and Microsoft operating system. So, the start of the S-curve was in the 1970s, with the bulge of the S happening in the 1980s and running into the 1990s – by which time Microsoft had effectively cornered the market and defined what a PC was. Just as the PC market was maturing and the S was flattening out again, along came the internet. This gave a completely

things are worse than the incumbent, it is not always obvious to the customer what that differentiator is, or they are not yet convinced that it's that important anyway. That was definitely true for Amazon. People were confused. They couldn't see the difference between shopping in Walmart and shopping on Amazon, except that Walmart had more stuff. And they couldn't see the point of Amazon because if they wanted more stuff, they could shop using a catalogue. The point of difference was that customers using Amazon had to place their order themselves online rather than call a customer order line and tell someone what to send. It didn't arrive any quicker at that point. The differentiator for Amazon – which would be, at least in time, access to pretty much anything at the touch of a button – was lost on them, and this is often one of the boobytraps of the Innovator's Dilemma. Customers will often look at the two solutions on offer and not appreciate the difference, or not yet value the difference. Fast forward even a few years and the difference is glaringly obvious to everyone.

Of course, this difference was not helped by Amazon's first website, which was pretty dire (see Figure 1.5), but today it is a global phenomenon where anyone with an internet connection can shop for just about anything, from anywhere, at any time of the day or night and have it shipped to their door within days. Today, Amazon's diversification into cloud services via Amazon Web Services (AWS) means that it also powers 50 per cent of the internet.

Amazon is a phenomenal success story of web1, although it really came into its own in web2. Its future is unknown in web3. This again is one of the interesting patterns of technological innovation. Those businesses that emerge in one wave of innovation tend to really come into their own and enjoy the ride in the second wave and then struggle or fail in the third wave.

We see this in privately owned family businesses too – there are universally understood aphorisms that indicate this pattern. For example, 'Shirtsleeves to shirtsleeves in three generations', or the Lancashire proverb, 'There's nobbut three generations atween a clog and clog'. In Italian it is, '*Dalle stalle alle stelle alle stalle*' ('From the stables to the stars to the stables'). In Mexico it's, '*Padre noble, hijo rico, nieto pobre*' ('Noble father, rich son, poor grandson'). In China, 富不过三代 ('*Fu bu guo san dai*') ('Wealth does not pass three generations').[12] In essence, the idea is that the wealth is made by the first generation,

FIGURE 1.5: THE FIRST AMAZON WEBSITE

Welcome to Amazon.com Books!

One million titles,
consistently low prices.

(If you explore just one thing, make it our personal notification service. We think it's very cool!)

SPOTLIGHT! -- AUGUST·16TH

These are the books we love, offered at Amazon.com low prices. The spotlight moves **EVERY** day so please come often.

ONE MILLION TITLES

Search Amazon.com's million title catalog by author, subject, title, keyword, and more... Or take a look at the books we recommend in over 20 categories... Check out our customer reviews and the award winners from the Hugo and Nebula to the Pulitzer and Nobel... and bestsellers are 30% off the publishers list...

EYES & EDITORS, A PERSONAL NOTIFICATION SERVICE

Like to know when that book you want comes out in paperback or when your favorite author releases a new title? Eyes, our tireless, automated search agent, will send you mail. Meanwhile, our human editors are busy previewing galleys and reading advance reviews. They can let you know when especially wonderful works are published in particular genres or subject areas. Come in, meet Eyes, and have it all explained.

YOUR ACCOUNT

Check the status of your orders or change the email address and password you have on file with us. Please note that you **do not** need an account to use the store. The first time you place an order, you will be given the opportunity to create an account.

enjoyed by the second and squandered by the third. Without smart, considered intervention that does not involve shoehorning old business models or outdated thinking into new tech or throwing money at it, the same occurs through waves of technological innovation.

GOOGLE

Google was about the thirty-fifth search engine. It was not a novel idea. By the time Google came along, or certainly its forerunner 'BackRub', there were already in excess of 75 million indexable HTML URLs. Other people had already realized that search was going to be really important for the internet.

From around 1990 to 1996, search as we know it just didn't exist, and there were still questions about whether the emerging search solutions really even made sense as the front page of the web. CompuServe and AOL were fighting hard to keep their customers inside their walled gardens. Meanwhile Yahoo, long before they did search as we understand it today, offered the Guide to WWW (Figure 1.6).

If you wanted to find out about something, you would go to Yahoo's Guide to WWW and select a category to explore but even with a few thousands listing in each category whether you found what you were looking for was more down to luck than great design. Having a place where we could access information was great, but even in the mainframe era it was recognized that it wasn't just about the hard drives and the databases; we needed a way to search that data so we could find what we needed when we needed it. Search as a concept

FIGURE 1.6: SCREENSHOT OF YAHOO'S GUIDE TO WWW

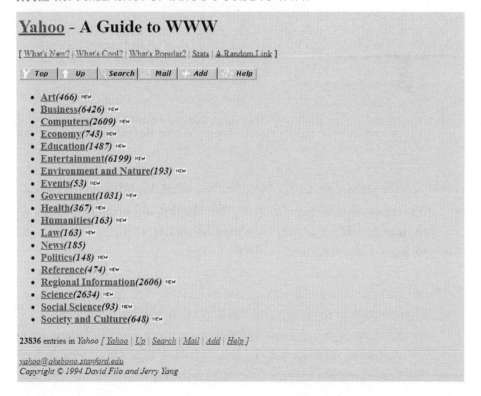

started in the mainframe computing era and migrated into PCs and eventually onto the internet too. Directories worked up to a point, but even when the internet had only a few thousand web pages, directories stopped being very effective. When the number of webpages on the internet reached 75 million, directories were no longer fit for purpose. In the interim, search became much more important. As mentioned earlier, Amazon was one of the early search tools – although that was limited to within the Amazon site. Other search facilities like AltaVista WebCrawler and Lycos were search tools, but in order to make money from the service they started to charge businesses to appear in the directory. As a result, the search results were not authentic. Users were not getting the best information or websites; they were instead getting the website that paid the most money to show up in the search results. The whole idea of free-flowing information was corrupted.

Meanwhile, Stanford University student Larry Page decided to write his dissertation on mathematical properties of the internet to better understand its link structures. He was interested in finding out which web pages linked to a given page and how the number and nature of 'backlinks' provided valuable information about the veracity and usefulness of that page. His process worked on the same principle as citations do in academic publishing: the more one paper is cited by another paper, the more valuable, valid and useful the cited paper is perceived to be.

It was this project that would lead to Google. How could people find things on the internet that were useful to them instead of just being given the information that was paid for by the businesses with the deepest pockets? The project started life in 1996 as 'BackRub' but thankfully was changed to Google. It's hard to imagine us saying, 'Hang on, just let me BackRub that!'

Page was joined by Sergey Brin shortly after and both worked on the Stanford Digital Library Project (SDLP), where the goal was 'to develop the enabling technologies for a single, integrated and universal digital library'; a mission that would become pretty close to Google's starting mission – to organize the world's information and make it universally accessible and useful.

Their resulting web crawler began exploring the internet in March 1996, and Page and Brin developed their now famous PageRank algorithm to convert the gathered data into meaningful results. The first version of Google was released in August 1996 on the Stanford website, and it used nearly half of the university's entire network bandwidth. Clearly they were on to something, and Google was officially launched in 1998 from another garage.

Like Bezos, Page and Brin had looked at what problems could be solved by the internet and created arguably the best search engine on the planet. I was a huge fan and, from coding HTML in my bedroom, once I graduated university, I joined Google. It was THE place to be.

People loved it. They loved the simple, clean interface and the integrity of the search results. Like so much of web1, they launched Google without any monetization model to start with. It was all very pure, striving to deliver the best information as fast as possible. Of course, all businesses need to make money, so they created a very clear section that displayed paid-for search results and another section that displayed organic search results.

•

As web1 drew to a close in the early 2000s there were many winners, but Amazon and Google were certainly two of them; Amazon for the purity of the concept and its utility, and Google for the purity of the information – both offering something that was truly different from anything else, while serving dense audiences.

The Demise of Web1

The impetus for the evolution of anything is survival. Something stops working or something starts to create more problems than it solves, and we are forced to adapt.

While a lot of people made a lot of money in web1, those profits were because the phenomenon of the internet was so powerful. As a result, business got greedy and rarely focused on utility or meeting the needs of the customer. It was the Wild West; again, an example of what can happen when old-world business models or modes of operating clash with new innovation. Countless companies in the gold rush went public with massive valuations based on very little substance or utility, and everything dot-com decoupled from reality.

Because of the phenomenon of web1, capital was flowing into new ventures all the time. This was the run-up to the dot-com crash of 2002, which effectively ended web1 and triggered the emergence of web2. At the time, investors were throwing money at anything with an online angle. Unsurprisingly this time was also synonymous with legendary dot-com parties! A bunch of engineers would come up with an idea, create a bad website, IPO for $100 million and have a lavish launch party at an exotic venue where a live band like Guns N' Roses would be paid $500,000 to play for a few hours.

> "THE DOT-COM CRASH OF 2002, EFFECTIVELY ENDED WEB1 AND TRIGGERED THE EMERGENCE OF WEB2."

Companies like pets.com, which sold pet supplies to retail customers, came and went remarkably quickly. Started in 1998, it IPO'd in February 2000, raising $82.5 million, and was defunct ten short months later. There are hundreds of stories like this.

But, as mentioned earlier, the main stumbling block of web1 was reach, density and accessibility. Even at the start of the twenty-first century only around 5 or 6 per cent of the global population had access to the internet. That was around 360 million people, which might sound like a lot, but it simply wasn't enough to support the plethora of web-based companies that flooded into the space to tap into the promise of web1. Even in the US only 45 per cent of the population had access to the internet. In the UK and Europe, it was nearer 15 per cent.[13] The density equation was all wrong. The end of web1 was essentially characterized by a profound performance oversupply against insufficient demand – great ideas but not enough customers yet. There were certainly winners, but there were also a lot of losers in this density battle. Too many businesses scaled up into extremely sparse, almost non-existent markets. High capital expenditure (capex) combined with customer sparsity killed off most of the dot-com businesses except a few such as Google and Amazon, who focused much more on dense user markets such as buying books or making it easier to trawl the vast number of web pages that had emerged.

Perhaps the poster child for the end of web1 was Global Crossing, a telecommunications company poised to take advantage of the phenomenal success story of web1. In 1999, during the dot-com bubble, the company was valued at $47 billion, but it never had a single profitable year. Hardly surprising – they were spending enormous amounts of money to put fiber optics in the ground for the future demand of the internet. And then it all imploded. In 2002 Global Crossing filed for one of the largest bankruptcies in history and its executives were accused of covering up an accounting scandal. Even Amazon's value was down 90 per cent in 2002, but it has subsequently risen to be one of the top five most valuable companies in the world.[14]

The dot-com crash exposed countless worthless companies. There just wasn't the demand that people hoped there would be. There were not enough PCs, not enough internet connections. It was all over. This performance over-supply and lack of density is another pattern, and we saw it again at the start of web3 – but more on that in Chapter 3.

As web1 drew to a close, the naysayers believed that the dot-com crash heralded the end of the internet and felt vindicated because they believed it was a flash in the pan anyway. Famously, Nobel Prize-winning economist Paul Krugman said, 'The growth of the internet will slow drastically, as the flaw in "Metcalfe's law" becomes apparent: most people have nothing to say to each other! By 2005, it will become clear that the internet's impact on the economy has been no greater than the fax machine's.'

Of course, the early users knew it wasn't over. The internet was now a fundamental part of humanity – it had just moved too fast for the market. Web1 started with individuals running their own server and creating a person-to-person (p2p) information system, and it ended with a few smart centralized leaders who focused on density. And it would be density that would character-ize, at least in part, the emergence and success of web2.

Business benefits of web1 (protocol era):
- Created new ways to find any information instantly and for nearly zero cost.
- Allowed us to communicate globally with anyone in the world in seconds for free.
- Disrupted distribution, making it possible to order anything in the world and have it sent directly to your house.
- Provided new ways to visualize information and interconnected databases.

Summary of Key Points

» We have to look to the past so we can appreciate and learn to recognize the constant and repeating patterns and trends that drive disruption.

» Innovation always leads to two diverging paths: one that focuses on augmenting the incumbent characteristics, and one that focuses on an as yet under-appreciated characteristic. This divergence is what creates the Innovator's Dilemma.

» The 'Dilemma Zone' is created where the new product or service is worse at pretty much everything except for one specific dimension or characteristic. Over time a new audience is attracted to that new product because of that feature, and it becomes the new incumbent.

» The easiest way to think about web1 is to think of it as the creation of an information exchange system.

» The database (ledger or record-keeping system) was at the heart of all the information exchange systems. The database and the ability to search that database were therefore critical to web1 and a common thread that runs through web2 and web3.

» In each era, there is always some sort of innovation plot twist, which acts as an accelerator to the innovation and adoption in that era.

» This innovation plot twist almost always creates a significant business risk to those who ignore it.

» Every new product or service travels through what is known as the adoption lifecycle and must 'cross the chasm' from innovators and early adopters to the mass market to be considered successful.

» Google and Amazon were the winners of web1 and certainly crossed the chasm. They were also instrumental in assisting web1 to cross the chasm.

Chapter 2

Web2: The Data Ownership Battle

Web1 was simply the digitization of analogue protocols at that time. And the easiest analogue protocols were digitized first. News became digitized. Music became digitized. In business, where once a letter was sent, now it is an email. Where once a brochure was printed, now there is a website. Google's and Facebook's adoption of ads as a revenue stream was simply the digitization of advertising that made newspapers and magazines money in the analogue era. They took the same model and applied it online.

Many of these digitizations did not change the outcome; it just made that outcome faster and more efficient. The recipient of a letter still received information or instruction; it's just that email did it faster. The newspaper still provided the news; it's just that newsfeeds did it faster and offered more news. CDs still provided music to the listener; it's just that Napster made it quicker and gave the listener more options.

From a business perspective, while this increased speed and efficiency was welcome, the cost and accessibility on the consumer side meant that consumers had not yet rushed to the online world. The result was the fire sale of the dot-com crash, which effectively killed web1.

While the businesspeople and the venture capitalists had run for the hills, lamenting the stupidity of the idea in the first place, the embers were still burning with the techies. And they were beginning to ask, 'What can we do beyond simply the digitization of commerce that is truly different?' While the market was too sparse to support the plethora of web1 companies (hence their collapse), having 360 million or so people globally connected to the internet was still significant. And it was likely to grow even further given the drop in PC costs and improved connectivity. What opportunities did that present?

> **THE EASIEST WAY TO THINK ABOUT WEB2 IS TO THINK OF IT AS A SHARED NETWORK FOR REDUCING TIME AND SPACE INEFFICIENCIES.**

The easiest way to think about web2 is to think of it as a shared network for reducing time and space inefficiencies in everything from servers to cars to spare bedrooms and local deliveries.

But before we dive into what happened in web2, it's worth exploring a little further this idea of how digital protocols emerge. It is another really important framework that can help us to better understand what has happened and what is therefore on the horizon. When we fully grasp these frameworks, we finally have the tools to predict future disruption and get ahead of it so we can see out to web4, web5 and beyond.

The Protocol–App Inversion

Between each iteration of the internet there is another evolutionary two-step between protocol development and the applications that are then built on top of those protocols. In truth, this inversion has been going on long before web-anything. The shipping container was a transportation protocol and globalization was the outcome of the application of that protocol. The Guttenberg press was an information protocol, and the dissemination of knowledge was the outcome of the application of that protocol. Protocols are like the train tracks being laid down, and the towns that emerged around these stations were the applications. Then new protocols emerge, such as roads and cars, and then the new apps are the shopping centers and malls. The cycle continues inverting ad infinitum.

In addition to the inversion between protocol development and application, there is also a progressive tension that is consistently held through each era. Web1 was 80 per cent protocol development with 20 per cent protocol application. The web1 winners, including Amazon and Google, essentially weaponized the open-source protocols that were developed in web1 to gain a commercial advantage through their application.

For example, one of the superpowers that Google developed was something called MapReduce. They figured out how to take a lot of cheap computers running Linux, an open-source operating system, to crawl the web to 'map' the internet and then bring that all together in a reduced format to make it useful. Linux was what made that possible. Although MapReduce originally referred to this proprietary Google technology, it has since been genericized and Google stopped using it in 2014 as their primary big-data processing model. But the fact remains that Google would not be Google without the application of these and other open-source web1 protocols.

As mentioned briefly in the last chapter, as the era moves up through its own S-curve, Stage 4 of the Innovator's Dilemma triggers an attacker's advantage where new entrants introduce the disruptive technology to small 'fringe' markets. This always creates some sort of innovation plot twist, which acts as an accelerator to the innovation and adoption in that era. This usually occurs somewhere in the middle of the S-curve, and for web1 that accelerator was HTML. This standard created a flurry of visualization that nudged the whole era forward into Stage 5 of the Innovator's Dilemma: disruptive technology moves 'upmarket'. All the web2 applications that changed our world were primarily built on web1 protocols but were able to attack entirely new concepts, such as the social graph.

> **AS WEB1 MOVED INTO WEB2 THE PROTOCOL–APP RATIO WAS INVERTED.**

As web1 moved into web2 the Protocol–App ratio was inverted, so that 80 per cent of web2 was protocol application and 20 per cent was protocol development. Simply put, the vast majority of capital and talent focused on application of the existing protocols instead of new protocol development. In web2 the innovation plot twist and attacker's advantage came in the form of Amazon Web Services and the Apple iPhone (and Android). These innovations became the accelerator for almost all web2 businesses (more on that shortly) as internet mobility and advances in user experience moved the technology of smartphones 'upmarket' to the masses. As web2 itself peters out, the inversion will happen again and move back to 80 per cent protocol development and 20 per cent protocol application. Only this time the digitization of analogue systems will move into areas that web1 couldn't touch. In web1 it was a simple and highly logical step to digitize information transfer from snail mail to email or newspapers to newsfeeds or CDs to music streaming. It was just about changing the delivery medium to make it faster and more efficient and to give the user access to more options. It would have been impossible to rewrite real estate contracts or loan agreements beyond simply making them available online. But the protocol development of web3 will make those things possible and much, much more. The literal transfer of the real world into digital protocol development is already happening in web3. Bitcoin is a protocol challenging what global central banking was designed to do, sweeping away a concept of currency and money that has stood for thousands of years. This sort of innovation simply wasn't possible in the protocol development of web1, but it is already happening in the protocol development of web3.

This is why so many application businesses are struggling to grapple with the emergence of web3. It's why it feels so disruptive. The web1 winners are so deeply entrenched in web1 protocols that they can't see a way to adapt to the new protocols being developed in web3. Remember, there is always a Protocol–App Inversion between eras. And the web2 companies are struggling too, but for different reasons – they are so deeply entrenched in the application of those web1 protocols that they can't see how to adapt their application to the emerging new protocols of web3.

This is why the flip from one era to the other is so fraught with commercial danger. Some companies that were successful in web1 succeeded in web2, but they are more likely to become increasingly irrelevant in web3 without significant change. Those who are successful in web2 may be able to move their application successfully towards web3, but it will still require a sizeable mindset shift.

In reality, any successful company in any era will require a significant mindset shift to survive as the world transitions between eras. But all business leaders should take heart – it is possible!

The Resurrection of Microsoft

When Microsoft started, pre-web1, their mission was simple: to put a computer on every desk and in every home. They nearly succeeded, and Microsoft is still a very successful company, but even the mighty Microsoft needed to adapt to survive. They very nearly slipped into irrelevance because they didn't understand the Protocol-App Inversion and what it meant for their business model.

Although web1 was built on collective open source protocols, Microsoft, like the Big Tech companies who dominate today, was monopolistic and very controlling. Microsoft worked against open source anything and the internet, because, initially at least, they believed that both posed a serious threat to their proprietary software model. They wanted to lock down ownership with Intel. Intel made the chips for the PC, and Microsoft created the operating system and the software. This approach effectively killed off the now-mighty Apple, at least for a while. It also nearly killed off Microsoft once web2 rolled around. The wars between Microsoft and Apple were well and truly won by Microsoft in the Nineties, but Google was its main challenger in the web2 era. From its heyday when almost everyone had a Wintel PC (Windows/Intel) on their desk, Microsoft became increasingly irrelevant as early web2 gathered momentum. As we covered in the Innovator's Dilemma pattern, as a pre-web1 company their strategic advantage and distribution models worked against them, and they couldn't get their head around how to monetize the web.

All that changed when Microsoft replaced their 'old world' CEO, Steve Ballmer, with Satya Nadella in 2014. Nadella had a completely different mindset to web2, and the company made a 180-degree shift in strategy. Instead of working against open source, they embraced it, buying GitHub, an open source code library and version control system used by developers, and making a few other strategic acquisitions. They did the opposite of what was in their corporate DNA and not only survived but roared back to prominence in web2 and are reasonably well placed for web3. They are now one of the three main cloud players (with Azure, which ironically uses Linux, one of the open source operating systems Microsoft railed against), along with Amazon's AWS and Google. Although, as I will explain at the end of this chapter, this is unlikely to be the advantage in web3 that these corporate titans are hoping for.

The key here, however, is that towards the mid to late web2 era Microsoft became relevant again. They were smart enough to see the writing on the wall and flexible enough to embrace the change to secure ongoing success in a world that was very different to the one of their glory years. That takes courage and smarts, but it is possible.

The Emergence of Web2

As mentioned earlier, web2 is all about shared networks that reduce time and space inefficiencies in everything from servers to cars to spare bedrooms and local deliveries.

It's unlikely that when 24 satellites were launched by the US Department of Defense to be used by the US military to improve navigation anyone imagined that exact same technology would allow us to call an Uber or have black pepper chicken and a cheeseburger delivered to our doorstep. Although the Global Positioning System (GPS) was started in the US in 1973, it wasn't fully operational until 1995. GPS provides geolocation and time information for a GPS receiver anywhere on or near the Earth. It doesn't require the user to transmit any data and it operates independently of any telephone or internet reception. Needless to say, it provides crucial location and positioning capabilities to military, civil and commercial users around the world. Once the smartphone gained traction it was then coupled with GPS, making a whole raft of new services possible.

GPS also serves as a brilliant reminder of what happens when the world does not standardize important innovations. There was no shipping container standardization with GPS. Far from it. Although the US opened up GPS to civilian use in the 1980s, it maintained control. During the 1990s GPS quality and functionality was deliberately degraded by the US Government in a program called 'Selective Availability'. Although this was discontinued in 2000, the damage to the protocol had already been done. Other countries realized that the US Government could deny access to GPS, which they did periodically, and started to create their own systems instead. Essentially, other countries, including Russia, China, Japan and the European Union, realized that they couldn't trust the US not to interfere with GPS when it suited them.

This is often one of the key drawbacks of web2 – the ownership of the data or innovation creates distrust. It is this breakdown of trust across many web2 innovations that laid the groundwork for web3.

GPS, until it was corrupted by Selective Availability, was also an example of network effect, a key component of web2. The internet itself is an example of a network effect.

Back in 1990 Bob Metcalfe, the co-inventor of Ethernet, studied network effects, which is the phenomenon whereby the more people who participate in or use a network, the more valuable and useful the network becomes. When the internet first emerged, it was pretty basic, certainly visually, so hardly anyone except techies used it. As more people started to use it, however, they produced more content, more information and services, and so more people started to use it in a virtuous cycle, which resulted in the internet being more useful and more valuable, leading to a network effect.

It was Metcalfe who created 'Metcalfe's law', the law that Paul Krugman got so very wrong as web1 began to implode. Metcalfe's law states that the value of a communication network is proportional to the square of the number of connected users of the system.[1] In other words, every time you add a new participant to the network, they square the effectiveness of the whole network. We've seen this occur from the telephone communication network onwards. When one person had a telephone, it wasn't very useful, but when there was a telephone in every home and office it was transformational because of the network effect. And each person helps to grow the network because the more people who can call each other, the more valuable the network becomes.

If web1 had been an information storage, search and exchange system, the game-changer in web2 was when open source collided with the network effects. As a result, the heart of web2 is anything to do with social networking, the sharing economy and the gig economy, which this collision made possible for the first time.

> **THE GAME-CHANGER IN WEB2 WAS WHEN OPEN SOURCE COLLIDED WITH THE NETWORK EFFECTS.**

All the big winners of web2 utilized network effects to facilitate sharing, which in turn reduced cost, increased efficiency and drastically reduced wasted time, capital and resources – whether that was sharing content and information with friends on Facebook, sharing the use of their car with Uber, sharing the use of their spare bedroom with Airbnb, sharing delivery drivers with takeaway venues via Deliveroo or sharing computer horsepower and functionality via cloud computing and software as a service (SaaS).

The sharing capability of cloud computing and SaaS have been particularly important for business and have, without question, helped to nudge the corporate mindset from needing to have their IT on the premises to being on the cloud, which will be key in the transition to web3. In reality, cloud-based software company Salesforce is directly analogous to Uber or Airbnb, but in the SaaS space. Where Uber takes an empty car and makes it more useful, and Airbnb takes an empty room and makes it more useful, Salesforce does the same with software. Instead of a business buying a software license for $3 million and using that software intermittently, the software is kept in the cloud. As such, it is shared by any business paying a small subscription, making it more accessible and more useful. These businesses may look very different on the outside, and appeal to different markets, but their DNA is the same. They all share a valuable resource – be that a car, home or software to squeeze all the unused value from that resource – making it more efficient, which in turn reduces the costs for the consumer while increasing the profit to the business.

It was because of the intentional concentration of network effects that these businesses did not make the fatal mistake that killed so many web1 companies – density.

Instead of focusing on the company and the product with little regard for the market, the successful web2 companies focused on density. Uber launched city by city, starting in San Francisco. Airbnb did the same, also starting in San Francisco. And Facebook did it, starting at Harvard University and then expanding to other Ivy League colleges in Boston to eventually most universities in the US and Canada. By getting one location right and building momentum in that location, the people already in the network helped to spread the word, therefore increasing the density and reach exponentially once critical mass had been achieved.

The really successful SaaS companies also employed this approach. Salesforce, for example, built a profile of their 'ideal customer' and targeted large companies who had the problem they solved. Slack, the corporate messaging service looking to replace email, is a great example of enterprise software and network effects coming together. Slack studied the size of the team that would need to use the product and how many messages that team would need to send to each other before they got ignition on the platform. Turns out the team needed to be sending a minimum of 2,000 messages. Founder Stewart Butterfield said that equated to about ten hours' worth of messages in a team of around 50 people. For a smaller, more typical team of ten people, that would be about a week's worth of messages. 'But it hit us that, regardless of any other factor, after 2,000 messages, 93 per cent of those customers are still using Slack today.'[2] So Slack focused on selling the platform into businesses that had highly active teams of at least six people. As a result, Slack is the fastest growing enterprise software company in the world. Perhaps unsurprisingly, Slack was bought by Salesforce in 2021 for $27.2 billion.

Although solving the density problem has been crucial for the web2 winners, it was virtualization that made the sharing economy we take for granted today possible.

> "IT WAS VIRTUALIZATION THAT MADE THE SHARING ECONOMY WE TAKE FOR GRANTED TODAY POSSIBLE."

Virtualization began in the 1960s, as a method of logically dividing the system resources provided by mainframe computers between different applications. As discussed in Chapter 1, mainframes were massive and extremely expensive. In the 1970s, time-sharing emerged as a way to squeeze more value from this expensive hardware. People would literally book to use the mainframe 24 hours a day, seven days a week to maximize the use of the resource. Since then, the meaning of virtualization has broadened, mainly because of the work done by Xen, a Cambridge University research project.

In 2003 Xen worked out how to allow multiple computer operating systems to execute on the same computer hardware concurrently. In other words, they figured out how to take a central processing unit (CPU), memory and hard disk and divide it up into parts and run an operating system on the parts. This was a massive departure even from physically sharing a single machine. It essentially allowed for the virtual sharing of every component part of the machine to squeeze all the shared value from each part, running hundreds of operating systems and processes at the same time, all connected through the network.

Meanwhile, around the same time in the US, Amazon's chief technical officer (CTO), Werner Vogels, was looking for greater efficiencies. This was after the dot-com crash and even Amazon took a battering. Their share price dropped from $91 to just over $15.[3] Since launching Marketplace in 2000, allowing third-party sellers on the platform, traffic had increased considerably. As a result, Amazon needed a huge bank of computers to successfully manage the spike in orders that occurred around Christmas. But all those computers were rarely utilized during the rest of the year. Putting that knowledge together with the breakthroughs in Cambridge, Amazon solved their under-utilization problem. By applying the insights of virtualization, Amazon was able to create their cloud solution Amazon Web Services (AWS). And AWS is now a bigger business than Amazon in terms of margins and profitability. Virtualization made the cloud boom possible.

The web2 focus on sharing was also further facilitated by the creation of application programming interfaces, or APIs – these are fundamental protocol connectors. As the name would suggest, APIs create an interface between bits of code that allow those bits of code to speak to each other and work as intended. The best explanation I've ever seen for an API is from Peter Lucas, founding principal of Maya Design, who likens the shipping container to an API – where the industry doesn't have to deal with what's inside the container, just the ability to move it around. When a developer writes a computer program, if they want that program to be reused by others, they keep most of the complexity hidden and expose a few very well-defined parameters that would allow that program to be used by others through the API. This is very similar to the shipping container. In fact, Lucas argues that the shipping container is an API between shippers and carriers. It doesn't matter what's inside the container, in the same way that it doesn't matter what's inside the computer program. All that matters is that there is a stand-ard agreement on how those containers are used and moved around.[4] So, APIs agree how two programs will interface and make that interface easy. And, just as the shipping container created a flourishing of productivity and global trade, the API created a flourishing of computer programs that could work together easily to further the sharing economy.

The winners of web2

The focus of web2 was how to avoid the density issues that killed web1 while building a commercialization strategy around datasets. The dominant mode was driven by creating useful products, with great user experience (UX), and providing this solution to the user 'for free'.

Over time, what happened in the digital era was that complex things were made increasingly simple. This is certainly a defining feature of web2 where the UX is light years from the UX of web1. Search is easy (Google). Getting a lift home is easy (Uber). Ordering take-out from five different restaurants is easy (Deliveroo). Figure 2.1 shows the relationship between UX and user ownership and control.

THE FOCUS OF WEB2 WAS AVOIDING THE DENSITY ISSUES THAT KILLED WEB1 WHILE COMMERCIALIZING DATASETS.

FIGURE 2.1: RELATIONSHIP BETWEEN UX AND USER OWNERSHIP AND CONTROL

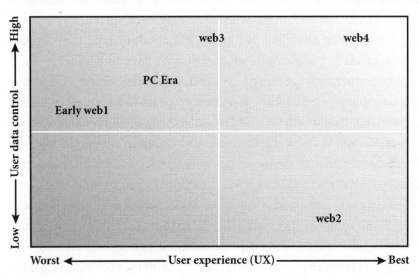

Source: GC Cooke

Early web1 users would build stuff on their own server using open-source protocols. It was fun, but the user experience was something that only a techie could appreciate. HTML made it possible to really visualize data, and so the UX improved in late web1, but there was a trade-off. Greater UX often came inside a company offering a platform. So, the internet was easier to use and nicer to look at and interact with, but we traded ownership and our data for that ease and simplicity. The PC era did the same thing via hardware and software that made the experience better, but we were tied to a company – usually Microsoft. There were so many innovations in web2, but from a user perspective web2 really nailed the UX.

In web2 there was a massive movement around user-centric design, and almost maniacal attention to detail about how to make something as easy as possible to use. Two of the key influencers in this area were Marty Cagan and Jony Ive.

Cagan defined and built products for some of the most successful companies in the world, including Hewlett-Packard, Netscape Communications and eBay. And he is the author of *Inspired: How to Create Tech Products Customers Love* (originally published in 2008), considered the product development and UX bible.[5] Founder of the Silicon Valley Product Group (SVPG), Cagan shares lessons learned and best practices to help companies build great products that users love.

Ive is the British-American industrial and product designer responsible for many of the Apple products we love. Joining the company in 1992, he was promoted to Senior Vice President of Industrial Design in the late 1990s, following the return of Steve Jobs, and became Chief Design Officer (CDO) in 2015. Working closely with Jobs, Ive played a vital role in the designs of the iMac, Power Mac G4 Cube, iPod, iPhone, iPad, MacBook, and parts of the user interface of Apple's mobile operating system iOS. Apple's products are truly beautiful. And it was that aesthetic quality combined with incredible functionality that made the UX so good and Apple so successful. Ive was instrumental in that and is part of the reason we flocked to Apple in such massive numbers, handing over a great deal of ownership and control over our data in the process.

Web2 really solved the UX issue, but in the process we became the product. Early moves in web3 pushed control back to the user, but the UX suffered as a result. It was back to the domain of the techies and early users where functionality has always trumped aesthetics. But UX is almost always the bridge, or at least part of the bridge, that allows anything new to cross the chasm from enthusiastic innovators and early adopters to early and late majority. As web3 accelerates, it is improved UX that will take it mainstream, triggering web4.

Two of the big winners of web2 were Facebook and Apple, because they both made life simpler and easier. Facebook made it simpler and easier to stay in touch with friends and family and share our lives. Apple made it easy to access a vast array of functionalities via their App Store.

FACEBOOK

As web1 came to a close, Mark Zuckerberg was at university. He's a smart guy so he knew that the internet was not going to disappear. The problem was density. Zuckerberg knew that the density issue would never be solved if everyone relied on people hosting their own website, social blog or chat server. But if he created a simple application on the web, a social graph where people could connect to and rank all their friends together, that might work. In 2003 Zuckerberg started Facebook (known then as FaceMash) to allow people to easily connect their social networks and share their world with their chosen friends and connections. People joined the platform for free and it immediately allowed them to engage in multidimensional social interaction with their community. Of course, this triggered network effects because once one person joined, they would get all their own friends to join because doing so made the platform more useful and valuable to that user (and Facebook).

Where web1 was very open, web2 companies protected their closed databases. The big winners, including Facebook, created very closed, highly protected databases of information that they then used to make money. Facebook is famous for having an insane amount of data. They won't let anybody access it without paying for it and you, the user, can't really touch it.

In truth, Facebook was not the first social network that attempted to connect people. Remember Friends Reunited, Bebo, MySpace? Google even tried with Open Social, but none of them came close to the success of Facebook. And the game changer for Facebook was the other big web2 winner – Apple. If

FIGURE 2.2: HISTORICAL GROWTH OF FACEBOOK

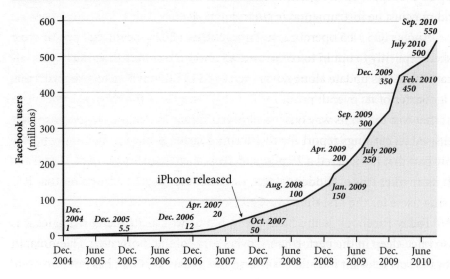

Source: Figures from firstmonday.org, blog.facebook.com, newsroom.fb.com/News and www.facebook.com/facebook

you look at Figure 2.2, Facebook really started to grow around the same time Apple launched the iPhone (2007).

Right from the start Facebook was taking advantage of web1 protocols by making a social network digital. As it moved through its own S-curve, a new entrant, in this case the Apple iPhone (and Android in other parts of the world), created an innovation plot twist, which acted as an accelerator to the adoption of Facebook by billions of people globally.

Every company either accelerates on this innovation plot twist or they die. And one of the reasons that Facebook accelerated so rapidly was that Mark Zuckerberg recognized its significance immediately and insisted that all his meetings discuss the mobile application of Facebook at least 90 per cent of the time. If anybody talked for more than 10 per cent of the time on the web application of Facebook, Zuckerberg would leave the meeting. In true Facebook fashion, however, they tried to do it their own way by building their own application first. Engineers created a really beautiful, very sophisticated mobile website that functioned like an app, but people didn't like it. They wanted the app from the App Store and so Facebook was forced to build the app in the Apple environment. That choice was instrumental in their growth and may just be instrumental in their downfall.

Apple's iOS 14.5 operating system update in 2021 meant that people were asked explicitly to opt in to companies that want to collect their data. It is estimated that this update alone cost Facebook $10 billion in advertising revenue – a quarter of its overall profit for the year! In one of the clearest indications yet that web2 is on its way out, Facebook is finally in decline. When Facebook released its earnings report for the fourth quarter of 2021 it was so unexpectedly bad that it triggered a 25 per cent drop in share price, taking $240 billion off its market value. Hidden in that same report was the admission that it is losing users for the first time in its history.[6]

Today Facebook is the incumbent, but as well as financial struggles it is also knee-deep in the performance oversupply of the Innovator's Dilemma. In a bid to stay relevant it could easily be argued that Facebook has become more complicated, thus making the user experience worse.

Facebook clearly sees the enormous power and distribution possibilities of web3. Their name change to Meta is a nod to the metaverse, which they believe is the future. But even there they are seeking to create a closed metaverse in much the same way that Facebook is closed, working as a walled garden system like AOL and CompuServe in the web1 era, despite indications that we're going to be in an open stage. They have also tried to venture into crypto but have been forced to exit, certainly for the time being. Federal regulators and law makers in the US effectively put a stop of Facebook's plans for Libra, later renamed Diem[7]. Facebook clearly sees how web3 is going to disrupt their future. The only question is whether Facebook will find a new way to navigate the new environment or whether they will become a much less relevant platform. This seems to be a very similar pattern that Microsoft went through against the open source movement only to eventually embrace the broader shift.

People are fed up with 'being the product' and today we see a backlash against Big Tech. Today, most businesses have to participate in those Big Tech gateways in one form or another. For example, if you want to make marketing work, you almost certainly have to engage with Facebook and Google. If you want to engage in e-commerce you have to engage with Amazon. Big Tech currently controls these gateways, but this is set to change with web3. People are unhappy that a handful of companies are so powerful, and they are so powerful because they have a huge amount of our data that they protect with force and use to increase profits.

APPLE

The game-changing innovation plot twist in the middle of web2's S-curve was the Apple iPhone – launched in 2007. The iPhone looked like no other phone that had ever come before it. It had a larger screen, clean lines and simple but intuitive functionality building on many of the successful functionalities of the iPod released six years earlier. The iPhone single-handedly

> ❝ THE GAME-CHANGING INNOVATION PLOT TWIST IN THE MIDDLE OF WEB2'S S-CURVE WAS THE APPLE IPHONE. ❞

democratized the internet and elevated UX to a whole new level, mainly through a 'multi-touch display' that was designed to 'work like magic' (see Figure 2.3). Overnight, not only could people get online without having a PC, but they could engage in apps and enjoy functionality that was genuinely beautiful – perhaps not by today's standards, but at the time the iPhone was a

FIGURE 2.3: STEVE JOBS LAUNCHING THE IPHONE IN HIS APPLE KEYNOTE

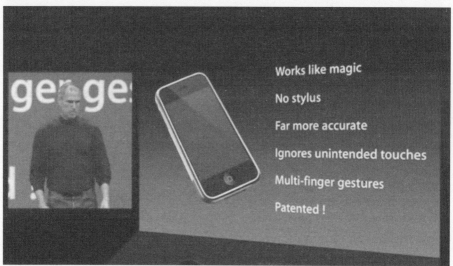

revelation and made all things internet prettier, better and easier to use. It is no coincidence that this innovation also marked the exponential rise of Facebook. People could use Facebook and all the other great web2 products and services via the phone in their pocket rather than having to own their own PC. And of course, this access meant an explosion in use. Waiting for a bus? You could scroll through Facebook or visit Amazon or read the news.

Apple revolutionized accessibility to the internet and so much of the value they have captured comes from the web2 ecosystem, its consumers showing that they want access to web2 in an easy-to-use way from anywhere. With the iPad and evolving versions of the iPhone, Apple made it incredibly simple to get online and use the many products and services that had begun to emerge in web2. There was no complex set-up, no need to host anything, no need for a PC or keyboard, and they didn't even need to be technically savvy – the iPhone connected its users to the internet straight out of the box. It also made the internet mobile, which itself created a flurry of additional innovations, such as Uber and Deliveroo, that used the GPS capability in the iPhone along with other sensors. These services that we all take for granted now would not exist without the iPhone.

Like the other web2 winner, Facebook, Apple is also running into issues around their market-dominant approach to the App Store. A class action lawsuit is forcing them to change the way their billing system works. They are also bumping up against performance oversupply. Most people can't really tell the difference between an iPhone 12 and an iPhone 13. Apple can't really improve the UX any further, certainly not without a revolutionary embedment of AI.

Interestingly, as web2 peaks, both Facebook and Apple and many of the other Big Tech companies are running into similar problems to those that Microsoft ran into at the end of web1. The big question is whether Big Tech will learn from Microsoft's lessons or not.

The Demise of Web2

It is clear that web2 has passed its peak and is at the tail end of its S-curve. We know this because innovation S-curves always overlap, and we have already experienced the start of the web3 S-curve.

Web1 ended in a blaze of glory during the dot-com crash, largely because of access and density. So how will web2 end? The pillars of web2 are UX (Apple), commerce (Amazon), social networks (Meta/Facebook), search (Google) and the cloud (Microsoft, Amazon and Google). These are the largest players in web2.

My prediction therefore is that web2 will end in a battle for cloud supremacy. Microsoft, Amazon and Google are going to buy a lot of businesses in an attempt to maintain their cloud leadership. Again, this is the classic endgame move in the Innovator's Dilemma where the established firms, in this case Amazon, Microsoft and Google, try to defend themselves. It's easy to see why they believe this makes sense: around 90 per cent of all the web2 applications are running on one of these three clouds. Like gladiators in the arena, they will likely make massive, history-making acquisitions of SaaS and app businesses in an effort to fund their cloud dominance.

The problem is that web3 is already disrupting the cloud. As web3 swings back to protocol development it is these distributed protocols that will become the new cloud.

As of early 2022, one of the largest, most powerful cloud computers in the world is Bitcoin. Ethereum (more on both in the next chapter) is probably the second-largest computing network in the world, and that's running 20,000 new applications (2022). Bitcoin, Ethereum and a few others are already the new decentralized cloud. While Bitcoin operates as a specific ledger for financial transactions, Ethereum is a much more generalized smart contract system, operating a little like Amazon Web Services (AWS) does for business cloud computing, but instead of paying dollars to use the network you pay in the native Ethereum currency.

Web3 is therefore going to make the current web2 winners less relevant. And many simply will not survive.

Business benefits of web2 (application era)
- Created the concept of the social graph, which introduced an entirely new way to advertise to consumers based on their interests and intent.
- Cloud computing revolutionized access to many different types of software solutions.
- Made it possible to share resources such as software or cars.
- Made it possible to connect to the internet anytime, anywhere.
- Ubiquitous access to the internet in your pocket thanks to the smartphone.

Summary of Key Points

» Web1 was 80 per cent protocol development with 20 per cent protocol application, whereas web2 was 80 per cent protocol application and 20 per cent protocol development. This is the Protocol–App Inversion and it flips with each era.

» The Protocol–App Inversion is fraught with commercial danger. Some companies that were successful in web1 succeeded in web2 but may struggle in web3 without significant change. Those who are successful in web2 may be better placed to adapt to web3, but it will still require a sizeable mindset shift.

» Web2 is a shared network for reducing time and space inefficiencies in everything from servers to cars to spare bedrooms and local deliveries.

» This sharing capability was made possible by network effects and virtualization.

» Network effects – the phenomenon whereby the more people who participate in or use a network, the more valuable and useful the network becomes – reduced cost in web2, increased efficiency and drastically reduced wasted time, capital and resources.

» And virtualization allowed multiple computer operating systems to execute on the same computer hardware concurrently. This also led to various cloud solutions, including Amazon's AWS.

» It is clear that web2 has passed its peak and is at the tail end of its S-curve. We know this because innovation S-curves always overlap, and we have already experienced the start of the web3 S-curve.

Chapter 3

Web3: Bitcoin Was Just the Start

In many ways, web1 and web2 have been logical progressions, moving the offline world online and making that process user-friendly and seamless through great UX and the sharing of resources. Web3 is something else entirely.

In 2014 Gavin Wood, co-founder of Ethereum, wrote a blog post where he sketched out his view of the new era. Web3, he said, is a 'reimagination of the sorts of things we already use the web for, but with a fundamentally different model for the interactions between parties'. He goes on to suggest that 'information that we assume to be public, we publish. Information that we assume to be agreed, we place on a consensus-ledger. Information that we assume to be private, we keep secret and never reveal.' In this vision, all communication is encrypted, and identities are hidden. 'In short, we engineer the system to mathematically enforce our prior assumptions, since no government or organization can reasonably be trusted.'[1]

> WEB1 AND WEB2 HAVE BEEN LOGICAL PROGRESSIONS, MOVING THE OFFLINE WORLD ONLINE.

If only a fraction of that vision comes to fruition, web3 will bring a seismic value inversion that will rip through society and business like a wildfire in bone-dry scrub. The scrub in this case being conventions that have stood unquestioned for thousands of years. In business that means everything currently associated with it, from the very notion of 'a company', 'shareholders' and what constitutes an 'employee' to every system and process in the business, the creation and distribution of value, exchange and remuneration. Many of these changes are already here.

As mentioned in the Introduction, the architecture, while not perfect, is functional ... right now. The genie is out of the bottle and it's never going back.

And what makes this story so remarkable and so ripe with business opportunity and humanity-improving potential is that the innovation plot twist accelerator of web3 was only just emerging as of the middle of 2022. That means we've not been able to completely define what the HTML or iPhone moment is for web3 yet. Just think about that for a moment. Both of these innovation plot twists resulted in an explosion in use, utility and engagement in web1 and web2 respectively. It's hard to even imagine a world where the internet was just text and files, or a world without the iPhone. And yet that same game-changing innovation plot twist for web3, with its explosive capabilities, has yet to fully reveal itself.

S-Curve Innovation Plot Twists and Explosive Growth

Remember in Chapter 1 we explored the Innovator's Dilemma and S-curves? Although looking at different aspects of innovation, the journey they describe is also mirrored by a theory proposed by US philosopher Ken Wilber. Wilber suggests that the evolution of anything can be traced back to three distinct phenomena: emergence, differentiation and integration. In many ways these phenomena track S-curves and the Innovator's Dilemma. They all speak of the same endlessly repeating pattern (see Figure 3.1).

When web1 emerged, only the techies and early users were interested because it required some knowledge to access, and that access was patchy and slow via a dial-up modem. Access was also actively prevented by the National Science Foundation's Acceptable Fair Use (NSFAFU) policy, which stated that access to the internet had to be restricted to academic and military use for fear that it would be swamped with porn and malware. Thankfully, that policy was repealed in 1992, and the internet as we know it really gathered momentum.

FIGURE 3.1: EMERGENCE – DIFFERENTIATION – INTEGRATION

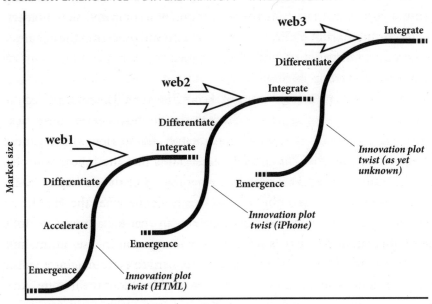

Source: GC Cooke

Of course, they were right about the porn and malware, but the positives of the internet still far outweigh the negatives.

As web1 progressed up the S-curve, it started to differentiate from its main rival at the time, the PC. The Innovator's Dilemma appeared where people really couldn't see why the internet was that interesting. You could do more on the PC and it looked better. The experience was slicker and faster. But then the innovation plot twist accelerator appeared in the shape of HTML. Not only did it help to visualize data online so that what was viewed looked better, but the code was open source and free for anyone to use. Products like Dreamweaver then created simple tools to help non-tech people use the protocols more easily. Every Innovator's Dilemma creates a divergence between the incumbent solution or approach and something new. In this case the innovation plot twist created by HTML triggered the emergence of web2, which started its own journey up its S-curve. All while web1 exploded up the S-curve by integrating more and more capability as a result of that accelerator. As web1 came to an end because there simply wasn't the density to support the business model, web2 took over. But again, linking back to the product lifecycle, at the start of each S-curve it's only the innovators and early adopters that care. At the start of web2, it was only the techies that could see that the internet wasn't finished.

As web2 moved up its S-curve it too started to differentiate. What were the specific characteristics and traits of web2? How could they be teased out and improved? How could we use the protocols of web1, solve the density problem and make the user experience better? The answer, although not the only answer, was the iPhone. As an innovation plot twist accelerator, the iPhone genuinely changed everything. Before the iPhone, if we wanted to get online, we needed to be at a PC, tethered to a phone line. The iPhone put the internet in our pocket and made it insanely easy to connect to, while elevating the user experience by a few light years. The thought that went into making the iPhone work so well was astounding. Even though we had 3G and fast internet on phones years before the iPhone, it was intended to be used for video calling – which never really took off at that time. Steve Jobs, on the other hand, was obsessed with controlling how the phone networks could deliver useful internet to these devices via a large screen, data plans and fast connection. This combination meant that not only internet use but the internet itself grew rapidly. The innovation plot twist of the 'connected touchscreen' led to app stores and an entirely new version of the internet we still use today. And again, this innovation plot twist created a divergence where web2 itself accelerated up the S-curve *and* at the same time the capability created by the iPhone forked into the emergence of web3. Once again, at the start of web3, it was only the innovators and early adopters who cared. The techies and early adopters in crypto forums were the only ones paying attention.

As of 2022, we are probably already in the middle of web3's Innovator's Dilemma. The part of web3 that most people grasp is Bitcoin, which we will explore in a moment. But even with Bitcoin, never mind the hundreds of other cryptocurrencies, there are plenty of people who just don't get the difference. 'But I have constant access to my money via my bank's online app. I can move money 24/7 – why is that different to the capabilities of crypto?'

This is an easy mistake to make and is the primary challenge of the Innovator's Dilemma. The capabilities of the new thing are not sufficiently differentiated in the mind of the market, certainly the early and late majority market, for them to fully grasp the difference and how that difference is going to impact them. Remember that when HTML emerged, there were plenty of people who didn't get it. Sure, it made things online look nicer, but it still wasn't as nice as a printed brochure. Or when the iPhone came out? There were plenty of people who didn't see the point of being able to access the internet and were more than happy to stick with their Nokia. It just seemed like a crazy idea, which is always a characteristic of the Innovator's Dilemma. It is the innovation plot twists that occur inside the Innovator's Dilemma that create explosive growth. And we are still waiting for confirmation of the innovation plot twist in web3.

This is both terrifying and exciting news. It's terrifying because we are already experiencing massive change and disruption, so what will the innovation plot twist accelerator do? And it's exciting because it still gives businesses time to prepare. Just as forward-thinking companies in the Industrial Revolution recruited people into Head of Electricity roles before electricity was rolled out, and companies recruited Heads of Mobile as the smartphone exploded, forward-looking business leaders have probably already recruited their Head of Web3. Business leaders need web3 expertise in their business before that innovation plot twist occurs and web3 accelerates rapidly up its S-curve while triggering the emergence of web4. If we leave it too late, there will be too much ground to cover, making it impossible to catch up, and irrelevance becomes inevitable.

Remember, web3 flips back from protocol application to protocol development again, and web3 protocols are already transforming business processes and foundations. This means that web3 protocols are going to be ten to a hundred times more disruptive than anything that's come before, including HTML, cloud computing or smartphones.

The Emergence of Web3

On 31 October 2008, Satoshi Nakamoto (a pseudonym) published a nine-page white paper titled, 'Bitcoin: A Peer-to-Peer Electronic Cash System'. The abstract of the paper, published to a cryptography mailing list, read:

A purely peer-to-peer version of electronic cash would allow online payments to be sent directly from one party to another without going through a financial institution. Digital signatures provide part of the solution, but the main benefits are lost if a trusted third party is still required to prevent double-spending. We propose a solution to the double-spending problem using a peer-to-peer network. The network timestamps transactions by hashing them into an ongoing chain of hash-based proof-of-work, forming a record that cannot be changed without redoing the proof-of-work.

What Nakamoto was doing was classic Stage 4 of the Innovator's Dilemma: new entrants introduce the disruptive technology to small 'fringe' markets. Cryptocurrency was very much a fringe market at the time. Only Nakamoto wasn't introducing a disruptive technology like a smaller hard drive or even an iPhone – he/she/they were disrupting a global monetary system that had stood for thousands of years. (Nakamoto's identity is still a mystery, so for ease of reading we will refer to 'they'.)

Allegedly Nakamoto had read *The Sovereign Individual: Mastering the Transition to the Information Age*, although this is almost certainly a guess because no one knows who Nakamoto is. In 1997 this book forecast, among other things, that a new technology of money would decentralize and disintermediate the structure of society. The authors, James Dale Davidson and William Rees-Mogg, argued, 'The Information Age implies another revolution in the character of money ... This new form of money will reset the odds, reducing the capacity of the world's nation-states to determine who becomes a Sovereign Individual.'[2]

This 'cybercash' should be 'unique, anonymous and verifiable' and able to 'accommodate the largest transactions' as well as 'be divisible into the tiniest fraction of value'. It would 'be tradable at a keystroke in a multi-trillion-dollar wholesale market without borders'.[3]

That idea was progressed from a hope or premonition to a technical possibility over a decade later by the 2008 white paper.

It is also important to bear in mind the backdrop to this emergence. First, although billions of people were now connected to the internet, cheap access to the world's knowledge had not been the 'magical, meritocratic elixir some expected'.[4] It had not led to the decentralization and disintermediation that was once prophesied. In fact, the opposite was more accurate. There was growing inequality and a deep division between the haves and the have-nots, a division that was brought into sharp and painful focus by the global financial crisis. Just as there is a backlash against Big Tech as their commercial tactics have been exposed, in 2008 there was a severe backlash against banking as *their* commercial tactics were exposed.

By some estimates as few as 50 individuals caused the global financial crisis (GFC) through a combination of greed and hubris.[5] The world's financial system was on its knees, millions of people were made redundant, and banks were being bailed out by governments despite years of obscene bonuses. Apart from the financial devastation felt by millions around the world, there was disbelief that trusted institutions like banks, many of whom had been around for centuries, could be so corrupt. It was clear to everyone paying even the slightest glimmer of attention that the system was rigged.

What if we could create monetary policy as an algorithm with scarcity built in? In other words, what if we didn't need to rely as heavily on a banking system that could create the conditions for a GFC? A few people thought that was an interesting idea and ignited open-source innovation again. Nakamoto wrote maybe 16,000 lines of code to create an entirely new financial system,[6] and announced that they were launching it on their computer, making it the first Bitcoin node. Nakamoto didn't say, 'OK, we're going to keep 20 per cent of Bitcoin and you keep 80 per cent.' They just started mining Bitcoin first.

> "NAKAMOTO WROTE MAYBE 16,000 LINES OF CODE TO CREATE AN ENTIRELY NEW FINANCIAL SYSTEM."

Mining Bitcoin

Although the term conjures up images of coal miners emerging from a tiny lift after a hard day underground, Bitcoin miners don't even get their hands dirty. They simply attach a device like the one shown in Figure 3.2 to their network. This device, and the more advanced ones developed later, use network software to solve increasingly difficult math problems, and issue a certain number of Bitcoin to the miner in exchange. There will only ever be 21 million Bitcoin mined, although each Bitcoin is divisible by 100 million, so that's 21 million multiplied by 100 million satoshis (a satoshi is to Bitcoin what pence is to the pound or cents are to the dollar). That 21

FIGURE 3.2: BITCOIN MINER

million Bitcoin, however, has to be created – and it is the miners who create it. Rather than a central bank printing money, people are incentivized to mine Bitcoin instead. And the miners have to approve the transaction, which makes the entire network more secure.

As more miners have jumped into the network, increasing the total processing power, the Bitcoin algorithm makes the math problem harder (by increasing the 'difficulty'), ensuring that the blocks are processed approximately every ten minutes. Bitcoin's inflation decreases every four years; the number of Bitcoin received has reduced over time in what is known as 'The Halving'. Initially miners received a thousand Bitcoin every ten minutes. At the beginning of 2022, it was 6.25 Bitcoin every ten minutes.

The first ever Bitcoin was mined in January 2009 by Nakamoto. Embedded in the genesis block of the Bitcoin blockchain is the text: 'The Times Jan/03/2009 Chancellor on brink of second bailout for banks'. Not only does this timestamp the genesis block of Bitcoin by making reference to an article in *The Times*, but it is also widely recognized as a deliberate swipe at the instability of the global financial system that the white paper hoped to disrupt. Billions of people the world over were disgusted at what had happened following the global financial crisis, and this reference is seen as a digital battle cry for something new that didn't need to rely on trust at all – Bitcoin.[7]

Blockchain

Bitcoin was the first example of a new element in our current techno-economic paradigm – blockchains. A blockchain is just a chain of blocks that contain information. Originally described by researchers in 1991 as a way to digitally timestamp information so that it could not be backdated or altered, it was resurrected by Nakamoto as a way of creating a distributed ledger that uses cryptographic protocols to allow for trust-minimized transactions between pseudonymous parties – that couldn't be hacked, stolen or changed.[8] Once the information is inside the block and connected to the block chain it's nearly impossible to change that information – the goal is to be immutable.

Along with their associated technologies, they allow for what computer scientist and cryptographer Nick Szabo has called social scalability: high levels of coordination with low levels of centralization.[9]

Each block is made up of three things: data, the hash of the block and the hash of the previous block. Hash being a unique digital identifier through the core Bitcoin SHA256 algorithm. Once the data is added to the block the hash is created, so it's very simple mathematically to detect attempted changes to the block because the hash will change. The data that is stored will depend on the blockchain. For Bitcoin, the data contains the details of a Bitcoin transaction. But other blockchains can store other types of information.

The hash of the previous block is what created the chain and makes the blockchain so secure. If someone tries to hack or tamper with one block it will change the hash, which will no longer then link to the subsequent block.

Proof-of-work (PoW), a mechanism for cryptographically validating transactions using significant amount of computing power adds another level of security by slowing down the time it takes to create a new block. For Bitcoin it takes ten minutes to calculate the required proof-of-work and add a new block to the chain. This makes it very hard to tamper with the block because if you tamper with one block, you will need to recalculate all proof-of-work for all the subsequent blocks.

But the security doesn't stop there. Instead of having the blocks on one machine, which is open to a single point of attack, the Bitcoin blockchain is distributed through an ecosystem of distributed ledgers. When someone joins the ecosystem (and anyone can because Bitcoin is open source) they get a full copy of the blockchain, and that node then verifies the full blockchain. When a new block is created, it is added to every node on the network simultaneously, and each node verifies the block to ensure it hasn't been tampered with.[10] All this is done via a mathematical algorithm, without the oversight of a human being. If the block checks out, it is added to the blockchain. If not, it is rejected. To successfully tamper with any blocks someone would therefore have to tamper with all the blocks on the chain, which is computationally impossible.

In web3 the abstract idea of interpersonal trust is replaced by concrete mathematical computations, algorithms and networks, which reduce the reliance of trust only in governments and businesses.

Going back to the GFC, many people believed, or at least hoped, that the GFC would be the start of something new, something better, that a system clearly no longer fit for purpose would be recast in a new form. And yet that never happened.

The wallet

Bitcoin invented the cryptocurrency wallet. And the concept around the wallet and how transactions occur is so brilliant that every other blockchain that's been developed since Bitcoin uses the principle of a wallet and public and private keys.

Really simply, the Bitcoin miners are the ones processing the transactions. They run and verify the ledger on the blockchain. Wallet to wallet is how Bitcoin is transferred. The public key is the address where the Bitcoin is transferred to. The private key is the signature of the current owner to prove the transfer.

Clearly, leaving human beings to reform the banking system and restore trust has not worked. This is not very surprising considering that there are around 23 lobbyists in the US for every member of congress.[11] These lobbyists are paid large sums of money to influence lawmakers not to impact respective industries in ways that would limit their ability to create profit. Expecting change from these individuals is a little like expecting turkeys to vote for Christmas. It will never happen. This type of 'dark money'[12] is not restricted to the US; it also happens in the UK and beyond. It will also never work because human beings are human beings.

This quandary is explained by the 'Byzantine Generals Problem'. Generals are besieging Byzantium and have surrounded the city, but they must collectively decide when to attack. If all the generals attack at the same time, they will win. But if they don't, they will lose. They have no secure method of communication because messages could be intercepted, so how do the generals organize to ensure they all attack at the same time?

> ONE OF THE MANTRAS OF WEB3 IS: 'DON'T TRUST. VERIFY!'

This is a game theory problem, which essentially describes the difficulty decentralized parties have in arriving at a consensus without relying on a trusted central party. In a network where no member can verify the identity of other members, how can members collectively agree on a certain truth?

Bitcoin solved this problem while removing the need for trust. One of the mantras of web3 is: 'Don't Trust. Verify!' Bitcoin doesn't trust; it verifies – thus removing the need for trust in the first place.

There are several things that make the emergence of Bitcoin so remarkable, and it is these characteristics that have spawned a never-ending array of potential capabilities. It is the integration of the very best of web1 combined with the peer-to-peer sharing of web2, with some extra innovations thrown in for good measure. Bitcoin is:

1. **Open source**. The Bitcoin source code is open source, which means it is published and available to everyone. Any programmer can read it. The Bitcoin software can't have a secret command or extra line of code that quietly sends all the Bitcoin to one person because that command would be seen by all the other reviewers and programmers, which would stop the verification of the Bitcoin.

2. **Operated on a peer-to-peer network**. Peer-to-peer first emerged with web1 file-sharing protocols but floundered in web2 as people did not want to host their own servers, and so everything centralized to the cloud. Using peer-to-peer means that Bitcoin creates Bitcoin incentives for serving the network and does not require trust in any centralized server for relaying information.

3. **Using cryptography**. Cryptographic proof is used to enforce the idea of possession in Bitcoin; only someone with knowledge of the private key (along with the public key) can spend their Bitcoin. Other cryptography is used in other ways – for example, proof-of-work.

4. **Decentralized**. It divides power widely across many people, so no single entity can reverse transactions or otherwise change the rules to suit themselves. No one can rig the system behind closed doors.

5. **Constantly verifying the rules**. Anyone can run the Bitcoin 'full node wallet' software, which verifies all the rules of Bitcoin. The user doesn't need to trust anybody else. For example, if somebody creates a Bitcoin transaction awarding 100,000 Bitcoin to themselves, the software will reject it as invalid in the same way a diamond trader would reject a cubic zirconia, only the rejection is done algorithmically and not by a human being.

Just 16 short months after the first Bitcoin was mined, it was used for the first time to make a purchase, of sorts. In May 2010, Jeremy Sturdivant, a 19-year-old student, noticed an offer by Laszlo Hanyecz to pay 10,000 Bitcoin to anyone who would bring him two large pizzas. Sturdivant fulfilled the order from Papa John's. Sadly, for Sturdivant, he went on to spend the Bitcoin, which would be worth hundreds of millions today.[13]

Effectively, Bitcoin started the web3 movement because it created the Bitcoin protocol, including the blockchain, which has far-reaching applications beyond a new global monetary system. The possibilities are endless, and we will explore those shortly. But web3 nearly didn't make it. What ended web1 was a lack of density. There were simply too many businesses jumping into the online world when the numbers of customers online didn't support that explosion. The winners of web2 learned that lesson and made sure that when they sought to apply the protocols developed in web1 they focused on density, and they grew their offering accordingly. By the time web3 was beginning its journey up its own S-curve, those density lessons were once again forgotten in the excitement over the protocol development and those endless possibilities. The result was the initial coin offering (ICO) bubble of 2017.

In mid-2017 a start-up called Tezos announced that it would create 'a new decentralized blockchain that governs itself by establishing a true digital commonwealth'. It raised $232 million (£178 million) for this endeavor via an emerging web3 funding model called a token sale. Also known as an 'initial coin offering' (ICO) as a play on the more traditional initial public offering (IPO), token sales were the new Wild West – the idea being that any company could create their own token or coin that could be exchanged for investment without the loss of equity.

The central concept was the creation of 'utility tokens', where a company issued tokens for participants to use in the network in the future. The utility token has a market value because it is transferable and therefore could be listed on an exchange with real-time demand and supply pricing set. Many ICOs issued tokens for their networks in exchange for Bitcoin or Ethereum so they could then use that to pay developers, marketing or other suppliers to build the networks. The principle works a little like a coffee shop that wants to open in your street, and they invite you to invest in their shop in exchange for tokens for coffee. You may invest $1,000 and get 300 coffee tokens to use in the coffee shop in the future. But what ended up happening in the ICO boom was that your 300 coffee tokens ended up being worth $10,000, so instead of keeping the tokens for coffees you sold them for Bitcoin or cash. The end of this crash meant that your 300 coffees were worth $50 in some cases. Most of these networks were built on issuing Ethereum-based tokens, which meant that it was instantly compatible with a lot of the existing ecosystem, such as exchanges. You also didn't need to sign paperwork or get lawyers involved because the contract was signed in the token transfer. This capability, known as smart contracts, is one of the core foundations of web3.

At their peak, ICOs were raising billions at lightning speed. Status.im, a browsing/messaging app, raised $100 million in under three hours. Brave, a browser start-up launched by former Mozilla CEO Brendan Eich, raised $35 million in under 30 seconds.[14] But again, there was insufficient density or people interested in the market to sustain many of the offerings over time. The ICO bubble popped in 2018 when the market cap of all cryptocurrencies fell by $700 billion, an 85 per cent drop from its peak.[15]

There simply wasn't enough usage in these networks to warrant the value of the tokens issued by all the ICOs. This meant that the tokens were not performing their intended utility, such as buying coffees, and instead became almost purely about speculation. Needless to say, web3 took a hit just like web1 did because of a lack of density and wild speculation. Luckily for web3, the hit was nowhere near as financially painful as the dot-com crash, but it did lead to another crypto-winter.

Bitcoin crosses the chasm

There are certainly signs that Bitcoin has crossed the chasm. J. P. Morgan and Goldman Sachs have both adopted bitcoin related services despite being vocally against it for many years. In September 2021, El Salvador made history by becoming the first country in the world to make Bitcoin an official currency alongside the US dollar. There is bound to have been some handwringing since, as the price has dropped. But even at its weakest, Bitcoin still has the equivalent market cap of a top-20 global company, so they probably don't need to worry too much.

The El Salvador Government also launched a dedicated mobile wallet that a majority of their citizens use or invest in their own Bitcoin reserve.[16] A year later El Salvador hosted a developing nation's central banking conference where they discussed Bitcoin as a treasury system.[17] This is particularly relevant because, while it would be easy to dismiss the actions of El Salvador as ill-advised or ill-informed, their actions speak to a perceived opportunity, shared by many smaller nation states, not to be so reliant on dominant global currencies and monetary policies. If small countries get this right, then large, less agile countries may be stuck with their broken central banking and antiquated welfare systems. There is still a long way to go for El Salvador and they were the first country to adopt this approach, but it is certainly indicative of a wider, global acceptance of Bitcoin. Only time will tell whether it was a good decision or not.

The trajectory of Bitcoin has been astonishing. In just 13 years Bitcoin went from an idea expressed in a nine-page white paper to being recognized alongside the US dollar in El Salvador.

There is little doubt that Bitcoin has crossed the chasm that Geoffrey Moore talked about in relation to the product lifecycle (see Figure 1.4).

A product or service, even a really brilliant one, is never adopted by consumers in a linear way. Not only were there different groups of people attracted to the product or service at different times for different reasons, but there was always a chasm between the early adopters and what could be considered the 'mass market'. There will always be psychological differences between the innovators and the early adopters and the rest of the market. The innovators are the people who will stand outside in the rain for ten hours to get the latest iPhone. They see themselves as risk-takers and pioneers, and they just want to be there at the start. They love being first. The early adopters are not quite as forgiving; they want more functionality and for at least some of the beta glitches to be ironed out. But both these markets are very different to the mainstream market of the early and late majority. A product or idea is only really successful when it crosses the chasm and captures the interest of that majority market. Bitcoin has crossed that chasm.

In 2021 Bitcoin went mainstream for people who don't care about being first. Those people want proven functionality. Bitcoin has done that because it adheres to a set of principles. And all changes and upgrades to the Bitcoin protocol will strive to maintain and reinforce these principles:

1. **Scarcity:** Only 21 million Bitcoin will ever be mined or created. All coins are equal and should be equally spendable.
2. **Trustless:** Irreversible transactions confirmed blocks should be set in stone. Blockchain history should be immutable.
3. **Open:** Bitcoin open-source code should always be open for anyone to read, modify, copy or share. No ID should be required to own or use Bitcoin – pseudonymous.
4. **Permissionless:** No arbitrary gatekeepers should ever prevent anybody from being part of the network (user, node, miner, etc.). Nobody should be able to prevent valid transactions from being confirmed.

•

At this point you might be asking yourself, 'OK, that was all very interesting, but what has Bitcoin got to do with my business?' The answer, regardless of what business you are in, is: everything.

What Bitcoin did was create a protocol that has far-reaching applications and uses that to go way beyond cryptocurrency. It demonstrated use, and that use will create even more protocols that will use parts of the Bitcoin protocol but apply them to different problems.

For example, blockchain capability has already been adopted where the blocks of information contain more than just crypto transaction records. The rigidity of the Bitcoin blockchain is simultaneously its greatest strength and its greatest weakness. It is a strength because this rigidity and sole cryptocurrency purpose makes it very secure, but this rigidity also limits alternate uses. Mining Bitcoin is also energy hungry, due to the computational complexity. As a result, it didn't take long for engineers to apply and adapt the Bitcoin protocol to a new protocol that offered more flexibility and more energy efficiency. That platform was Ethereum.

What is Ethereum?

Gavin Wood, one of its co-founders, described Ethereum as 'one computer for the entire planet', with computing power distributed across the globe and controlled nowhere.[18]

Ethereum builds on Bitcoin's innovation, with some big differences. Both let you use digital money without payment providers or banks. In Ethereum's case, that currency is ether (ETH). But Ethereum is the world's first programmable blockchain, so you can also use it for lots of different digital assets, including Bitcoin. As such, it already boasts around 20,000 applications that anyone can use and no one can take down.

This also means Ethereum is for more than just payment-related applications. It's a much broader smart contract system for financial services, games and apps, with greater versatility, which can't steal your data or censor you.

Bitcoin is still a smart contract, but it is incredibly rigid. This rigidity relates to the underlying principle of block space scarcity. Bitcoin is the scarcest block space. Ethereum is probably the second. And then you get newer blockchains such as Solana, Fantom, NEAR or Polkadot, which are a lot less scarce. The greater the flexibility, the lower the cost of creation and, in theory, the higher the risk. This is why Bitcoin is so secure; it has low flexibility, high cost to mine and low risk. But not everything needs the security of a currency, and that's where these different blockchain solutions can trade off security with versatility and a less decentralized set of nodes that end up running the network. There are real benefits to assessing these sorts of trade-offs, and this is common in any technology decision. When it comes to enterprise software, when I've met customers who want the 'everything platform', I always relate this to, 'Oh, you want the digger truck that can drive as fast as a Ferrari?' In truth, no one needs a high-speed digger truck, and a closer look at needs over want will usually illuminate that. The same is true for blockchains.

To fully grasp just how much web3 is going to disrupt business-as-usual, we have to look beyond the technology to what it enables or makes possible, often for the first time. Web3:

1. Removes the need to *only* rely on trusted entities.
2. Facilitates verifiable, secure digital ownership.
3. Creates community through open and permissionless incentives to participate.

REMOVES THE NEED TO ONLY RELY ON TRUSTED ENTITIES

Since human beings first started making and recording transactions in various ledgers, whether the Incas or the Babylonians, the accuracy and legitimacy of the recorded information came down to the integrity and trust of the record keeper.

There was always a human being doing the data entry. As such, our need to trust that human being was baked into the system at a local level (see Figure 3.3). Over time, institutional trust emerged when entities such as banks, government departments, lawyers or trusted third parties gave us more assurance of the accuracy, certainty and trustworthiness of those transactions or agreements. The high-profile web3 collapses I mentioned in the Prologue may have been web3 centric, but they were still relying on institutional trust and were not therefore true web3. Web3 moves to distributed trust. Right now, we spend enormous amounts of time and money regulating these institutional trust management systems, and still mistakes are made. Web3 codes the trust into a smart contract on the blockchain that can't be tampered with or negotiated with after the fact.

Almost every system we interact with is a trust management system.

FIGURE 3.3: EVOLUTION OF TRUST

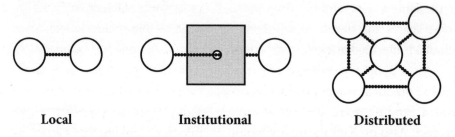

| Local | Institutional | Distributed |

Source: Who can you Trust? by Rachel Botsman

We are still very much in a world of institutional trust. Human beings are still making judgements inside those trust management systems. And, as we saw during the aftermath of the global financial crisis, those human beings are still susceptible to manipulation, greed, hubris and outright corruption.

Human beings are human beings. Even with the best will in the world, if the chips are down or they are presented with an opportunity for personal advancement, most people will take it, even at the expense of the collective good. This is why there has been no meaningful banking reform. And why many experts believe that a new crash is now inevitable.

For the first time in human history, the Bitcoin protocol removes the need to trust a human being at any point in the cryptocurrency system. The trust management system of Bitcoin is done entirely by the protocol. The information is stored in the blockchain, and peer-to-peer networks make it impossible to tamper with the information in the blockchain. Even when human beings try to rig the system – which they have been doing for centuries – they can't.

The Bitcoin protocol nullifies one aspect of human nature, the need for trust, while tapping into cooperative competition – an entirely new phenomenon. Participants in the Bitcoin network are still incentivized – they can still make money – but they will always make more money if they cooperate in the network, rather than trying to corrupt the network.

One of the most recent protocol developments based on the principles of the Bitcoin protocol is the creation of smart contracts. Although a smart contract acts like a legally drawn-up paper contract, it is purely digital and is actually a tiny computer program that is stored in the blockchain. This means that anything can be agreed in a smart contract without the need for trusted third parties or middlemen. You 'sign' the transaction with your crypto-wallet, in the same way as sending currency. And it's incredibly efficient. Say you own some shares and decide to sell them, on average, selling that asset involved about 11 intermediaries. A smart contract is enacted in one transaction.

Most people have heard of Kickstarter, for example. It is a large fund-raising platform where product teams can visit the website, create a project and a funding goal, and see if anyone is interested in supporting that project. Also on Kickstarter are would-be investors looking for interesting projects to invest in. Those who then believe in the idea contribute to the project's financial target. If the target is reached, then both parties have to trust the middleman – in this case Kickstarter – to do the right thing and send the monies on to the project. If the target is not reached, then they need be trusted to send the money back to the investor. But smart contracts could easily replace Kickstarter by programming the smart contract to hold all the received funds until a certain goal is reached. If the goal is reached, the money is automatically passed to the project team; if not, it is automatically refunded to the supporters. No need to sit on a customer service call to Kickstarter or fire off a terse email. The algorithm carries out the pre-agreed actions automatically. Plus, those instructions are stored in the blockchain so they can't be tampered with – they are immutable and distributed, adding even more security to an already very secure system. No one can force the contract to release the funds because every node on the network will flag this and reject it as unverified.[19]

It may be that many of the elements of the smart contract are the innovation plot twist of web3, but it's probably too early to tell for sure. What we do know for sure is that smart contracts will securely connect end users with creators or participants and obliterate the need for trusted third parties, middlemen or central entities. They will remove the need for one human being to trust another at every point in the process.

Please understand, this is not to say that trust isn't a useful concept and something we should all still strive for in our lives. It is still human to trust our family and our friendships – all examples of local trust systems. We still need local trust in order to maintain close connections and functional relationships. But in business and society, history has shown us time and time again that if you mix human nature with opportunities for self-interest, trust is often the casualty. And the institution trust systems we have adopted as a solution have repeatedly failed. If we look back through the rise and fall of various empires from the Ottoman to the Roman to the British, they fell largely because of the breakdown of institutional trust between the ruling elite and the people who were meant to trust them. Web3 simply evolves trust away from institutional trust (which is a burden to efficiency and cost and often just doesn't work) to independently, algorithmically verified distributed trust.

What this means for all business leaders ...

» If your business 'moat' is dependent on heavy forms of regulation to keep competition out, then you are in trouble. Like a castle uses a moat to protect its walls, a business moat protects the business from its competition and makes it hard for new entrants.

» If your business is currently viewed as a trusted third party, you are in trouble.

» If part of your USP or competitive advantage is built around trust, you are likely to end up severely competing with much more objective web3 smart contracts.

FACILITATES VERIFIABLE, SECURE DIGITAL OWNERSHIP

This capability is clearly connected to the first capability. In truth, they are all connected (see Figure 3.4).

Right now, ownership is regulated by the rule of law in each jurisdiction. Not only will smart contracts remove the need for trust in the human beings involved in various transactions and ownership, but they will also remove the need for the industry that created those contracts and manages the disputes that arise when people disagree on ownership.

FIGURE 3.4: THREE CHARACTERISTICS OF WEB3

Source: GC Cooke

With smart contracts those disagreements will be impossible. The agreed outcomes of the contract will be followed through on, based on the algorithm. There is no room to determine whether you will follow through on the agreement because it's coded and signed by both parties.

Smart contracts demonstrate that it's possible to agree on something and for it to be delivered, and the Bitcoin protocol showed us that it was possible to own something that is indisputable, immutable and tamperproof.

Up until now, governments and organizations have held information about us as citizens or customers in-house because it's not really been possible for us to hold that information ourselves – or considered wise. (For example, it is still very hard to get your own medical records.) There was no other way. Organizations would create a record and store information about us on that record and they then discovered they could use that information to sell us more products.

Part of the backlash against web2 is the idea of 'surveillance capitalism' – an economic system centered around the commodification of personal data with the core purpose of profit-making.[20] People are sick of being the product and there is a growing call for data sovereignty.

The Bitcoin protocol demonstrated that data sovereignty is possible. The use of private and public keys already means that it is possible for us to store our own data about ourselves and only provide access to that data via a public key to those we want to have it. Perhaps we will choose whether to sell the right to access some or all of that data in the future.

What this means for all business leaders ...
»   If your business is currently profiting from personal data, you are in trouble.
»   If your business is currently involved in the mitigation of disputes over ownership and transactions, you are in trouble.
»   If your business is seeking to hold onto and protect your databases and keep them centralized, you're focused on the wrong direction, and you are in trouble.

CREATES COMMUNITY THROUGH OPEN AND PERMISSIONLESS INCENTIVES TO PARTICIPATE

At the moment, the people who benefit most from business are the shareholders. They invest money, sit back and enjoy the spoils. The next group of beneficiaries are the employees, but their benefit has often been eroded with the rise in prominence of shareholder maximization. There may now be talk of stakeholder capitalism, but web3 calls time on even that more progressive idea.

The problem with stakeholder capitalism is that it still relies on trust. A company is having a bumper year, so they embrace purpose, limit their carbon footprint and bump wages up to the living wage or beyond. But if that business then runs into problems, costs, including wages, are clawed back. The fiduciary duty is to the shareholders, especially in public companies, and all the rest just gets 'Greenwashed' out of existence. The current system therefore relies on the executive team doing what they said they would do.

The Bitcoin protocol and the countless protocols that have followed will upend that system completely. It will no longer be enough just to invest money into a company as a shareholder, sit back and watch the return flow back. Instead, more of the spoils and rewards will flow to the supplier talent, including operational talent as well as those who are participating in the network.

Covid has already kickstarted our move to new ways of working, and the world of work will never fully go back to the way it was before Covid. Not only have people realized that they can be very productive without the soul-sapping need for a busy commute, but people – your employees – have also decided that they don't want to go back to the way life was, and don't financially need to. One of the biggest lessons of Covid was that it made us, as a species, less materialistic. Millions of people have already left their jobs in what has been dubbed 'the Great Resignation'.

A Microsoft survey of more than 30,000 global workers showed that 41 per cent of workers were considering quitting or changing professions this year. A separate study in the UK and Ireland showed 38 per cent of those surveyed planned to quit in the next six months to a year. In the US alone, April 2021 saw more than four million people quit their jobs: the biggest spike on record, according to the Department of Labor.[21] Obviously, people leave work for different reasons, but a common theme is that those who are moving on are seeking new ways of living and working, and that is unlikely to spring back to pre-Covid reality.

As American physician, poet and polymath Oliver Wendell Holmes once said, 'A mind that is stretched by a new experience can never go back to its old dimensions.'

It's worth noting, however, that the shifts in employment of the Great Resignation have largely been spurred on because of a desire for more flexible working arrangements versus the onsite nine to five. This redistribution of labor is going to look like an HR blip compared to what's coming as a result of web3. Would-be employees already have a growing array of web2 money making options available to them that simply didn't exist even five years ago. Think TikTok influencers and vloggers. Never mind the explosion of additional opportunities that are emerging in web3 which will increase even more with easier access in web4. If the choice is minimum wage on a zero hour contract with no breaks or benefits versus figuring out a few web3 capabilities that bring in more money without the commute or the stress, then the gig economy and any business that has viewed people as replaceable widgets might in be in trouble.[22]

And this shift is across the board. When your high-potentials and fought-for 'talent' work out that they can come

> **" BUSINESS IS GOING TO FACE A MASS EXODUS OF TALENT. "**

together in small groups and work with other small teams to create value, while also being better incentivized than they are as an employee, business is going to face a mass exodus of talent. When ordinary workers realize that they can participate in these web3 networks and make money in ways that were not even possible ten years ago, then where is business going to get its staff?

Web3 offers everyone except, ironically, shareholders real financial options. The rewards in web3 will go to the creators, the talent and the participants. For the first time, ordinary people will be rewarded for participation rather than endlessly ignored, squeezed or downsized.

What this means for all business leaders ...
»   If you currently have problems attracting and keeping staff, you are
     in trouble.

» If you rely on your high potentials and talent to run your business, you are in trouble.
» If you still think bonuses will solve your problems, you are in trouble.

At the heart of web3 are decentralized information systems: Bitcoin as a monetary system, and Ethereum for everything else. But even more protocols will emerge.

Web3 has the game-changing capabilities of the shipping container and will revolutionize every process in your business, from whether it even stays as a business all the way to how you buy things and pay for input.

It will allow you to take any contractual process in your business product or service supply chain and put it into an automated decentralized system – everything from funding to payments to salaries to teams working together. It's what cloud computing did for business, but it's going to go much further into how people cooperate to create products and services. It's going to change the way people come together and work on projects. It will allow us to cooperate and work in a completely new way. Traditionally, we as employees, shareholders or customers have interacted with companies, but the construct of a company is now being disrupted. Bitcoin is not a company. There are no shareholders, employees, a board of directors or a CEO. We don't even know the true identity of the person or group of people who created it!

And yet the Bitcoin protocol is just the beginning.

When the Internet Protocol of web1 was invented, most people didn't know about it and, of those who did, most didn't really care. And yet today you probably don't spend a single waking hour in the day without interacting with Internet Protocol in some way. It doesn't matter whether you understand it or not; almost everything you do during the day relies on that protocol: the video calls you make, the emails you send, the Uber you get home, the takeout you get delivered and the Netflix show you watch in the evening. It was all built on Internet Protocol. Bitcoin works on the Internet Protocol, and yet what will be built as a result of the Bitcoin Protocol is as yet unknown. As with the Internet Protocol, you won't need to understand it, but chances are, in time, you will use it every day. It's hard to even imagine what we will be taking for granted in a few short years because of what the Bitcoin Protocol made possible and because of all the other protocols that are built on top.

Business benefits of web3 (protocol era again)
- Removes the need to *only* rely on trusted entities.
- Facilitates verifiable, secure digital ownership.
- Creates community through open and permissionless incentives to participate. These communities will be central to web3 and beyond.

Summary of Key Points

» Web3 will bring a seismic value inversion that will massively disrupt the status quo leaders of today. That means everything from the very notion of 'a company', 'shareholders' and what constitutes an 'employee' to every system and process in the business, the creation and distribution of value, exchange and remuneration. Many of these changes are already here.

» And what makes this story so remarkable is that the innovation plot twist accelerator of web3 was still unconfirmed in mid-2022. This gives business time to prepare.

» Web3 first emerged, if only as a cryptocurrency concept, on 31 October 2008, when Satoshi Nakamoto published a nine-page white paper entitled, 'Bitcoin: A Peer-to-Peer Electronic Cash System'. Nakamoto later created an entirely new financial system.

» In just 13 years Bitcoin went from an idea in a white paper to being recognized alongside the US dollar in a developing country.

» In web3, the abstract idea of interpersonal trust is replaced by concrete mathematical computations, algorithms and networks that reduce the reliance of trust only in governments and businesses. One of the mantras of web3 is 'Don't Trust. Verify!'

» What Bitcoin did was create a protocol that has far-reaching web3 applications and uses that to go way beyond cryptocurrency. These game-changing capabilities will revolutionize every process in your business.

PART 2
THE FUTURE IS HERE

Chapter 4

The Evolution of Business-as-Usual

The author William Gibson was right: 'The future's here already. It's just unevenly distributed.'

Using mainly Messari, a leading provider in crypto market intelligence, and Crunchbase, a leading destination for company insights for private and public companies (2022), I've taken a number of the largest crypto projects based on market capitalization to illustrate this fact. It's worth noting again that some of these projects may not cross the chasm into mainstream use, but the capability they point to almost certainly will, perhaps in another form or a different vehicle or platform.

But before we take a closer look at the future that is already here and how web3 is disrupting business-as-usual, it's worth anchoring the disruption we face in some comforting historical context, while also unpacking the building blocks of business that are about to change.

Cooperation and competition have always been different sides of the same 'human' coin. Human beings are primarily social animals, and it is our ability to cooperate that has been the key to our survival and prosperity as a species. But that cooperation has always had limits. Dunbar's number, named after anthropologist Robin Dunbar, suggests that 150 is the maximum number of people with whom any individual is able to sustain a stable or meaningful social relationship. Beyond 150, cooperation is only possible through some shared story such as religion or nationality.

Business is also a shared story that has been used to elicit effective cooperation. Human beings have been trading since the barter system. In medieval times, society was structured around feudalism and the relationships that were derived from the holding of land in exchange for service or labor. Mercantilism arrived next and became the dominant school of economic thought in Europe throughout the late Renaissance and the early-modern period, from the fifteenth to the eighteenth centuries. In the run-up to the Industrial Revolution, economists such as Adam Smith proposed what is known as classical economics, and the idea of the free market came to prominence. Instead of subsidies and tariffs and government 'overreach', the market would regulate itself via the 'invisible hand'.

Although Smith is widely seen as the father of modern capitalism, he was much more interested in the greater good than many give him credit for. The invisible hand he referred to is an economic concept that describes the unintended greater social benefits and public good brought about by individuals acting in their own self-interests. Often that self-interest was expressed through business of some sort.

Business itself has evolved from those early trading societies to sole traders or partnerships, both of which are still common today and both are far older than corporations, which are characterized by some form of limited liability. Today when we think of business, especially big businesses or public limited companies, we are referring to corporations. And yet this type of business is, in the entire scheme of history, a very recent invention.

It was the expansion of the US railway in the 1800s that created the idea of a corporation that we take for granted today. In 1857 John Pierpont (J. P.) Morgan was working as an unpaid clerk at a New York investment firm linked to his father's US private bank. The investment firm specialized in finding European investment to finance railroads. At the time, the railroads were full of eager builders who were haphazardly laying track across America. They would build until they ran out of money and would therefore have to raise more capital to continue. It was impossible for any one builder to have enough money, so J. P. Morgan would convince people, mainly in Europe, to buy fractional ownership units called 'shares' of stock to raise the massive sums of money needed to complete the railway. This was the first time resources were pooled like this to make larger projects possible. This 'share' became the new way to invest in the future profits of large enterprises. The notion of shares was a revelation, but it's only a couple of hundred years old.

Being offered shares in the US railway when you were an aristocrat in London probably felt as speculative and distant as cryptocurrency still feels to most people today.

As the idea took off, it became necessary to look out for the interests of these holders of shares, and corporate governance evolved over time to include a board of directors elected by the shareholders, a CEO chosen by the board, and the rest of the organization reporting to the CEO through various layers of management.

There is little doubt that business in all its forms has been a boon for humanity. It has facilitated far greater productivity, and the resulting stock market has created significant value. At the start of 2022, the total value of the world's stock markets stood at $116.78 trillion,[1] and GDP per capita increased 14-fold in real terms from 1800 to 2000. In the US GDP per capita has increased significantly since web1 began (see Figure 4.1).

FIGURE 4.1: US REAL GDP PER CAPITA

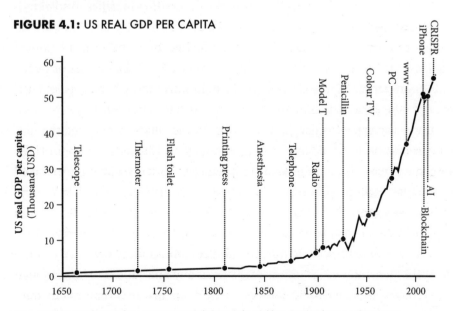

Source: Maddison Project Database. version 2018. Bolt, Jutta. Robert Inklaar, Herman de Jong and Jan Luiten van Zanden (2018). "Rebasing 'Maddison': new income comparisons and the shape of long-run economic development" Maddison Project Working Paper. nr.10 and Alger.

It is easy to underestimate what a miracle the last 200-plus years have been for the global standard of living. According to Laurence Boone, Chief Economist of the Organization for Economic Co-operation and Development (OECD), over one-third of the population of the planet has been lifted out of extreme poverty since the early 1990s.[2] It's even easier to forget that the idea of a company that we currently recognize as obvious and logical hasn't actually been around that long.[3] Business-as-usual has served us well – it has been a brilliant model for growth, productivity and escalating prosperity – but web3 heralds a significant upgrade. It can feel daunting because it's entirely new. The upgrades to the business models we have taken for granted for so long will be far greater than the incremental (albeit significant) upgrades that emerged from web1 and web2.

The emergence of 'cooperation protocols' will almost certainly render the existing model of corporations obsolete. Human beings have always found ways to cooperate but beyond 150 people, it's just not been possible to create those close, trustworthy connections that allow ventures to flourish. Business circumvented that barrier by becoming a vehicle with a shared story where hundreds, thousands or, in some cases, hundreds of thousands of people would come together to cooperate around the delivery of a product or service in exchange for wages (self-interest).

"THE EMERGENCE OF 'COOPERATION PROTOCOLS' WILL ALMOST CERTAINLY RENDER THE EXISTING MODEL OF CORPORATIONS OBSOLETE."

Although Adam Smith first wrote about the 'invisible hand' in 1759, the world did not yet have a mechanism to deliver the greater social good he talked of, certainly not alongside self-interest. Instead, cooperation clustered around self-interest alone and capitalism flourished with little regard for the greater good. This was inevitable. Smith's prophecy is, however, finally coming of age. Web3 is the mechanism to deliver Smith's 'invisible hand'.

Web3 will facilitate unintended greater social benefits and public good brought about by individuals acting in their own self-interests because web3 facilitates cooperation *and* competition in a way that has never been possible before.

It's also important to remember that Smith was not a lone voice. John Maynard Keynes, Karl Marx and John Stuart Mill could all see the challenges of pure self-interested capitalism when taken to its logical conclusion. Capitalism, in its current form, operates largely on a centralized scarcity model because there was no alternative.

But now web3 is making it possible for everyone to participate and everyone to benefit from what economic and social theorist Jeremy Rifkin calls a 'collaborative commons'. Cooperation can flourish far beyond small groups of 150 because trust or even personal connection is no longer required to participate, contribute and make money from the commons.

Again, this 'commons' or cooperative community idea is not new. Economist Elinor Ostrom suggests that this 'commons' can create huge value if a set of rules are consistently applied and respected by all members.[4] And while she compiled eight specific rules for managing the commons, work she won a Nobel Prize in Economics for in 2009, the beauty of web3 is that it creates those rules algorithmically, thus removing the need for trust from the cooperation process. This is truly groundbreaking, as we will see as we explore the industries in the rest of Part II and tomorrow's world in Part III.

Supply and Demand Disruption

Smith's invisible hand was proposed in relation to the law of supply and demand. What we all must grasp as we look to and embrace web3 is that where web1 and web2 completely changed the demand side of the economic equation, web3 and web4 are going to upend the supply side.

Let's just take a moment to time travel back to pre-web1. Prior to web1 a business could mainly compete locally, and so long as they delivered a good product or service that was in demand and no new entrants arrived in the territory, business was relatively straightforward. Strong brands kept demand high, and good distribution networks meant customers were served. Marketing was via print and TV advertising, direct mail or the *Yellow Pages*. Demand was local, which meant that locality drove property prices and the demand for prime locations. Businesses needed to have a physical presence in a location to successfully compete in that market. Locality-based demand also existed at an informational level, where customers would go to their local department store and all they could get was access to the store's information and 'experts'. The store held the power and thus controlled demand.

And then the internet or web1 emerged. If you were around, you may remember some of the speculation and furor, especially from techies! If you were not, then there were 'wild' predictions that the internet was going to completely change the way business interacted with its customers. All the distribution advantages that businesses may have spent years accumulating and fine tuning were about to disappear, or at the very least be seriously disrupted. Businesses were going to have to embrace web1 and service their customers in a new way and find new ways to deliver what those customers wanted across a digital medium.

The thing about technological disruption is that there are always two camps. Those who pay attention to the disruption and seek to pivot to embrace it and those who ignore the disruption or imagine that the changes won't affect them or that it's just some fad that will fizzle out.

Those who pivot can thrive among the disruption. Instead of wasting time looking backwards and lamenting over what they've lost, they accept the inevitability of the change and embrace it. Some of the catalogue companies pre-web1 did this brilliantly. They could see how the internet was going to change their business model and put their catalogues online, and many are still around today as a result. As for the companies who actively seek to fight the changes, they rarely survive. Even if they do survive, they are forever diminished by the battle. We saw that when the music industry fought Napster (more on that in Chapter 5).

Although this reaction of disbelief and reluctance to engage with the change is understandable, it's futile. You may be tempted to slide quietly into the second camp. I get it, you are already busy, and the first camp almost certainly requires a pretty major shift in strategic direction and operational processes. But if you do, you are falling for the same mistake the music industry fell for. Pre-web1 business leaders in that second camp were adamant that the disruption didn't affect them. No one is ever going to buy a luxury handbag or a car online! No one is ever going to buy clothes without visiting a shop and trying them on. No one is ever going to get their fruit and vegetables delivered directly to their home. And yet we do. Today it's commonplace and obvious.

Sure, if there is no burning platform, if the numbers are still solid and the business is doing well it can be easier to put this technological advance on the backburner. But just think about the impact of the internet on your business today. Those wild predictions were tame compared to reality. The size, scope and scale of change brought about by even web1 was phenomenal.

Web1 changed everything about the demand side of business. It opened up markets and 'levelled the playing field'. A sole trader with a website could now compete with a 100-year-old business, thus giving customers more choice. Information was also free flowing so people could get access to more experts and compare prices for the first time – massively disrupting demand for some businesses. Globalization meant that prices dropped, which further altered demand. Depending on the offering, any business operating anywhere in the world could sell to anyone. Demand for everything exploded.

This demand side of disruption also changed the commercial business models, or the way businesses made money. In web1, online advertising became an important part of business revenue generation, as most of web1 maintained the media playbook. Markets opened up far beyond locality, and online advertising allowed any business to reach and service more of those customers, regardless of geography.

Web2 simplified and streamlined delivery, sharing and UX, and it improved everything, but web2 was still focused on the demand side of the economic equation: 'What can we do to make this better, easier, faster, cheaper, so more people will want it?'

Commercially, the emergence of web2 and centralized data capture, big data analytics, predictive modeling and online tracking made the advertising capability started in web1 incredibly effective. Sites like Facebook and Google, who knew more about us than we knew about ourselves, made vast sums of money leveraging that knowledge through advertising. Needless to say, advertising costs also rose, and companies started to look around for other ways to make money. Towards the end of web1/early web2 the subscription model started to gain traction. If a customer could be enticed to join an ongoing subscription, then the business would not have to keep shelling out indefinitely on advertising.

In addition, the cost to advertise was rising steadily *and* people started to get sick of advertising. Consumers also learned just how much data some of these companies held about them and found out about misuse of that data. Demands for greater online privacy increased, culminating in the high-water mark for highly targeted advertising at the expense of consumer privacy. Apple's iOS 14.5 update brought about some of that increased privacy and meant that, if anyone visited a website or social platform, they were asked if they wanted to opt-in to tracking. Needless to say, millions of people, now alerted to the tracking in the first place, declined. As mentioned in Chapter 2, that one update cost Facebook $10 billion in advertising revenue – a quarter of its overall profit for the year.[5]

In web2 the dominant business model, certainly of the most successful companies, became the subscription model. The high-quality UX of web2 combined with vast numbers and data sets made it possible to offer real value at a 'no-brainer' monthly cost. For example, Spotify has 365 million active monthly users, 165 million of whom pay $9.99 a month. That's a staggering amount of guaranteed monthly income.

It's likely that the subscription model will continue to prosper as a money-making option although there is already a new kid on the block – tokens and micro-transactions. Tokens are a web3 innovation, although they did first emerge in late web2 (see Figure 4.2). We'll explore these tokens when we look at different industries shortly, but alongside tokens will also be an

FIGURE 4.2: BUSINESS MODELS BY ERA

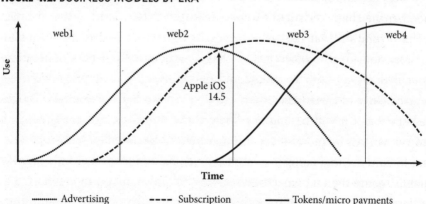

Source: GC Cooke

94

explosion in micro-payments that are distributed for participation, creation or some other role in the community.

Web2 maxed out the improvements that could be made and revenue that could be squeezed from the demand side.

Now, web3 and beyond is going to start upending the supply side. This Supply-side Revolution is going to disrupt the supply side of talent, capital and operations as well as further disrupt demand. Where web1 and web2 completely changed how businesses sold their products and services, web3 is going to completely change how those products and services are created and offered to customers in the first place!

This book is issuing the same clarion call of impending disruption that experts and engineers were making pre-web1. And if those web1 and web2 predictions now look tame against reality, know that web3 is going to be a hundred times more mind-boggling.

Remember, web3 is a protocol era again and web4 will be the app era where apps emerge to make the web3 protocols easier to access and use by the masses. This is hugely problematic for businesses that have sought, often over many decades, to erect barriers to entry and 'moats' designed to protect their competitive advantage over time. These moats were designed to keep the database closed and private; the data business's hold on customers is protected fiercely and the business often seeks ways to lock talent in place via golden handcuff deals and non-compete agreements. Those barriers, all built on the supply side, are about to turn into a serious liability as everything opens up. Remember the characteristics of web3 (see Figure 3.4).

The revolution that the web3 protocols have facilitated is the means to cooperate, non-locally, without any of the corporate barriers. Cooperation will occur in large numbers without the need to even have trust in others or the shared story of a business as we understand it today. There may still be a shared story, but it will be one of mutually advantageous collaborations and not top-down command and control hierarchies. Web3 will allow talent and capital to connect to a collective or straight to the end user while facilitating verifiable, secure digital ownership – and it will allow anyone to get involved. These large-scale collaborations have already solved really complex problems such as a secure digital currency. Governments issue money for banks to exist, and yet Bitcoin emerged out of thin air. An entire industry of bank-like services is now coming together to change the supply of capital dramatically (more on that in Chapter 6).

This is incredibly disruptive because up until now, people have still come together on the supply side of business to cooperate and produce goods and services, either as shareholders, employees or freelancers (talented creators and operational experts such as tax accountants). The ownership of what's created has always remained with the business. Web3 is already changing all that.

Many commentators see web3 as some sort of mechanism for the redistribution of wealth and greater equality, and while that may be true over the long term, web3 (like the other two internet iterations before it) is still a platform for wealth and value creation. What it does that was not possible in web1 or web2 is making those wealth and value creation opportunities available to more people. It may even be the mechanism through which genuine – as opposed to lip-service – stakeholder capitalism can emerge.

Communities will be the new companies

In web3 people will come together to produce goods and services in a completely different way. And all the complexity that goes into making that a reality via various corporate departments, such as HR, Legal, Sales, Operations, and various aspects of the supply chain will be taken care of by other platforms within the web3 'stack'. This stack being the deconstructed, unbundled components of the supply chain reconstituted into a bespoke interconnected solution. So just as corporations have leveraged cloud computing, individuals will have the tools to leverage web3 to produce goods and services and be paid for their participation in a myriad of new ways. The building blocks for cooperating to produce these goods and services will be as easy as adopting services from a cloud platform and will potentially create a productivity boost that will make the shipping container phenomenon look like a blip.

Web3 will be the end of corporations as we know them today. Communities will be the new

> **IN WEB3 PEOPLE WILL COME TOGETHER TO PRODUCE GOODS AND SERVICES IN A COMPLETELY DIFFERENT WAY.**

Decentralized autonomous organization (DAO)

The DAO (pronounced 'dow') acts like a form of company where the rules or 'articles' and 'shareholder agreement' are coded into a smart contract using a platform such as the Ethereum network. There is no management structure, board of directors, employees or shareholders in the typical sense. Instead, membership is recorded on the blockchain (digital ledger), and members meet via chat apps like Discord and vote to govern decisions. Joining a DAO is signaled by some sort of 'financial cooperation' in the form of tokens, via a crypto-wallet, which provides members with owner's tokens – which correspond to voting rights. The more tokens someone owns the more voting power in the DAO. Smart contracts determine deliverables between creators or investors who are incentivized to participate.

The architecture of these new entities is not perfect yet and there has been significant criticism of them because of a 2016 hack resulting in the loss of 3.6 million ETH, worth about $50 million at the time. But there is still a great deal of interest in DAOs and it is likely that, with time and improvements, this type of organization will eventually come to prominence, perhaps even replacing traditionally structured businesses (see Figure 4.3).

FIGURE 4.3: DAO VERSUS COMPANY

Source: Awesome People DowMasters

companies and the new community-focused construct that will replace the corporation is already here in the form of a decentralized autonomous organization, or DAO. The DAO is already creating a new way to organize resources and talent towards an agreed objective where more of the spoils are distributed more evenly based on capital, talent or participation.

Deconstruction and the End of Business-as-Usual

Have you ever been to a restaurant and ordered a 'deconstructed tiramisu'? When it arrives, you realize that it has all the expected elements of a classic tiramisu, but they are separated and displayed elegantly on the plate. There is the sponge, coffee 'soil', mascarpone whip and a little shot glass of coffee, along with some chocolate shavings. This is what's going to happen to business in web3 – complete deconstruction. Everything that currently goes into making your product or service will be unpacked and unbundled from 'the company.' This unbundling is essentially where the business is deconstructed into its component parts and disseminated out into separate but connected and interdependent services within the community. This is why the community will be the new company.

Figure 4.4 shows the various functions of a business. All of these and more will drop out of the corporation structure and be separate deconstructed capabilities that users can plug into in the creation process.

Not only that, but these separated ingredients are also going to come together in novel and bizarre ways to create completely new capabilities and, often, completely new markets. As is always the way in the Innovator's Dilemma, at first some of the web3 innovations and capabilities will appear similar to what already exists. They may look like new ways of creating the same outcome – so what? This ironically helps to soothe those business leaders holding firm in the 'let's ignore this and hope it fizzles out' camp. 'Nothing to see here – it's just a different flavor of what already exists.' Only it's not. As more protocols are developed and proved, it has already morphed into something very different and is creating new ways to facilitate completely fresh outcomes. So, while web3 is heralding a deconstruction of business-as-usual where all the component parts are separated out and offered into the market in novel

FIGURE 4.4: PRIMARY FUNCTIONS OF BUSINESS

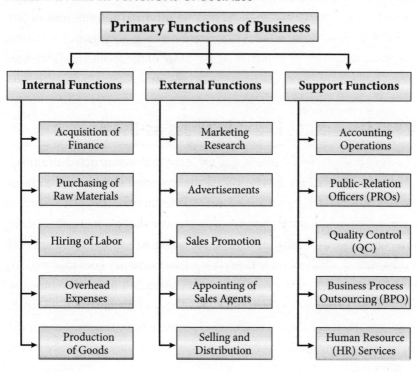

Source: Gaurav Akrani

ways, it is also facilitating a reconstruction that is going to tilt everything we currently take for granted about business on its axis. Web3 is not a new flavor of the internet, it is a brand-new internet.

There is little doubt that the very idea of a company is going through its own S-curve and the innovation plot twist accelerator is very likely to be the DAO (see Figure 4.5).

The Innovator's Dilemma for business is itself part of a much bigger shift as humanity has evolved over 10,000 years from the Agricultural Age (value created from producing food or tools) to the Industrial Age (value created by industrialization and machinery) to where we are now in the Information Age (value created from information). The Imagination Age will be where creativity and imagination will become the primary creators of economic value. Web3 is likely to make the Imagination Age a reality (see Figure 4.6).

FIGURE 4.5: THE INNOVATOR'S DILEMMA OF BUSINESS-AS-USUAL

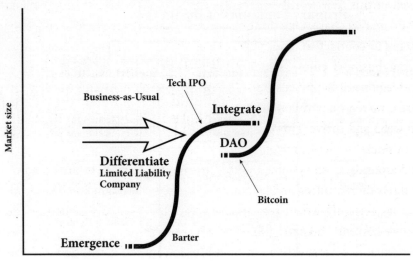

Source: GC Cooke

FIGURE 4.6: EVOLUTION OVER THE AGES

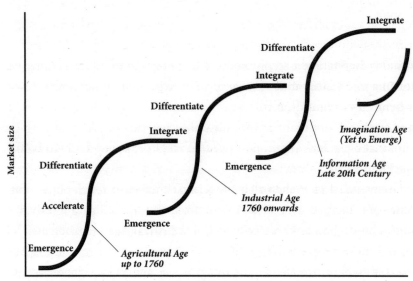

Source: GC Cooke

These are exciting times to be in business. Established businesses can do really well in this new world, especially if they already have strong demand and a solid market share. One thing that web3 won't change is the need for the new supply to connect to demand. So, if your business enjoys strong sales and legions of happy customers, there is no reason why you can't pivot to web3 and thrive. However, if your business model is currently designed around closed systems that profit from large datasets, are based on trust and rely on recruiting and keeping talent, then you might still be in trouble. And it's certainly worth remembering that the 'business' structure and function we currently take for granted is not that old.

> **ONE THING THAT WEB3 WON'T CHANGE IS THE NEED FOR THE NEW SUPPLY TO CONNECT TO DEMAND.**

This expanded perspective can be useful in times of disruption and was explained brilliantly by Sir David Attenborough during his TV show *Life on Earth*. If we shrink the evolution of the planet and all living things into one year, living organisms didn't emerge until August. At the beginning of November, backboned creatures emerged and left the water to colonize the land. By the beginning of December those backboned creatures broke their dependence on water and by the middle of the same month they could generate heat in their body and the scales turned to feathers. On 25 December the dinosaurs disappeared and mammals and furry animals emerged. In the early morning of 31 December apes arrived, and human beings arrived two minutes before midnight.[6] On this basis companies have been around for a fraction of a second.

It's not that big a deal to change a system that's been around for a fraction of a second, and it certainly shouldn't be causing the levels of anxiety that web3 seems to be engendering. Web3 will bring change, there is no doubt about that, but the change is likely to be a boon to humanity in much the same way that the limited liability company was, only with this evolution more people will be involved, and more people will benefit. Finally, the invisible hand that Adam Smith referred to back in 1759 will deliver what he predicted – greater social benefits and public good brought about by individuals acting [collectively] in their own self-interests.

Please don't ignore web3. Don't decide to worry about it later 'once it's a little more established'. Don't make the same mistake so many did pre-web1 and -web2 who are no longer around to tell the tale. While I completely understand the desire to maintain the status quo and resist the changes, web3 is here and it's happening, and it IS going to completely disrupt your business whether you are ready for it or not. Pay attention and pivot while you can, and you will win. Refuse to or ignore it and you are on your way to irrelevance. It really is that simple.

Summary of Key Points

» William Gibson was right: 'The future's here already. It's just unevenly distributed.' What's going to disrupt your business is already here right now.

» Business-as-usual has brought growth, productivity and escalating prosperity, but web3 heralds a significant upgrade.

» The emergence of 'cooperation protocols' will almost certainly render the corporation obsolete.

» Although Adam Smith first wrote about the 'invisible hand' in 1759, the world did not yet have a mechanism to deliver it (greater social good facilitated by self-interest). Web3 will facilitate unintended greater social benefits and public good brought about by individuals acting in their own self-interests because web3 facilitates cooperation *and* competition in a way that has never been possible before.

» What we all must grasp as we look to and embrace web3 is that where web1 and web2 completely changed the demand side of the economic equation, web3 and web4 are going to upend the supply side in the Supply-side Revolution.

» Web1 and web2 completely changed how businesses sold their products and services; web3 is going to completely change how those products and services are created and offered to customers in the first place!

» Web3 will allow talent and capital to connect to a collective or straight to the end user while facilitating verifiable, secure digital ownership.

» Communities will be the new companies and the new community-focused construct is already here in the form of a decentralized autonomous organization, or DAO.

» Everything that currently goes into making your product or service will be unpacked and unbundled from 'the company' and disseminated out into separate but connected and interdependent services within the community.

» These separated ingredients are also going to come together in novel and bizarre ways to create completely new capabilities and often completely new markets.

Chapter 5

The Next Battle for Talent

In 1997 management consultancy firm McKinsey & Company launched an initiative called the War for Talent to find out what made top-performing American companies different when it came to hiring, firing and promotion. The term 'war for talent' has been part of business language and discussion ever since. One of the most consistent challenges facing any business is the ability to find, attract and keep good people. Those challenges are not going away. Far from it. Web3 is already changing the way innovators, creators, engineers, coders and other talented individuals are engaging with, and providing their input to, projects or businesses.

In order to unpack the depth of the talent disruption occurring because of web3, let's explore three traditionally talent-rich creative industries: music, entertainment and publishing. You may be tempted to think, 'I'm not in the music, entertainment or publishing business, this won't be relevant to me.' But I assure you it is.

Music has always led the way.

Throughout history, the only way to experience music was to go to a live performance and listen to musicians and singers in person. In 1877 Thomas Edison, the man of a thousand patents, invented the phonograph. But it was poor quality and impractical, and Edison soon moved on to other inventions. Ten years later, Emile Berliner invented the gramophone, making sure to avoid the notoriously litigious Edison and his various patents. Instead of using a cylinder, Berliner used a disc, and a stylus moved across the recording to play the sound.

He went on to start what would become HMV, choosing a painting by Francis Barraud as its trademark (the picture with the dog looking into the horn). Berliner's disc became the standard medium for sound recording, and it dominated the domestic audio market until the end of the twentieth century. The 'Acoustic Era' (1877–1925) gave way to the 'Electrical Era' (1925–1945), with an integrated system of electrical microphones, signal amplifiers and recorders, which was adopted by major US record labels. Sound could now be captured, amplified, filtered and balanced electronically, and the disc-cutting head was now electrically powered. The recording process stayed the same, but the listening experience was exponentially improved.

The 'Magnetic Era' (1945–1975) arrived after the Second World War when the world found out about the German invention that had been around since the 1930s: magnetic tape recording. It provided a dramatic improvement again to audio quality and quickly became the standard medium for audio master recording in radio and the music and film industries. Magnetic tape led to the development of the first hi-fi stereo recording for the domestic market. It also radically changed the recording process because it became possible to record for longer, improve the editing and produce a far higher-quality recording than ever before. Other advances in audio technology created a whole new audience, with different audio formats and devices opening up music to the masses. There was the invention of the 33rpm, 12-inch long-play (LP) discs, 45rpm 7-inch 'single' and domestic and professional portable tape recorders and 4-track cartridges and compact cassette format.

From 1975 onwards we've been in the 'Digital Era'. In the space of about 20 years, a century's worth of innovation was superseded. Ry Cooder recorded the first all-digitally recorded album in 1979, and it quickly became the new standard. The same year, the Sony Walkman came out. Music became mobile for the first time, and it was a revelation.

Sony, together with Philips, also developed the digital compact disc (CD) in 1979, which rapidly replaced both LPs and singles as the new standard consumer format. When they were first launched, consumers were told they were virtually indestructible (they were not). The suggestion was logical because the CD was read optically using a laser beam rather than a stylus on vinyl, which causes scratching, but you still needed to take care of CDs, otherwise they stopped working too. CDs did, however, solve the 'tape chewing' issue that any avid music fan over 40 years old will probably remember. CDs were smaller and could hold more music, but they were not as good for mobile music playing. The cassette was still superior for music on the move – it didn't skip because the laser was moving too much.

Vinyl, CDs, cassettes and the MiniDisc all became virtually redundant with the advent of web1. The MiniDisc especially was a triumph, one of the most sophisticated approaches to recorded music ever made, but it was none-theless annihilated by a completely new S-curve of innovation in music.

If you look past the industry specific innovations of entertainment and publishing, the journey from initial capability to where we are now is essentially the same as it is in music. It's just that the music industry was the trailblazer.

Prior to the end of the nineteenth century if you wanted to be entertained you needed to go to a live performance, theatre or the opera. That all changed in Paris in 1895 when a series of silent 50-second scenes were shown to a stunned audience. The images, including a train arriving at a station, a wave breaking and children engaged in a snowball fight (we've come a long way) were recorded by the Lumière brothers and were the start of recorded enter-tainment. Sound was added once the quality became good enough, and the first 'talkie' came out in 1927 – *The Jazz Singer* with Al Jolson. As for publish-ing, prior to the Gutenberg press, most people didn't read. If they did read, what they read was controlled by the Church.

Once the capability existed, entertainment and publishing flourished. But making a movie or publishing a book was expensive, just like making an album. Inevitably, large businesses built up to manage that process, raise funds and maintain control over the output – just like record labels. These entities completely controlled the supply side. The talent (actors, authors or musicians) were at the mercy of these large businesses. A man in a suit, or a panel of men in suits, decided if that talent was worthy of a contract and the creator was paid a small fee or tiny royalty for their efforts.

If you wanted to watch a movie you went to the cinema. If you wanted to read a book you could only buy a book produced by one of the large publishers.

All the capabilities that we explored in music from the gramophone onwards have of course had an impact on film and the ability to capture and replay any type of performance, from live performances to some type of innovation that allows us to experience that performance – in this case, VHS video and eventually DVDs. But as soon as digital emerged, Blockbuster was in trouble. And so were the publishers. Like the music industry before them, and the large publishing houses, Blockbuster didn't want to acknowledge the writing on the wall.

When I was halfway through university I could see just how rapidly the demand side was shifting, so I created a business called Media Portal Technologies, which distributed video on demand. It was basically Netflix when Netflix went into streaming. When Netflix started, they were sending DVDs via the post, not over the internet. I won the Entrepreneur of the Year Award for it and was awarded a grant to help build it. The prototype allowed the user to plug it in at home and get videos on demand over the internet, but it was a business ahead of its time, specifically ahead of the technology to make it really sing. Although I solved the problem of how to provide high-quality video over slow internet connections, I was faced with an insurmountable challenge around licensing content for streaming. Licensing was impossible because no one I spoke to could see the future that was already here. I even took the business to Blockbuster, but they were also so deeply entrenched in their old ways that they didn't see the potential. What's ironic is that Netflix also approached Blockbuster in 2001 with the offer to sell for $50 million and they turned it down again. It is now one of the most famous missed opportunities of all time and yet they actually turned down the idea twice!

This is always one of the challenges as web1 moves to web2, which in time moves to web3: how to separate the hype from the technological capabilities that are here to stay. Like streamed music, streamed movies and TV shows were inevitable; it's just that few people saw it before it arrived. I did, but the technology just wasn't quite there to support 'my Netflix'. The same is true in publishing. Once the e-reader arrived and it was possible to buy a book and have it delivered to your Kindle, Kobo or NOOK in seconds, the incumbent publishers were in trouble. But it wasn't just the distribution that was disrupted. Their grip on supply was also slipping with the rapid advance of self-publishing. It was no longer men in suits that were deciding if authors could publish their books; authors could just do it themselves. Of course, the same thing happened in music and, to a lesser but still significant extent, in entertainment.

If you look at the evolution of music, entertainment and publishing, it leads us as a society (by example) to what comes next. They all followed the same path from initial capability to inventions around the medium, from Berliner's disc, which allowed for three minutes of music, to LPs of ten songs, to CDs with even more songs, to digital music with an infinite playlist. Digital changed everything for each of these industries because the library of potential became infinite for the user and the price for access dropped significantly.

Disruption in Web1

Up until web1, if you wanted music you needed to go to your local music store and buy the music you wanted in whatever format you wanted to listen to it. People still went to live concerts, but if you wanted to listen to music at home or on the go, you needed to buy a vinyl record, cassette or CD. If you wanted to watch a movie you needed to go to the cinema, watch TV, rent a video or later a DVD, and if you wanted to read a book you went to the library or your local bookshop.

And then, along came the digital audio file. The Waveform Audio File (.WAV), developed by IBM and Microsoft, and MP3 format, developed largely by the Fraunhofer Society in Germany, both emerged in 1991 – although they were not the only formats. When combined with newly developed compression algorithms that reduced the file size, digital music as we know it today became possible for the first time.

And all this coincided with the rise of home-computing and the emergence of the internet. The protocol development era of web1 had already created game-changing protocols such as the Internet Protocol and File Transfer Protocol.

In many ways Napster was an inevitable convergence of disparate innovations. This is always the case; each new innovation stands on the shoulders of previous innovations or puts unconnected innovations together to create new functionality. Uber would not have been possible without the iPhone; the iPhone wasn't possible before GPS, etc.

In web1 we had more and more people using a home PC, we had digital audio files that could contain music, we had compression capability so that each song didn't take up huge amounts of space, and we had the capacity to share files in a peer-to-peer network.

Napster was a simple application built on a peer-to-peer file-sharing protocol of web1, which allowed people to share information from a PC hard drive. In a few keystrokes you could access just about any song you wanted to listen to. As such, web1 completely disrupted the distribution of music. If you wanted to listen to music, you didn't need to get a bus into town and browse through hundreds of album covers to find something you wanted to listen to. Instead, you could just fire up the dial-up internet connection and listen to music that someone else had bought and 'ripped' to their PC. And it was free. Again, following the Innovator's Dilemma logic, the ripped music wasn't as good quality as the record or the CD, but some users still preferred it because the new distribution method made it instant and free.

Although it was possible to search for and download digital music files before Napster, it was awkward, and it didn't always work. Shawn Fanning, then a 17-year-old student at Northeastern University in Boston, who went by the username 'napster' in chat rooms, built an app that would streamline the whole process. It was launched on 1 June 1999, with $50,000 raised by business partner Sean Parker. Napster didn't host any music. Each user downloaded the app and designated a folder of music files as shared. Users who logged into the app could search for a song and then Napster would search all the shared files living on thousands of personal computers to find a match and the user could then copy the song to their PC.

For the first time in history, you could listen to any song you wanted, immediately (or at least within ten minutes), and it was free. Needless to say, Napster exploded in popularity. In just five months, four million songs were available. A year after launch, 14,000 songs were being downloaded every minute. At its peak Napster had 57 million users.

That meant that 57 million people were no longer buying music. After a couple of lawsuits by artists including Metallica and Dr Dre, the Recording Industry Association of America (RIAA), the trade group for the collective music business, filed a $20 billion copyright infringement suit against Napster.

What followed was an epic legal battle. And the whole sorry saga is often repeated in business schools as a case study of what not to do when your industry is going through seismic change!

On 12 February 2001, the United States Court of Appeals found in favor of the RIAA. On 6 March, Napster began complying with the federal court order. Three months later, it shut Napster down. In the end the RIAA may have won the battle, but they lost the war. The industry was forced to change its business model and Napster also changed the way we consume music forever.

Instead of fighting Napster, the music industry should have recognized that the genie was out of the distribution bottle. The same can easily be said for entertainment and publishing. Consumers had been complaining for years about the way music, entertainment and books were made available. If people wanted to buy a single, they could on vinyl, but as vinyl lost its appeal it was no longer possible to buy one song. Not every consumer wanted to pay for an album when all they really wanted was one or two songs from the album. Napster worked because it gave people access to music the way they wanted it. In entertainment, people were fed up with hiring videos for the weekend, not being able to get the ones they wanted because the store didn't have enough copies, and getting stung by late fees. Although streaming of sorts emerged in web1 when ESPN SportsZone streamed a live radio broadcast of a baseball game to thousands of subscribers, it was challenging to say the least over dial-up internet connection. And that was without video! It was only when broadband improved that streaming as an idea could really flourish. As for books, they were still viewed as too expensive, with rigid genres. Publishers decided what would be published and so niche genres were almost always overlooked.

This should be a cautionary tale for all businesses as we look to embrace web3. Music, entertainment and publishing all had an opportunity to adapt during web1 and embrace the changes their customer base was pointing to, but they didn't and have been severely impacted as a result.

Disruption in Web2

Napster changed the music industry forever, but by today's standards it was pretty basic. Once a song you wanted was located, the download process was often grueling as the user tracked the download onto their machine bit by bit. And the transfers didn't always work. Although the search was useful, the user experience was poor.

This is another important distinction to bear in mind as you figure out web3. Protocol development eras are profoundly important, but they are often not easy to use, so the capabilities stay with the innovators and the early adopters (the techies and early users). The protocol capability rarely crosses the valley of death between the early adopters and the mass market. It is only when great user-friendly apps are built on top of the protocols that they make the leap across the chasm. Think HTML versus Dreamweaver. Dreamweaver made HTML easy and so it exploded in popularity, thus taking HTML to the masses. We see this pattern repeat over and over again. Web3 is a protocol era again and the protocols being developed are mind-blowing, but it's likely that it won't be until web4 that access to these protocols is simplified via easy-to-use apps. That's when capabilities will explode. However, if you are thinking that it buys you a little more time to get your head around web3, you're mistaken. The shortening timescale of this innovation is exponential. It took 20 years for web1 to mature, ten years for web2 to mature and it's likely to be five years for web3, which means those apps that make web3 unavoidable are already being developed and will be commonplace by the end of this decade.

Napster did manage to cross the chasm, or at least get partway across it, before the legal system shut them down. Their ability to get so far was largely down to the fact that Napster gave access to free and instant music – a potent combination for consumers.

Another major innovation that rocked the music industry was iTunes and the iPod. In the same year that Napster was closed down, Apple, clearly recognizing something the music industry did not, launched iTunes on their Mac. Initially iTunes was a simple music player for Mac computers, giving paid-for access to digital music. Over time, iTunes developed into a sophisticated multimedia content manager, hardware synchronization manager and e-commerce platform. In 2001 Apple also launched the iPod, a miraculously small, beautiful, intuitive device, not much bigger than a cigarette packet, that could hold hundreds of songs and other content. When Apple rolled that capability into their iPhone then good-quality music on the move became ubiquitous almost overnight. In 2008 the business model for music evolved again, with streaming versus buying a single song for $1. Streaming was appealing to the music industry because it captured the people who were still stealing music and not paying Apple $1 per song.

And, of course, then Spotify came along. Spotify, which launched in 2008, took what had been learned by Napster in the protocol era of web1 and Apple's iPod functionality, and built a slick, easy-to-use app on top of the protocol to simplify and improve the user experience. Agreements with artists were reached so they were paid for their music, thus solving the legal issues that effectively killed Napster. And there were search features and suggestions around what the listener might also like based on their current playlist. This was very web2: sharing but with better UX. And they succeeded because they solved Napster's main bugbear – poor-quality music. Early Spotify even built on peer-to-peer protocols initially, but peer-to-peer ended up mattering a lot less than portability and great UX on a smartphone. Today, streaming is the dominant business model, and for Spotify this happened at the right time because in 2007 the iPhone launched, meaning a smartphone with an eventual app store could make music portable on your phone. It is not a coincidence that Spotify launched the year after the iPhone. Adding Spotify to the iPhone transformed our access to music. The iPhone and the invention of high-speed, stable internet connection also significantly improved streaming capabilities and access in the entertainment industry. Turns out it was possible to create something that rewarded artists and record companies for their content, but which still tapped into the zeitgeist of music sharing.

In the publishing world, there were a number of breakthrough innovations that altered the landscape. First, in late web1, electronic paper was invented, which allowed a display screen to reflect light like ordinary paper without the need for a backlight. Sony's Data Discman was the first commercial e-reader, but the Sony Libre was the first to use electronic paper in 2004. Amazon's Kindle launched in 2007 and the rest, as they say, is history. Amazon, probably more than any other company, has decimated the traditional publishing model on pretty much every front. Amazon has facilitated end-to-end supply *and* demand disruption. Authors can self-publish on their platform and receive royalties significantly larger than anything offered by traditional publishing companies; they can engage in Amazon ads to promote their book, and the book is available as print on demand, fulfilled by Amazon, or available on their Kindle. They also offer subscribers to Amazon Prime access to millions of books, like a library, with users gaining access to around ten books a month for their monthly subscription. Authors are then paid on page views. In essence, Amazon did to the publishing industry what web3 is going to do to all industries – complete deconstruction. Amazon unbundled the various aspects of publishing from the supply and demand side and made it available to anyone.

Disruption in Web3

Whereas web1 and web2 disrupted the demand side of business via altered distribution channels, routes to market and access to customers, web3 will upend the supply side of talent, capital and operations.

This was a challenging section to write because I wanted to tell the story of the revolution that is already underway, but there is no way to cover the community capability and game-changing interconnectivity of web3 without the book being so long that no one would read it. The danger, therefore, is that you read it and think, 'Yeah, but that doesn't impact me or my business.' The trick is to stop and think about how it might. I have tried to pull those parallels out as I go, but again there is no way to do that adequately because I don't know your industry. So, this is going to be a joint effort. I will seek to draw out what this means for business as much as possible and you will need to consider what else it may mean for your business. Make no mistake – the change is seismic.

It's also important to recognize the demographics in the stories I share. This is very deliberate. The new types of cooperation protocols that are emerging are especially appealing to millennials and Gen Z – your future workforce. Web3 is going to make it easier for those individuals to collaborate on multiple projects that fit around their life than it is to apply for a job. The next generation war for talent you will experience is being disrupted from the younger generation up. As such I have sought to tell the stories from a younger perspective (Alice) and from an older perspective (Bob). That way you can hopefully appreciate the technological shift and the demographic shift at the same time.

To tell the story of how the war for talent will change, let's look at the story of a musician. Alice is a deliberately precocious singer-songwriter who also plays acoustic guitar. I've also given her some surprising levels of financial acumen! This is in part so I can better explore her story in a relevant way to business leaders and is also a nod to the fact that her generation are insanely familiar and comfortable with tech.

Like all musicians, including her dad, Bob, she wants to break through and make a living as a musician. Her dad felt the same and for years he and his band played the local pubs and weddings, and would record and send demo tapes to record labels. They were far 'luckier' than most and even got signed to a UK label. Bob still remembers the euphoria – they had made it. Only it didn't really work out that way. They had a bruising touring schedule for the year and were expected to do radio shows and media pretty much constantly. By the time the record label had produced their album and recouped their costs, together with the touring costs, the band ended up with significantly less than the equivalent of the minimum wage. It was heartbreaking, and although Bob was the songwriter (so he was paid royalties on the songs), they never made a Christmas song that is on repeat every December, so he ends up getting enough for a nice meal out with the family every year. In the end the dream died, and Bob went back to his dad's family business and became an accountant.

Alice has heard all the stories of woe, and Bob has repeatedly tried to warn Alice off a life in music. 'It's a con, Alice – the people who have all the talent and make all the songs always get shafted.'

But Alice is a web3 native.

Alice is a millennial. She has grown up with tech. She doesn't even remember a world without the internet and is undaunted and unfazed by it; unlike her dad, who struggles to use email! This is an important distinction for business to grasp. Baby Boomers and even Gen X were happy to slot into the corporate structure and work their way up the legendary corporate ladder. Gen Y and Gen Z, however, have very little interest in following that path. They saw how hard their parents worked for very little real reward. The company demanded loyalty, but employees could rarely expect it in return. This younger demographic is also acutely aware of the world's many wicked problems and want to be part of the solution, not part of the problem. They want purpose and genuine work–life balance, and they have zero qualms about changing jobs or roles countless times to find that right mix. That means business is going to find it increasingly difficult to attract and keep this demographic in employment, especially when web3 is opening up untold opportunities for portfolio careers and multiple streams of income that the individual is in control of, not some HR department. When there is a demographic cohort the size of Gen Y and Gen Z who are already extremely comfortable with technology, with no tech fear or trepidation, web3 is going to be second nature for them in a matter of years. And that is going to create a massive hole in the talent recruitment pool for companies, especially those hell-bent on maintaining top-down hierarchy who believe high salaries and bonuses will be enough.

Alice already knows that the music industry is being deconstructed. In Figure 5.1, each box represents something that a record label used to do, control or manage, which is now offered as a distinct deconstructed product or service in the web3 stack.

FIGURE 5.1: MUSIC DECONSTRUCTED

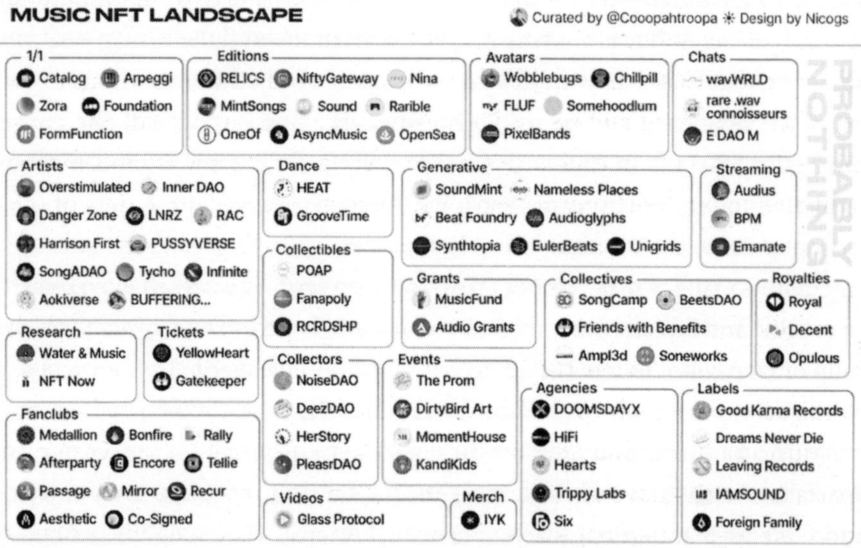

MUSIC NFT LANDSCAPE — Curated by @Cooopahtroopa ✳ Design by Nicogs

The music, entertainment and publishing industries are collectively worth $800 billion, and Alice is confident she can find multiple ways to access her share of that revenue – on her own terms. Instead of creating a band and producing hundreds of demo tapes like her dad, Alice joined SongCamp, which runs month-long online 'camps' that are a cross between songwriting camps and web3 hackathons (an event where a number of developers work together collaboratively in a short time frame to release a production ready application). Each camp brings together new artists, songwriters, producers and hackers from all over the world. Together, they collaborate on music, visual art and NFTs. Alice collaborated with a couple of other musicians and a producer to create a new track.

Only Alice didn't add the track to a demo tape. She joined Royal. In the traditional business model in the music industry (and publishing), the talent (either musician or author) gets a royalty, which is usually a tiny portion of net receipts (what the label or publisher makes per unit after costs).

At time of writing in 2022, Royal, the music NFT platform that has received the most VC investment, is still in the beta testing stage, but this and other similar platforms that will follow are set to change the landscape by potentially unbundling various parts of the record industry with fans and 'prosumers'. There are many emerging solutions that will create opportunities for these fans and prosumers to support the future work of artists and earn royalties. This future starts to create opportunities for Alice to tell her community and all her followers on her YouTube channel and social channels that she's going to release a new track and invites them and other music fans to own part of the new song and be paid a royalty every time it's played! She creates an NFT for $50,000, in exchange for a percentage of her royalty income; fans are invited to buy portions of that NFT. Alice decides on three tiers of offer, starting at $200, each entitling the owner to a slightly bigger royalty and also some additional goodies. Her top tier is $5,000 and is worth 0.5 per cent of the royalty, and anyone who buys that will also get access to a special Discord group or chat room where they can chat to Alice and other fans. They will also get first access to new NFTs and be put on the VIP guest list for any live show.

Music platform Sound allows Alice to sell access and exclusivity to her superfans. Artists have always relied on the labels to manage their monetization, taking a scaled approach to touring and music sales. Web3 is offering the chance to monetize differently, where superfans become the primary revenue source to ensure more artists are able to make the living wage or better. The record industry is filled with many talented individuals with decades of experience. Developing new artists is an extremely complex endeavor that will make parts of these new marketplaces challenging.

Using a third-party platform, Alice uploads her new song to Spotify and also web3 platforms such as Audius, which is a fully decentralized digital music streaming service built with public blockchain infrastructure and other decentralized technologies. It is owned and run by an open-source community of artists, fans and developers from around the world and is the largest non-financial crypto application ever built. Audius allows artists to distribute their music and get paid directly from their fans via tokens in Audius's own currency called the $AUDIO. As of early 2022 there was $332 million worth of $AUDIO in active use. And while in true Innovator's Dilemma fashion this may look like Spotify, it owns the network; whereas in Audius the participants own the network and are incentivized to participate by the tokens.

Every time her new song is played Alice will be paid and so will everyone who bought a share of the NFT. So, for a little upfront investment her fans get a bunch of cool stuff, support their favorite artist and potentially make money if that track is successful. And those tracks still plug into the existing distribution network, which makes them more likely to be successful.

Although web3 is going to upend the supply side, the distribution side is still hugely important, so the existing demand-side winners such as Spotify in the music space will continue to prosper because they still have the markets. For anything to be successful it still has to go where the people are. Music consumers are still on Spotify and will probably stay there for the foreseeable future. But how those tracks are created to end up on Spotify is changing.

Clearly in this scenario the record labels are again facing major change, this time in the supply side and not the demand side. All the component parts of the music industry are being deconstructed and Alice is then able to plug into the ones she wants to access. The fans are listening to the music they want and if any of the fans who bought a portion of the NFT want to sell it then they can do so on OpenSea, which is eBay for NFTs.

This disruption may also be relevant in your business. Take a moment to think about who is involved in producing your product or service. If those people have specific sought-after talents, then it is very likely that they will migrate to a web3 stack and offer those services to businesses and projects that are meaningful to them. Generation Y are also known as Generation Why because they are looking for more than money – they are motivated by purpose. If your business can't provide that purpose, flexibility and incentive, then web3 can and will.

As for Alice, she is also scheduling gigs in the metaverse. The metaverse is a rapidly growing digital native entertainment channel where people spend their discretionary time. The idea is that, eventually, everything you can do in the real world you will be able to do in the metaverse.

Alice has chosen Decentraland for her gigs, a virtual reality platform built on the Ethereum blockchain where users can explore a virtual world where they can create, experience and monetize content and applications. At this point, Decentraland still looks like a fairly low-tech 3D video game, but the platform allows users to create unique environments in a virtual world. Alice has bought some virtual real estate and her fans can come to her shop and buy digital merchandise. If she's a bit bored, she will pop into Decentraland and busk outside her shop. Transactions and interactions are real, and ownership is secured by cryptocurrency, where the digital ownership exists in a smart contract on the blockchain. Everyone who enters Decentraland emerges into Genesis Plaza. And from there you can explore and visit various shops or have various experiences. Her fans can interact directly with her in Decentraland and she can try out new music ideas with them.

Currently, users gather, interact, share content and play games primarily on large proprietary platforms like Facebook. The decentralized model of Decentraland will allow participants to realize several benefits over that type of closed platform. Alice and her fans will be able to benefit from transactions that occur on the platform, instead of allowing some or all of the revenue to flow to a single party. Furthermore, a decentralized platform will reduce the risk of censorship and vulnerabilities due to infrastructure failures or security breaches.

Bob thinks this is all very strange, but as Alice explains to him the concept is pretty simple. We all have a limited amount of spare time and attention.

Where do we spend it? On an app or playing a video game, reading a book or going to the movies? Or will we spend our time in the metaverse? Alice is betting on the latter.

Even now, in what is still the early days for Decentraland, there are people who make their living designing or creating products or accessories in this virtual world. When Alice entered Decentraland she was asked to create an avatar, and bought herself a 'brilliant guitar and punky rock outfit' for 3.5 MANA (about $9). (MANA are one of two tokens in Decentraland.) M Social, part of the Singapore-based Millennium Hotels brand, opened the world's first virtual hotel in Decentraland in May 2022.[1] Alice is not sure where this platform will go, but as of early 2022 Decentraland is already an economy worth in excess of $4 billion.

So again, what might Decentraland or similar technology do for your business? Do you already have bricks-and-mortar shops? Because if you do, you may need to secure some retail space in the metaverse sooner rather than later.

Bottomline: There is enormous opportunity for Alice to monetize her creativity while connecting with fans. But Alice's creativity doesn't stop at music. She also spends time on Axie Infinity, which is a pet-training game inspired by Pokémon. Again, this is a virtual world built on the Ethereum blockchain. Players can collect, breed, battle and trade in-game pets called Axies. However, unlike traditional web2 gaming, Axie leverages blockchain incentives to reward players financially for their contribution to the ecosystem. In web2 the mantra was 'If the service is free, you are the product'; in web3 the mantra is 'play-to-earn'. This philosophy has grown increasingly popular in developing nations like the Philippines, Argentina and Venezuela. In some of these places, the economic opportunities presented by the game exceed those available in the real world. This is because Axie Infinity minted its own token called Axie Infinity Shard (AXS) and set aside tens of millions of AXS to effectively pay gamers to play. Originally worth a few cents, shards have traded at close to $80, giving players a literal and economic stake in the game's success, which further fuels and drives the whole Axie ecosystem, including demand for Alice's pet.[2]

This too is a significant shift that will spread as web3 protocols become more accessible, probably via easy-to-use web4 apps. Because of the decentralized nature of web3 and beyond, individuals like Alice, within these new established communities, will have many more opportunities to make money via various different web3 capabilities. Where it is more common now to have a portfolio career than to start and retire with the same company, web3 will almost certainly facilitate portfolio income – multiple avenues of income via micro-transitions that collectively give people like Alice (and not necessarily companies) greater power and more flexibility and control than being an employee, especially in an era of zero-hours contracts and diminishing workers' rights.

If your business currently sees employees as a necessary cost that needs to be kept low then you will almost certainly hit significant recruitment problems as more and more people turn their backs on traditional employment for a vast array of web3 opportunities that also give them more freedom. They may not make as much money, but for millennials and Gen Z, quality of life and purpose is much more important.

It was Axie that served as an on-ramp into crypto for Alice, and this has been true for thousands of users. According to Messari, a leading crypto market intelligence platform, as of July 2021 Axie has 568,000 Discord users and 450,000 daily average users, but, unlike centralized games such as Fortnite, where the value generated by the game is accrued solely by the platform owners, Axie hands the keys of the virtual world to the users, allowing them to modify the digital topography and maintain full sovereignty over their arithmetically scarce assets.

> **WHERE WEB1 WAS FUNDED BY ADVERTISING AND WEB2 WAS FUNDED BY SUBSCRIPTIONS, WEB3 WILL BE TOKENS OR MICRO-TRANSACTIONS.**

Where web1 was funded by advertising and web2 was funded by subscriptions, web3 will be tokens or micro-transactions. Tokenomics is therefore the economics behind these web3 innovations and how people like Alice can make money.

For a very long time, the talent in their industries – artists and musicians, actors and authors – have received a tiny share of the revenue they generate. Granted, producing an album, movie or TV show or publishing a book was expensive so there were a lot of people to pay before the creator or talent. But that is already changing. Alice is setting up multiple streams of income where she is paid in tokens that can be exchanged or borrowed against (more on that in the next chapter). She is in control of her creative output, has found multiple ways to be paid for it and is engaged in projects she believes in, on her own terms.

Digital art NFTs

Clearly, this deconstruction is also reconstructing to create completely new opportunities and markets for Alice and other creators. Take digital art NFTs as an example.

In 2021 Beeple caused a sensation when an NFT of his artwork sold at Christie's for $69 million.[3] A year later the digital art NFT market ballooned to $41 billion, out of thin air. The conventional art market was worth about $50 billion.[4] Just think about that for a moment. A market that didn't even exist a decade ago is almost worth as much as a market that has been around for centuries.

The first known NFT, 'Quantum', was created by Kevin McCoy and Anil Dash in May 2014. It consists of a short video clip made by McCoy's wife. Quantum was the first demonstration of 'monetized graphics' and was registered on the Namecoin blockchain. McCoy sold it to Dash for $4; a bargain, considering a version of that original NFT was sold by Sotheby's in 2021 for $1.4 million.[5]

And it was only made possible because of the invention of Bitcoin as the most widely used blockchain, which eventually led to Ethereum. This technology allows, for the first time, to prove digital ownership. Up until web3 the internet has been a copying machine. Copying websites, copying images, copying text. The term 'NFT' only achieved wider usage with the ERC-721 standard, first proposed in 2017, which coincided with the launch of several NFT projects, including CryptoPunks, which trades unique cartoon characters released by the American studio Larva Labs on the Ethereum blockchain. ERC-721 allows someone to create a unique piece of digital art and cryptographically sign that image with their key, which says that this is the first and only original image.

And then along came the Bored Ape Yacht Club (BAYC) – a collection of 10,000 unique NFTs, each depicting a profile picture of cartoon apes in various outfits. Each unique NFT exists on the Ethereum blockchain and is procedurally generated by an algorithm (known as 'generative art').

According to the BAYC website, the NFT collection was created by four friends who 'set out to make some dope apes, test [their] skills, and try to build something (ridiculous)'. It's safe to say they succeeded. Each NFT also functions as a membership card to the Yacht Club, which includes access to 'The Bathroom', a digital graffiti board and exclusive in-person events.

Originally sold for 0.08 ether each, around $190 at the time of their April 2021 launch, Bored Ape NFTs are now selling for millions. In January 2022 Bored Ape #232 sold for 1,080.69 ETH (approximately $2.85 million).[6] The same month, total sales of BAYC passed $1 billion on OpenSea.

What's even more bizarre and potentially disruptive to all the creative industries is that BAYC NFT holders have full commercial rights to their ape. This represents one of those bizarre twists I was telling you about on what is already the bizarre twist of NFTs. Major NFT players, such as NBA Top Shot and CryptoPunk, prohibit owners from commercial use. BAYC doesn't. Whoever owns a Bored Ape can spin it into whatever film, music, TV, book or media project they want.[7] They don't just own the digital art, but the full intellectual property for that ape.

Remember there are 10,000 Bored Ape NFTs. So far, owners have been quick to jump into traditional merchandising of everything from clothes to kites to IPA beer.

And then there is the non-traditional, left-field business moves that are truly unique. One collector has partnered with a music company to create a new label to manage four of his Bored Ape packages into a band called Kingship. Celine Joshua, the founder of the label, said, 'Whether you're a major [player] or someone in your bedroom, pay attention. It can only go as far as your imagination will allow, because finally the tech and the time is in the right place.' Another owner has created a metaverse entertainment company that will discover and amplify artists who are Bored Ape owners.

As Nick Adler, former SVP of business development at marketing collective Cashmere Agency and Snoop Dogg's business partner, said, 'People can go out and control their digital rights and own their digital footprint. We've given so much of our IP away to the big web2 brands, and now we get to take that back.'

In the publishing sphere, an anonymous collective has signed with a talent agency to develop projects for their Bored Ape named 'Jenkins the Valet' (he currently has more than 26,000 followers on Twitter). Together Jenkins and the agency have created their own NFT that grants holders access to the Writer's Room, a platform where the 2,700-plus members vote on the creative direction for the character of Jenkins in his debut novel, written by a bestselling author. Members can submit their proposals for ideas, and if they have a Bored Ape NFT, they can also license their apes to be included in the novel.[8]

And this characterization has been taken into the movies too. In April 2022, Coinbase, the cryptocurrency exchange, announced a film that will feature the Bored Ape Yacht Club and ApeCoin. Whoever owns the Bored Apes that are cast in the movie will be paid royalties. According to Adler, we are going to see 'a new studio model and new industries and new places where [NFTs] come out. I can't just think about how I traditionally build IP and sell it to Netflix. It's more like, what is the new Netflix? What is the blockchain decentralized distribution model?'

Bored Ape Yacht Club is decentralizing rights of ownership and is, as such, creating a completely new commercial landscape. Already the same source material is being recast and repurposed into different commercial endeavors with very different visions.

In another project, actress and producer Mila Kunis raised $8.4 million in less than 35 minutes selling 10,000 NFTs tied to an animated cartoon series called *Stoner Cats*. The show, featuring voiceovers from Kunis, Ashton Kutcher, Jane Fonda, Chris Rock, Seth MacFarlane and even Ethereum co-founder Vitalik Buterin will give only token holders the ability to watch it.[9]

All Talent Will Be Disrupted

The supply-side disruption of talent will impact every industry and all business because it puts even more power in the hands of that talent to decide not just terms, but the very way they provide and monetize their input.

It has already started in service and information-based businesses, but it will spread to every industry, even capital-intensive manufacturing businesses.

It just might take a little longer and look a little different. A car will still need to roll off a production line, but the talent that went into that production may work as part of a collective. The operational talent required in that production process may also be provided within that community and the capital may have come from new web3 sources. It may be hard to imagine how an NFT can be applied to manufacturing or companies that have produced physical goods for centuries, but as you will see in Chapter 8, it's already happening. It is inevitable as the topography of producing anything changes.

THE SUPPLY-SIDE DISRUPTION OF TALENT WILL IMPACT EVERY INDUSTRY.

If you think of Apple, are they a manufacturing company or is it really a design and R&D business that outsources its manufacture to Foxconn in China? Instead of 'Designed in California, made in China', it may change to 'Designed by AppleDAO, made in China'. Apple has a rock-solid brand today and plenty of talent keen to work for the company as a result, but what if that changes? It's already happening in Facebook, Google and Amazon, where there is a serious exodus of talent to web3 ventures.[10] And a non-compete clause in the talent contract won't help! What if the talent behind Apple decided to take their abilities elsewhere and join various DAOs?

This is the reality all business faces. And business leaders need to figure out what to do about it … now.

Summary of Key Points

» One of the most consistent challenges facing any business is the ability to find, attract and keep good people. Web3 is already changing the way innovators, creators, engineers, coders and other talented individuals are engaging with and providing their input to projects or businesses.

» Protocol development eras such as web1 and web3 are profoundly important, but they are often not easy to use. It is only when great user-friendly apps are built on top of the protocols that they make the leap across the chasm.

» If your business currently sees employees as a necessary cost that needs to be kept low then you will almost certainly hit significant recruitment problems as more and more people turn their back on traditional employment for a smorgasbord of web3 opportunities that give them more freedom. They may not make as much money, but for millennials and Gen Z quality of life and purpose is much more important.

» Web3 will allow talent to set up multiple streams of income where they are paid tokens that can be exchanged or borrowed against. The talent will be in control of their creative output, with multiple ways to be paid while only engaging in projects they believe in.

» This deconstruction is also reconstructing to create completely new opportunities and markets for talent and creators such as digital art NFTs.

» The Supply-side Revolution of talent will impact every industry because it puts even more power in the hands of that talent to decide not just terms, but the way they provide and monetize their input.

Chapter 6

Capital and Finance

Financial services in some form or another have been around for about 40,000 years. Starting in the Upper Paleolithic period, hunter-gatherers used barter systems where people would swap items they had for items they wanted or needed.[1] Of course, bartering has its limits as it's pretty hard to trade half a chicken or determine what is more valuable between a pig and a sack of wheat. It depends on demand. Money in some form started out as natural objects such as shells, salt, then metallic coins and evolved over time into paper money, credit and digital money.

However, regardless of the form money takes, all monetary systems share three characteristics:

» A unit of account.
» A store of value.
» A means of exchange.

Although we tend to think of banks when we think of financial systems, banks developed relatively late compared to currencies. Currencies could be stolen, so banks emerged as a place to protect wealth. Banks also worked with governments, royalty and wealthy families to pool resources for larger projects. They were in many ways the predecessors to the corporations that we know today. Banks often facilitated large projects like the railways, which spawned so much commercial activity and made some sort of management of these projects necessary.

Of course, this pool of money allowed banks to get creative, and loans and debt entered the economic process. Essentially, the bank would use the money pooled by customers to lend to other customers, and the system worked because the interest paid to savers was always smaller than the interest charged to lenders. And as long as the loans were paid back, the system worked.

Until it didn't. In 2007 the system stopped working because the banks had been doing all sorts of things outside of that remit. The cycle is always the same. Over time, regulation, much of which is implemented in the first place in the wake of a previous financial crash, is watered down as a way to keep out competition, reduce innovation and allow the existing players to bend the rules to their advantage again. Remember, there are around 23 lobbyists in the US for every member of congress.[2] And it's not much better in the UK. As such, there is a lot of money being spent getting to the ear of policymakers, who then influence regulation. Plus, the political process is itself cyclical, with politicians often agreeing to all sorts of manifesto promises in order to get elected and promptly forgetting about those promises once in office. Each raft of regulation can be, and often is, wiped out when the political leadership changes or the flavor of politics changes from right to left or vice versa.

Just look at the sanctions imposed on Russia following their invasion of Ukraine. Never in history have so many sanctions been enacted so quickly by so many countries, or gone so far. Regardless of your views on those sanctions, they show the political power of the central banking systems. And the measures taken against Russia are making many countries around the world nervous about holding US dollars in their treasury in case one day the US decides to turn those sanctions on them for some reason.[3]

As for 2007, the financial services industry had been deregulated, which led to all sorts of questionable behavior. According to the International Monetary Fund (IMF), 'The crisis that began as the US "subprime" crisis in the summer of 2007 spread to a number of other advanced economies through a combination of direct exposures to subprime assets, the gradual loss of confidence in a number of asset classes and the drying-up of wholesale financial markets. In this process it came to expose "home-grown" financial imbalances in a number of advanced economies, typically characterized by an overreliance on wholesale funding sources by the banking system and asset bubbles in residential property markets.'[4]

In other words, banks started to lend massive amounts of money to people who had no way of ever paying it back (subprime) on the assumption that the property market would continue to rise so the underlying asset, the person's home, would serve as adequate collateral. So, when the property market started to go south, they were in trouble. Many of those loans, as it turned out, had been divided up and peppered throughout other, more stable asset classes. Think of this like little bits of rotten apple being hidden in large apple pies. The good masked the bad. Until it didn't. The 'big three' credit rating agencies, Standard & Poor's, Moody's and Fitch – all formerly trusted sources of financial knowledge and integrity – were seen as key players in the crisis because rather than help investors evaluate the safety of the various complex investment vehicles, they were paid handsomely to provide favorable ratings.[5] When the real estate bubble inevitably burst, it came to light that these agencies had allocated AAA ratings to investments that were stuffed full of that bad apple in the collateralized debt obligation (CDO) market. People trusted this rating as indicating safety when it didn't, and investors large and small lost millions.

As you probably know all too well, what caused the crash was a massive oversupply of housing, which should have and would have broken the banking system had central banks not stepped in to save it. But, in doing so, they created the conditions for another systemic collapse even larger than the GFC – confidence in central banking. We can see this already. Even now, most of the regulation, including the Dodd–Frank Act, signed into law to prevent a repeat of the 2007 crisis, has already been watered down or repealed. In 2022 banking industry bonuses were the biggest since the crash.[6] The fact that banks were considered 'too big to fail' and repeatedly bailed out by governments meant that the banking industry benefited way beyond just survival. They were also innately protected by what is known as the 'Fed put'. Investors have not needed to worry too much about the performance of the financial markets because the GFC taught them that the US Federal Reserve (and other central banks) will not allow the markets to fall beyond a certain threshold – say 20 to 25 per cent – before riding to the rescue with lower rates and more quantitative easing. The logic is simple: there is so much in the global financial system that the markets cannot be allowed to fall any further because a bigger drop could set off a chain reaction of bad debts that could destabilize the biggest banks and cause a crisis that would make 2007 look mild.[7] Hence the Fed put, 'put' being an option trading term that allows investors to make money when the market goes down. In this scenario the Fed is ensuring that there really isn't that much risk that the market will go down too much. This has, of course, inflated the market still further to a point that bears almost no resemblance to the daily realities of people's lives.

The fallout from the global financial crisis was severe and far reach-

> **SINCE THE GREAT DEPRESSION THERE HAVE BEEN 28 FINANCIAL CRASHES OR 'CORRECTIONS'.**

ing, but it wasn't new. The Great Depression, which started in 1929 and lasted most of the 1930s, was the longest, deepest and most widespread depression of the twentieth century. Triggered or at least accelerated by the stock market collapse of 29 October 1929, known as Black Tuesday, the Great Depression saw personal incomes, tax revenue, profit and prices plummet. International trade fell by more than 50 per cent and unemployment in the US rose to 23 per cent, reaching 33 per cent in other countries.[8]

In response to the harrowing reality caused by the Great Depression, President Franklin D. Roosevelt (FDR) enacted the 'New Deal', starting in 1933. It consisted of a series of programs, public works projects, financial reforms and regulations to constrain the banking industry and inflate the economy. Focusing on what historians have since referred to as the 'three Rs', it delivered 'relief' to the victims of the Depression, 'recovery' of the economy back to pre-crash levels and 'reform' of the financial system to prevent it happening again.

Only it did happen again. Since the Great Depression there have been 28 financial crashes or 'corrections', including the GFC, felt around the world.[9] And it will continue to happen as long as human beings are central to the financial system. Even with the best will in the world, and FDR-style interventions, human beings have always found ways to circumvent regulation in the pursuit of shareholder return and self-interest.

This is called the 'Minsky cycle', named after economist Hyman Minsky, who noted that bankers, traders and other financiers periodically played the role of arsonists, setting the entire economy ablaze. In a repetitive chain of Minsky moments, a period of stability encourages risk-taking, which leads to a period of instability when risks are realized as losses, which quickly flips into risk-aversion, thus restoring the stability for it all to happen again.[10]

Hence why financial services have been so ripe for disruption. That, and the fact that the global financial services industry is worth around $1.3 trillion. Crypto is a back-up plan to the next systemic failure, because it is increasingly clear that human beings can't or won't solve this problem.

Disruption in Web1

Financial services looked different for the first time in web1, but it was all just window dressing. For example, instead of just sending customers statements, banks built a fairly basic HTML website with some security where customers could log in and look at their statement online. It was all exactly the same processes and centralized banking system; it just gave the appearance of more control for the user. They could organize payments, but the payment requests were usually just sent to a branch for someone to execute.

Remember, web1 and web2 completely disrupted the demand side of business. The search capability of web1, for example, empowered customers looking for financial products such as mortgages or credit cards for the first time. Prior to web1 insurance salesmen, financial planners, mortgage brokers and bankers would tell their customers about their offering and the customer would pretty much have to decide if they trusted the person and the pitch in order to make a buying decision. Search and the emergence of comparison sites completely changed that and allowed customers to compare that offering to those of other providers and therefore shop around for a better deal. Although Andersen Consulting (now Accenture) created the first comparison-shopping site called BargainFinder as an experiment in 1995,

> "THE SEARCH CAPABILITY OF WEB1 EMPOWERED CUSTOMERS LOOKING FOR FINANCIAL PRODUCTS SUCH AS MORTGAGES OR CREDIT CARDS FOR THE FIRST TIME."

the first comparison site for financial services was probably Moneysupermarket.com, which was launched in late web1 (1999).

Disruption in Web2

By the time web2 rolled around, banking and financial services were ripe for even greater disruption, and that took the form of the challenger banks such as Revolut and Monzo. But these offerings are not window-dressed banking as usual. Instead, they provide digital native banking on a mobile phone, made incredibly intuitive, fast and easy to use. These challenger banks and financial services integrated all their services into a single system. For the bank, there were significantly fewer overheads, as there were rarely any physical branches; everything was digital – mobile money management on the go.

The surge in challenger banks that emerged in web2 was not just about the evolution of technological capability; their popularity was also a backlash against the legacy banking system following the GFC of 2007. It was clear who was to blame for the crisis. People were disgusted when the full story of the greed and hubris were laid bare and they sought alternative banking solutions.

Disruption in Web3

Remember, web3 will upend the supply side of talent, capital and operations. Let's look at what that actually means for capital through the extension of our story about Alice and her dad, Bob.

Bob trained as an accountant after his musical dreams were dashed, and he has invested into his pension ever since. He's got a stocks and shares individual retirement account (IRA), to which he adds any spare cash he has. Even Bob knows that 'cash is trash' when it comes to investments. Alice has been encouraging him to get into crypto, but he thinks it's just crazy speculation. In truth, he's right. And so is Alice. There is a world of difference between investing in Bitcoin, which is now considered a 'blue chip' cryptocurrency, and some of the newer, less secure cryptocurrencies. But that is true of the stock market. There is always greater risk attached to shares of unproven companies than those that have proven year-on-year returns. As Alice also likes to point out, the stock market is also incredibly volatile, and it's impacted by all sorts of madness. 'Come on, Dad, it's all based on nonsense. How come Kylie Jenner can tweet that she doesn't like Snapchat's new redesign and it wipes $1.3 billion off Snap Inc.'s stock price?[11] That's crazy. It makes zero sense. I'm not getting involved in that.'

Alice is not investing in traditional capital markets; she is becoming her own capital market. That is why this supply-side disruption is so profound. She still has stocks and an IRA just because the tax advantages make it hard to ignore – certainly for now. But she's not investing in a pension, and she's certainly not got a high-street bank current account that charges her a fee to use her own money and gives zero interest on savings. She knows that web3 is already making a significant impact on global financial services far beyond how someone accesses their money.

Alice read an interesting blog post that asked readers to imagine that the centralized global financial services system is a giant lake, full to the brim with water (money). Web3, starting with Bitcoin, opened the dam and the water is just pouring out of the centralized dam, to lots of decentralized lakes and rivers. It is this outpouring of money from the centralized system that is making traditional institutions nervous *and* fueling the speculation in cryptocurrency and NFTs. We are potentially experiencing the digitization of our entire global economic system, with a total market size of $300 trillion.

Governments are nervous because they have traditionally used monetary policy as levers to control supply and demand and therefore the economy. Although many of these levers have now been politicized, governments still often increase interest rates so that people have less money in their pocket, which reduces demand and dampens inflation. At the time of writing, we're currently seeing this lever being pulled after over a decade of 'quantitative easing', or printing money to buy corporate assets. There are obviously some pros and cons to this centralized capability, but it is still open to abuse. If money becomes decentralized, governments and central banks lose these powers. This is probably the biggest existential threat to web3 realizing its full potential. It would be naive not to recognize some of the enormous benefits of a centralized system, yet at the same time, there is still significant lobbying power working on behalf of the capital-based status quo. As such, the threat of governmental intervention, regulation and legislation is significant and could stifle web3 innovations in the shorter term, especially in financial markets, which are currently extremely centralized and equally lucrative.

The problem that those seeking to maintain power have right now is that the dam has already burst. People, including Alice, are already grabbing some of that money flowing out of the ultra-centralized model. What makes what's happening in web3 different from anything that has come before is the removal of trust from the system – everything is now an algorithm, which can be openly verified. 'Don't Trust. Verify.' We no longer need to hope that politicians will do the right thing, which is just as well considering past performance. We don't have to hope they will enact the right legislation and regulation to prevent the next crash. Digital ownership is algorithmically secured on the blockchain, making the rules of the game much more transparent. Middlemen and those seeking to game the system won't be able to in the same way as they do today. Needless to say, those middlemen (i.e. traditional banks) are worried and many are making web3 moves, although most of the effort is window dressing. Think J. P. Morgan's move to Decentraland or crypto mortgages, which are really just mortgages with crypto collateral. Nothing particularly innovative about that! Although web3 started with capital (in the form of Bitcoin), now, as web3 matures up its own S-curve, it's showing us that it's much more sophisticated than taking one analogue concept and digitizing it. And the options it presents are going to liberate everyone, including Alice.

> **EVERYTHING IS NOW AN ALGORITHM, WHICH CAN BE OPENLY VERIFIED.**

Alice is already acting as a supplier of capital, replacing a bank, by becoming her own bank, and is making money from that supply-side shift. She doesn't have a lot of money, but she still has the capacity to use what little she has in novel ways as a supplier of capital or a contributor to the ecosystem. Even small amounts of capital are a contribution. Alice knows that the world of money is already being massively deconstructed. In Figure 6.1 each box represents something that a bank or financial services company currently offers, controls or manages that is now offered by individuals all coming together in

FIGURE 6.1: DECENTRALIZED FINANCE (DEFI) DECONSTRUCTION

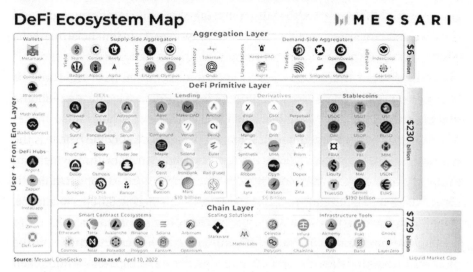

Source: Messari, CoinGecko   Data as of: April 10, 2022

the web3 stack to provide those same products or services to other individuals or companies, thus cutting out the centralized banking middlemen.

Alice has several crypto-wallets that hold various cryptocurrencies, including Bitcoin. None are as secure or as well established as Bitcoin, but there is little doubt that, by the time web3 tips into web4, cryptocurrency will include many different currencies, just as there are currently many national currencies. In a crypto native world, Bitcoin is likely to maintain its dominance in the same way that the US dollar is widely viewed as the king of currencies. For me personally, I was attracted to crypto because of Bitcoin, and it led me to discover everything else that was possible. A lot of people come for Bitcoin and stay for web3.

Alice has already converted some of her more volatile crypto into stablecoins. Stablecoins are a class of cryptocurrency that offer price stability by pegging the currency to a reserve asset. So, for example, USD coin (USDC) takes a real US dollar and digitizes it. So, the dollar itself is held in a bank account or treasury bond but not used or accessed in any way, and its equivalent digital counterpart is simultaneously 'minted' as a USDC crypto coin on Ethereum. PAX Gold is a stablecoin that uses gold as the reserve asset, where you can take your crypto-wallet to redeem physical gold stored in a London vault. Gold is a 6,000-year-old asset for storing value, so it's not likely to go away overnight. There are also stablecoins linked to all major currencies.

When it comes to money or the creation of digital currency, Bitcoin is by design very limited. It is a cryptocurrency and that's all it is. This limitation is one of its greatest strengths because it makes it very secure. As such, Bitcoin has proved itself to be an awesome store of value over the last decade, but as a unit of account and a medium of exchange, it hasn't been as good.

Ethereum emerged as a much more versatile smart contract system. The cost to build the DeFi and other markets in the Bitcoin blockchain are prohibitively high because of the block space. The trade-off for more versatility is security risk and centralization. But these innovations, including stablecoins, solve the unit of account and medium of exchange problem.

Stablecoins provide the benefits of the integration and transportability of crypto with the stability of a currency as the medium of exchange. You wouldn't necessarily want to hold a lot of money in stablecoins because of the risk of the reserve asset depreciating, but it manages crypto's current volatility well.

At the time of writing there was $51.9 billion in USDC, and that is just one stablecoin. The challenge with these types of stablecoins is two-fold. They still rely on traditional banking, so if the world saw another GFC, which is highly possible, the currency backing these stablecoins could disappear or else be significantly devalued. Plus, these providers still need to be a trusted third party to function properly. Therefore, they still rely on institutional trust to function. Another provider, called Tether, was busted for not being trustworthy when it was discovered that they were not holding one real dollar per one tether (USDT). They, along with exchange Bitfinex, were fined $18.5 million for allegedly not holding the stated 1:1 ratio.[12] When you're dealing with these sorts of 'on-chain' to 'off-chain' solutions you're once again relying on institutional trust of the intermediary.

These types of solutions have created enormous efficiency in the crypto economy. Remember the characteristics of money. One is the medium of exchange, but with crypto that is very complicated. Stablecoins have made that medium of exchange much easier. But even the good ones, like USDC, still carry counterparty risk. And that's where collateralized stablecoin comes in.

MakerDAO has created a stablecoin dollar called a DAI. One dollar equals one DAI, just like USDC, but it's backed by collateralized crypto. So instead of the counterparty risk of a provider such as USDC, who users have to trust to put the corresponding paper dollars into a bank account for safekeeping, MakerDAO has created a model for collateralization. Alice put her Bitcoin into a smart contract and that, along with other people's Bitcoin, collectively collateralized the entire system instead of needing to trust a third party. As such, Alice is supplying her capital to others in a secure way that protects her capital and allows others who need money access to it, and she also receives interest, which is yet another stream of income for her. It might not be huge, but it all mounts up. If the dollar is unpegging off the DAI, their algorithms adjust the collateral, and the collateral provider (Alice) earns interest for providing that collateral. Because it's all in a smart contract on the blockchain there is only algorithmic counterparty risk. DAI is a much more decentralized stablecoin with decentralized trust.

This is truly profound because in the history of humanity this has always been left to a centralized institutional trusted third party like a central bank whose job it was to ensure that a currency was stable. It's been up to the central bank who can access capital, how much they can access and under what rules. In the MakerDAO ecosystem an algorithm is creating that stability with the help of collateralized cryptocurrency, which comes from thousands of individuals like Alice who are allowing their capital to be used in exchange for an interest payment.

As already mentioned in the Prologue, Terraform Labs' TerraUSD (UST) was the 'third way' for stablecoins attempting to create benefits of decentralization with the efficiency of not having to 'lock up' and over collateralize other assets to peg the currency. There are two types of algorithmic stablecoin – rebase and seigniorage. Rebase stablecoins control the supply of a stablecoin to maintain its one-to-one peg to fiat currencies, in other words $1 digital token has $1 of actual money in the bank account. The protocol mints (adds) or burns (removes) coins in line with the price movement of the stablecoin to ensure the price stays 1:1. If the price of the stablecoins slips below $1, coins are removed from circulation, or they are added if it goes above $1. Seigniorage stablecoins work in a similar way, only they also pair the stablecoin with other cryptocurrencies to have more control over its valuation. These currencies offer 'market makers' incentives to participate in their cryptocurrency and generate profits. Terra was an example of a seigniorage stablecoin. It uses Terra's native cryptocurrency, LUNA, to maintain its valuation with the USD. However, this innovative pegging approach also led to its downfall,[13] and lost the 1:1 peg.

For Alice, if she did not know better and was attracted to the 20 per cent yield she could be earning on her UST on Anchor, it would have meant she lost almost everything. Although there was algorithmic transparency in how UST operated, and it did not rely on a trusted third party, there is still systemic risk and the possibility that you can lose everything. Fortunately, Alice has taken a diversified approach with her crypto strategy and didn't put all her eggs in one basket. Leveraging peer-to-peer lending platforms such as Compound or Aave, Alice has been able to lend her coins out to a market of borrowers using algorithmic smart contracts and over-collateralization to reduce the risk earning on average through the year between 5 and 10 per cent. Over-collateralization in this context is where the lending platform requires something in the region of 150 per cent of what the user wants to borrow as collateral – thus the loan is over-collateralized.

Thinking about your business, what implications would these capabilities have for you? Are you able to better use the capital assets of your business or to access money in different ways and create new types of treasury models? Could you be less reliant on banks? You are probably thinking this is all just pie in the sky. Many of these platforms are offering rates of return that traditional banks have not offered in decades, if ever. These sorts of numbers make it easy to dismiss the deconstruction that is currently happening to financial services, but this deconstruction is so complete that you can also insure those returns.

Insurance is another very easy concept to decentralize because it is basically people coming together and saying there's a risk that certain events will happen, and calculating the likelihood of that risk so as to cost it. Nexus Mutual is a DAO that pools together capital in exchange for a return and, so far, it only insures in the crypto space, but it's likely to include all types of insurance over time. Essentially it covers algorithm failures or custodian risks.

Before heading off on tour, Alice decided that she could make the USDC she still held work for her a bit harder while she was gone. So, she lent her USDC on a decentralized lending platform, which was offering a 10 per cent return, and she used Nexus Mutual to insure that return for 2.6 per cent, meaning she was guaranteed a 7.4 per cent return – almost risk free. It would be easy to draw parallels between the portfolios that were insured prior to the GFC and how those insurance policies ended up being worthless, and it would be naive to say those parallels don't exist. But Nexus Mutual limits the amount of insurance they provide so the chances of that happening are minimized. The decision to pay out on policies is decided by a decentralized network of claim assessors and members, and so far Nexus Mutual has paid out in many of the hacks where their members had insurance.

When Alice was explaining her plans to her dad and telling him about her moves to fund the tour, including using the money she already had, he couldn't believe the returns she was talking about. Bob has a current account with a high-street bank and even on his designated savings account he's only getting 0.4 per cent. Even his stocks and shares IRA is not consistently making 7.4 per cent and it's certainly not guaranteed. Bob is beginning to think he should get his daughter to handle his retirement annuity.

For decades large companies have become proficient in 'sweating their assets' – getting the most out of what they already possess or own. That may include moving cash reserves to other places or moving operations. What web3 does is allow individuals like Alice to do the same. Instead of investing her savings in banks paying lousy interest so the bank can use her money to make their shareholders wealthy, web3 creates a decentralized free-flowing system where Alice can use her own money to find value, insure against any risk and sweat her assets so they benefit her, not the bank or shareholder. And stablecoins have certainly accelerated that capability.

> **WEB3 ALSO GIVES BUSINESSES MANY MORE NEW WAYS TO SWEAT THEIR ASSETS.**

Web3 also gives businesses many more new ways to sweat their assets.

Before she leaves for Asia, Alice is going to need to borrow some money for some equipment upgrades. She did look at selling some of her assets but decided against it because there are so many really interesting web3 options open to her already that means she doesn't have to sell anything.

When Bob needed a bank loan to help get his band started pre-web1, he had to make an appointment at his local bank for a robust meeting with Mr Mallory, his bank manager, who grilled him on his plans and effectively decided whether he was worthy of the money or not. A huge amount of power in the hands of one man (and it always was one man). Bob got the money, but what if the bank manager didn't like the look of him or had an argument with his wife that morning? Bob might have been denied based on nothing more than natural bias or a bad mood. It was profoundly unfair. The concept of credit scores started in 1989 as a way to bring more objectivity to the lending process and make it fairer. It's highly questionable whether that has happened. There are still far too many people who need money whose options are severely limited when it comes to credit or forced to use unscrupulous lenders charging exorbitant interest payments.

Web3 is set to change all that. Alice doesn't have to bother with bank managers or credit scores; she goes straight to web3 platforms like Aave or Compound, which connect people who have money to the people who need money without any middlemen or scoring.

Both are built on Ethereum. At the time of writing Aave had $22 billion available to lend and Compound had $11 billion. People with money to lend to others can connect their wallet to either platform and select what crypto or stablecoin they will invest from their wallet. They can see upfront what percentage return they will receive on their loan. And they can also see what that currency or stablecoin is being lent out at. The borrower – in this case, Alice – uploads her collateral (Bitcoin) from her own crypto-wallet and the agreement is recorded in a smart contract on the blockchain. With projects like Goldfinch this type of capability is being extended to entrepreneurs in the developing world with lenders spreading the risk over the thousands of small, micro loans to entrepreneurs such as farmers in Africa or well builders in India.

As of early 2022, this type of platform is used mainly by people like Alice who own Bitcoin but don't want to sell it and will simply use it to secure a loan. Or by traders and speculators who want to increase their exposure to crypto assets when they are highly volatile. In time, as crypto becomes second nature to us, we will all have a crypto-wallet, which will give us access to these and many other web3 applications. The vast amounts of money that are currently pouring out of the centralized financial system will flow into countless platforms in the web3 stack. Millions of people like Alice will use these platforms to offer up their own capital securely for others to use in the same way banks still do today, and they will find novel ways to access money when they need it, all secured algorithmically on the Ethereum blockchain and insured to reduce risk. In the future it's these sorts of platforms that will provide the finance and treasury capabilities to the largest businesses.

Alice is fully aware that she is fortunate; she got into Bitcoin really early and never sold what she bought. That said, she doesn't own a lot, just enough to give her some very interesting options. For example, when Alice was in Asia, she realized that everywhere she was going or places she was staying in also accepted Bitcoin Lightning as well as the usual Visa and Mastercard.

As mentioned, Bitcoin is an amazing store of value, but as a medium of exchange and unit of account it is cumbersome to put it mildly. Bitcoin Lightning is a 'Layer 2' payment protocol, which sits on top of Bitcoin and solves those last two problems. It enables instant transactions between different nodes who agree to participate in the Lightning Network. This in turn allowed Alice to make purchases instantly without the need for the Bitcoin transaction to be processed in a specific block by the miners at that moment. Instead, it looks to the network to validate the transaction and then eventually registers the transaction to the core blockchain. This small step is potentially the beginning of a payments revolution, as it creates a globally instant, highly scalable, yet completely decentralized peer-to-peer payment system. It is just as fast as using a credit card. Only with Bitcoin Lightning Alice was offered lower prices, didn't have issues with her bank blocking her card because she was traveling in places that were off the beaten track and didn't pay ridiculously high currency exchange rates. Every time she paid for something it was almost instant. This is undoubtedly the future – a payment network that works on a global basis, from her phone, over the internet with low fees and no central intermediary.

Before Alice left for her trip, her family went out to dinner. Bob was talking to Alice's mum about retirement and what the financial planner had suggested with his pension. But Alice was having none of it. 'Dad, can you just wait until I get home and we can go through it together? I've been doing a ton of research and there are so many more options for you now.' She went on to tell him about TokenSets, as an example. TokenSets is a web3 platform, also built on Ethereum, that gives anyone with a crypto-wallet access to an investment manager who will manage their assets for them without actually giving them the keys of those assets. The assets, like most web3 innovations, are secured by the crypto in their wallets and a smart contract that outlines the investment sets Bob wishes to invest in.

As such, they don't have to trust that the asset manager won't run off with the assets or embezzle funds. This substantially changes the risk profile, as Bob can have several asset managers without taking counterparty risk, and he can insure against smart contract failure, just for extra peace of mind.

All Capital Will Be Disrupted

The nature of capital has meant that we have relied on trusted third parties to store our wealth and protect it while monitoring the services that we purchase. The banks held all the power and we held very little, beyond shopping around for the best deal. High-street banks were the only place most people could access capital or secure financial services. They encouraged parents to open an account for their children because they knew that once they had, that individual would probably stay with that bank their entire lives. There have, however, been very few alternatives, which has made the banking and financial services sector lazy, with little regard for customer satisfaction. No point worrying too much about losing customers when all the other options are just as bad! Even the challenger banks of web2, while significantly better, are just variations on the same theme. Namely, the bank holds the power and you as the consumer can choose from a suite of products that make more money for the bank, but not necessarily for you.

Web3 is going to change all that because participants in the web3 network will hold the power, and you as a consumer can choose from a suite of products that make you more money. Even the very act of holding the assets via private keys means that you are part of the network that is creating this new financial system. Not only will we have many more financial services to choose from that put us in the driving seat, but individuals will be able to sweat their assets in the same way a large corporation already does to maximize value and increase revenue over time. People will no longer be locked into a set financial system or forced into certain products; they will have far more options and the ability to insure those options to further minimize risk.

These same expanded choices will also be available to businesses. Instead of through banks or venture funding, they could access capital in new ways. There are already some companies that give shares to their employees, but why not invite employees to invest for a certain return? Not only do they get a return, but the business benefits twice over from the cash injection and the renewed engagement of that employee to make the business successful.

The assumption that there will always be those willing to invest in their shares may be about to change anyway, as web3 offers those with money far more options and control over where they invest, while limiting risk. Modern portfolio theory (MPT) employs the core idea of diversification: that owning a portfolio of assets from different classes is less risky than holding a portfolio of similar assets. What web3 is already doing is creating new asset classes and allowing people access to novel ways to increase their diversification, thus reducing the risk even further. And those that need money, individuals and businesses, will also have far more options for how to secure the capital they need.

The issue of how money is pooled together in the future for projects or business expansion is also going to be changed by web3. Traditionally, if a business wanted more money it would have to approach a traditional lender, but significant sums are now being raised via a DAO for all sorts of projects.

For example, in November 2021, Sotheby's announced that it was going to auction off a rare copy of the US Constitution, one of only 13 in existence. A bunch of people interested in purchasing the Constitution created a DAO called ConstitutionDAO and invited others to join. Within 48 hours the DAO had raised $5 million, going on to raise a total of $34,025,859 in a matter of weeks.[14] This is quite a contrast from the drafting process of the US Constitution, which took 55 delegates nearly four months to complete.[15] It is also in stark contrast to how millions of dollars used to be raised via pedigreed financiers and lawyers locked in endless meetings over weeks or months. ConstitutionDAO was unsuccessful in its bid, but it's certainly a glimpse of the future of what can happen extremely quickly when a strong purpose meets web3.

Summary of Key Points

» Regardless of the form money takes, all monetary systems provide a unit of account, a store of value and a means of exchange.

» Since the Great Depression there have been 28 financial crashes, or 'corrections', including the GFC, felt around the world. And it will continue to happen as long as human beings are central to the financial system.

» In web1 financial services looked different, but it was largely window dressing. The search capability of web1 did, however, empower customers to find the best financial products, such as mortgages or credit cards, for the first time.

» Web2 saw the emergence of challenger banks that offered fast, intuitive, digital native banking on a mobile phone.

» Web3 provides individuals and businesses new ways to 'sweat their assets' – getting the most out of what they already own.

» The assumption that there will always be people willing to invest in shares may also be changing, as web3 offers those with money far more options and greater control over where they invest, while limiting risk.

» The issue of how money is pooled together in the future for projects or business expansion is also going to be changed by web3. Money is now being raised via a DAO for all sorts of projects.

Chapter 7

Deconstructed Operational Supply

They say necessity is the mother of invention. If we look back at the history of commerce, business and production, we can see that the various functions, departments and processes that make up modern business have evolved out of necessity.

Before there were towns and cities, most people lived in rural areas, in small settlements. Work was often sporadic, and life was precarious. Most people were employed on the land, and what was created from the land was then turned into goods by artisans and craftspeople who made entire products either themselves or within small collectives or families. These craftspeople also provided services to others such as weaving, dyeing, bookbinding, painting, masonry, baking, leatherwork, embroidery, cobbling and candle making. But it was all primarily small-scale production, selling what a family or small collective didn't need for themselves.

The Industrial Revolution changed all that.

The emergence of steam power and later electricity transformed production capability, which in turn created the 'factory system' in the late eighteenth century. The factory system created the 'industrial' of the Industrial Revolution. Richard Arkwright built his first cotton mill in Nottingham and by 1833 his mill complex in Belper employed 2,000 people. Several factories in Manchester employed over 1,000 workers. The exploding demand for labor saw hundreds of thousands of people leave the land and flock to the factories in search of a better life. Few found one. Conditions were brutal. Men, women and children worked incredibly long shifts in unsafe, unhealthy and mind-numbing environments.

Historian and author Joshua Freeman paints a bleak picture of the reality of the factory system at the time: 'The noise and motion of the machinery; the stifling air, full of cotton dust, in many mills kept oppressively warm to reduce breakage; the pervasive stench from whale oil and animal grease used to lubricate the machinery … and the sweat from hundreds of laboring people, the pale countenances and sickly bodies of the workers; the fierce demeanor of the overseers, some of whom carried belts and whips to enforce their discipline.'[1]

But these changes transformed the economy because they produced a boom in productivity. The study of economics also emerged as a new branch of knowledge concerned with the production, consumption and transfer of wealth. This was Adam Smith's time. His 'division of labor' described how productivity could be increased if the production process into different stages was broken down to allow workers to focus on specific (albeit monotonous) tasks. The idea was that if workers become better at one small aspect of production, it would increase overall output – so long as there was sufficient volume and quantity produced.[2] Alfred Marshall, another noted economist of the time, brought the ideas of marginal utility and costs of production to business for the first time.[3] Together, Smith and Marshall were instrumental in not only the emergence of operations as we understand it today around how goods are produced, but also the connection between production and profit. Hence the finance department, charged with paying for inputs and wages, usually paid as little as they could get away with. Division of labor together with increased scale, facilitated by mechanization, reduced marginal costs and increased profits, hence the revolution that followed industrialization.

> **DIVISION OF LABOR TOGETHER WITH INCREASED SCALE, FACILITATED BY MECHANIZATION, REDUCED MARGINAL COSTS.**

The impact on productivity and society was profound. According to Freeman, 'The average annual per capita growth of global economic output from the birth of Jesus to the first factory was essentially zero. After the introduction of the factory system in the eighteenth century, it approached 1 per cent per annum, and from the mid-twentieth century 3 per cent per annum.'[4]

But it also came at a cost. The drive to reduce costs led to some very unsavory practices, such as 'employing' pauper apprentices. Employed implies payment and yet these poor children or orphans, often under the age of ten, were unpaid, bound apprentices until the age of 21. These children would be locked in, doing 12-hour shifts, and would 'hot bunk' in an upper floor of the factory. It was known as hot bunking because as one shift ended those children would climb into warm beds just vacated by children off to do the next 12 hours. Free labor certainly helps profits.

Thankfully, the Health and Morals of Apprentices Act was passed in 1802 outlawing such practices, and the 1833 Factory Act further protected children, although the provision still seems harsh by today's standards. No child under 9 years old could work in a factory, but from age 9 to 13 children could work 9 hours a day, and over 13 years old, 12 hours a day!

However, this was the beginning of ensuring effective welfare and management of people – today's HR or talent management. The Acts also facilitated education, a forerunner to the talent management learning and development activities in most businesses. As Freeman notes, 'The giant cotton factory had led to new ways of organizing production, new sets of social relations, and new ways of thinking about the world.'[5]

It was increasingly clear that the factory system needed to develop a people-management system not only to coordinate vast work forces, but also to get the most out of that workforce to maximize productivity.

The focus on productivity evolved from two directions. First, mill owners like Richard Arkwright built housing and mill villages close to his factories to bring the workforce closer. In the US, the famous Lowell mills established boarding houses in the mid-1800s to house their female workers. But this was mainly a way to get more people to work at the mills. It was strategic rather than focused on worker welfare and engagement.

Welshman Robert Owen saw worker welfare as being inextricably linked to productivity. He was also a driving force behind the first Factory Acts. Owen was convinced that a person's character was shaped by their environment. The factory system was a horrendous environment for most workers, with inevitable consequences. Owen believed that the problems so many mill owners were experiencing with their workforce could be solved by improving the environment. His New Lanark Mill in Scotland, which employed 1,700 people at its height, was a revelation. Not only did he build a village for mill workers, but he significantly improved education, made provisions for the sick and provided pension and welfare funds.

Looking after the workforce and treating them like human beings rather than cogs in a machine was certainly one way to improve productivity – now the domain of HR. In 1913 the Welfare Workers' Association (WWA) was formed at an employee conference in York. Thirty-four employers in attendance, including Rowntree's, Boots and Cadbury, declared the WWA an 'association of employers interested in industrial betterment and [the] welfare [of] workers engaged by them'. The WWA is now known as the Chartered Institute of Personnel and Development (CIPD), which many HR professionals are part of today.[6]

Many other mill owners, seeing the productivity uplift and often feeling a deep moral duty (many were Quakers), followed suit, including Joseph Rowntree, the Lever Brothers and George Cadbury. Cadbury built the Bourneville village at his own expense in 1895. His mission was 'to alleviate the evils of modern, more cramped living conditions'. He believed if the workers were happier outside work and had a good place to live and access to fresh food, they would be more productive inside work. Bournville village included 313 cottages, each with a large garden to grow fresh food, and the houses were set on 330 acres of land, including a park and recreation areas.[7]

Today these ideas are clustered around employee engagement. Some companies that are getting this right are reaping significant rewards not only in terms of productivity, profitability and market capitalization, but also innovation and problem solving. Enlightened leaders know that the best output they can get from their employees is not measured in hours

> **THE BEST OUTPUT YOU CAN GET FROM YOUR EMPLOYEES IS NOT MEASURED IN HOURS.**

worked, but the freedom of thought they are given to come up with good solutions. There are, however, still far too many companies where employee engagement is viewed as irrelevant, as evidenced by Gallup's State of the Global

Workplace report. Just 20 per cent of the full-time global workforce is actively engaged, leaving 80 per cent watching the clock or actively working against the business![8] Disengaged workers are not productive, they are not innovative, and they will not deliver organizational change. Engagement is always going to be important as we try to access discretionary effort and elevate productivity, but web3 bakes engagement into the system through open participation and incentives to cooperate.

The other direction came from process innovation and greater drive for efficiency. And this was largely the brainchild of Frederick Winslow Taylor. Taylor professionalized management – another important part of operations. He started his career as an apprentice machinist and patternmaker, despite coming from an affluent Philadelphia family – probably a little like Bill Gates or Sergey Brin dropping out of university to go to where the action was in personal computing or the internet respectively. Where the action was at the start of the twentieth century was factories, and Taylor eventually moved into factory management. Most managers in factories at the time were educated men who had no hands-on experience of the production processes they were managing. Taylor did. While working at Midvale Steel Works, near Philadelphia, and later at Andrew Carnegie's Bethlehem Steel in Pennsylvania, Taylor applied his engineer's mind to the mechanics of steel production and metalworking, leading to innovations in cost accounting, inventory control, tool standardization and shop-floor layout – all important considerations in modern operations.

Taylor believed that if a task in a production process was observed and measured, quality and productivity could be systematically improved. His approach, 'scientific management', was a revelation for productivity, although it wasn't always well received by workers. Before scientific management workers would tell their boss what was possible in terms of work rate and maximum output. But Taylor knew from his work as an apprentice that what was possible and what was delivered were often two very different things. Most managers didn't. For the first time ever, Taylor's approach split planning from execution. Taylor took Smith's division of labor to a whole new level. Not only were employees expected to work on only one small task, they were then given detailed instructions on how to best complete that task for maximum efficiency based on detailed observation and testing. Pay was then calculated by a piecework system that rewarded higher productivity for those who met agreed production norms.[9]

Taylorism, as scientific management became known, spread across continental USA, Europe and Soviet Russia, and even entered Mao's China. It gave us work study, or the men in white coats with a clipboard assessing operational processes to eke out greater efficiencies. Every business that has a standard operating procedure, systems and a set of operational protocols can thank Taylor for the innovation.

When we see this progression laid out over time, we are essentially witnessing the emergence of what is commonly called 'operations'. Operations is the administration of business practices to successfully convert various inputs, such as materials, labor, technology or equipment, into outputs the market wants, as efficiently as possible. And all this must be done while managing revenues and costs to maximize profit.

In many ways everything about what we now consider business-as-usual can be traced back to the Industrial Revolution. It built the framework for what commerce and enterprise was. It laid down the rails on which all businesses from that point operated on. So ubiquitous were those rails that we didn't even see them anymore, but they included corporate structure, various departments such as legal, talent management (HR), finance, supply chain management, logistics and sales and marketing. People were employed to produce the products and services the business created, and those were then sold to the market. This is business-as-usual whether a business creates diggers or software or bread.

But the Industrial Revolution is long gone and so are the factories. Figure 7.1 shows the decline of US factory-based manufacturing jobs from 1930.

Between 1995 and 2002, 22 million manufacturing jobs were eliminated in the global economy while production increased by more than 30 per cent worldwide.[10] Those jobs were not being moved to different locations; they were gone forever, largely because of automation. For example, 128 robotic arms at a Philips factory in Holland make the same number of products as their Chinese factory with one-tenth of the workforce.[11]

The same decline in factory-based manufacturing can be seen in all industrialized countries. And yet we are still largely running business on rails set up in the Industrial Revolution and treating workers like cogs in a factory

FIGURE 7.1: DECLINE IN MANUFACTURING JOBS IN THE US

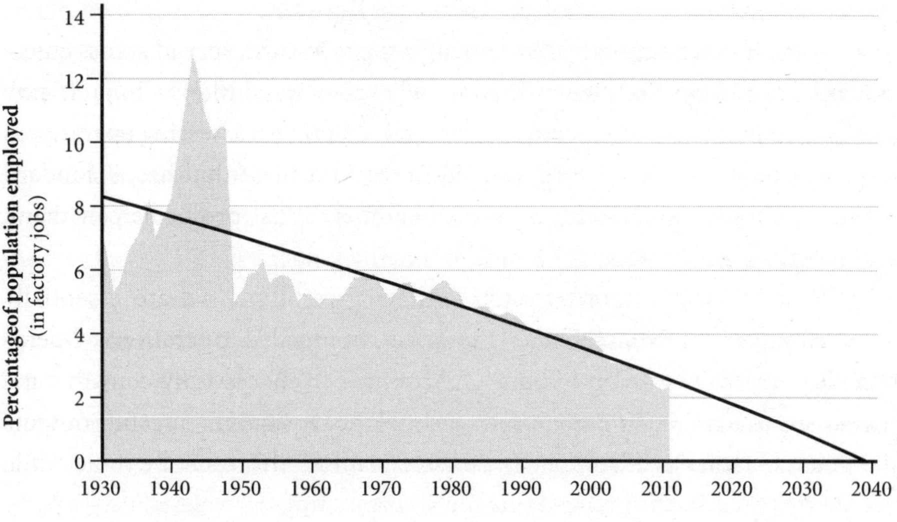

Source: U.S. Bureau of Economic Analysis. www.FutureTimeline.net

machine when the vast majority of those workers are now knowledge workers in the Information Age.

Where machinery and new forms of energy replaced millions of workers during and after the Industrial Revolution, digital technology and the internet started to replace millions more in the Information Age.

Evolving Education

It is also interesting to note that those rails that were set up in the Industrial Revolution included education. The formula for the current education system in the US and UK came out of the observations of a young Anglican chaplain, Andrew Bell. Originally stationed in India, he studied how Hindus arranged training for the lower castes. About 5 per cent of the Hindu population are born into the upper social classes or castes, including the industrial caste, the warrior or administrative caste and the elite Brahmins – those trained in law, medicine, teaching and other professional occupations. The other 95 per cent of the population were divided into the menial caste and the 'untouchables'. Whatever caste someone was born into was their lot in life.

Bell could immediately see the parallels between this system and the vast workforce that was needed for the Industrial Revolution. This Indian system was therefore extremely attractive because it proposed a very efficient way of churning out individuals who would do what they were told in dirty, difficult and poorly paid jobs. The changes to the law to prevent children from working when they were too young also led to the idea of compulsory schooling. Although it was, rightly, seen as largely beneficial to the children and society, compulsory schooling for children who were no longer legally allowed to work also allowed their mothers to continue working in the factories.

Bell suggested that 'schooled ignorance was more useful than unschooled stupidity'. In other words, if young children were schooled in a way that got them used to long, boring monotonous 'work', they would slip seamlessly into the mills, factories and workplaces of industrialized Britain.[12]

In the US something similar was also happening. In what could easily be described as early lobbying, wealthy industrialists and influential financiers were investing more money into 'education' than the government. As late as 1915, Andrew Carnegie and John D. Rockefeller, both financial titans even by today's standards, were individually spending more on education than the entire US Government. The following excerpt from the first mission statement of Rockefeller's General Education Board may give an indication as to why:

In our dreams ... people yield themselves with perfect docility to our molding hands. The present educational conventions [intellectual and character education] fade from our minds, and unhampered by tradition we work our own good will upon a grateful and responsive folk. We shall not try to make these people or any of their children into philosophers or men of learning or men of science. We have not to raise up from among them authors, educators, poets or men of letters. We shall not search for embryo great artists, painters, musicians, nor lawyers, doctors, preachers, politicians, statesmen, of whom we have ample supply. The task we set before ourselves is very simple ... we will organize children ... and teach them to do in a perfect way the things their fathers and mothers are doing in an imperfect way.[13]

In other words, education was not about creating educated individuals; it was about creating an obedient army of workers who would learn to do what their parents did before them – only better! No wonder the current education system, which is still largely running on those tracks, is no longer fit for purpose. It is 'teaching' for a world that no longer exists.

What makes web3 so transformational is that it will bring the industrial era to an end, or at least massively reduce its relevance in the global economy. Web3 effectively creates brand-new rails to which all future businesses will attach themselves. And those rails will also include an evolution to the education system. We must teach children how to navigate the Supply-side Revolution and how they and others will come together to produce goods and services.

However, those rails are not straight, connecting one input to one output or one department neatly to another. Web3 will be a smorgasbord of distinct operational and educational efficiency that a business can then plug into as and when it needs. The business itself will no longer be a business, but a DAO. It is in effect a brand-new way of doing things that changes the very nature and infrastructure of business-as-usual. This includes the educational on-ramps into business and operational supply (how to administer business practices to successfully collaborate with multiple inputs who are no longer directly connected, owned or employed by the managing entity).

Disruption in Web1

The operational disruption brought about by web1 was essentially the speed in operational efficiency brought about by better communication via email. It was possible to transfer documents instantly regardless of geography.

Greater access to more information also helped with research and development, product development and sourcing better, more favorable suppliers – all of which increased efficiency of operations. The companies that thrived were able to leverage the ubiquitous access to information and media faster than their counterparties. It's a well-known fact that organizations driven by leaders who can embrace data-driven decisions grow much faster.

Disruption in Web2

The operational improvements brought about by web2 have been significant. The entire software as a service (SaaS) industry came from the web2 cloud computing capability.

Countless companies emerged during this period to improve operations, everything from cloud computing to Salesforce to Slack to Workday. Salesforce is an integrated customer relationship management (CRM) solution that gives all departments a single shared view of every customer. Slack is where teams, regardless of location, can come together to get stuff done. And Workday is essentially an HR management platform that is used by some of the world's largest employers, including Walmart.

> **ONE OF THE MOST THOROUGHLY PROVEN FINDINGS IN SOCIAL SCIENCE IS THAT BONUSES AND INCENTIVE PACKAGES DON'T IMPROVE PERFORMANCE.**

There is little doubt that the Covid-19 pandemic massively accelerated these and many other web2 platforms as millions of people were working from home, globally. Not only did web2 make the transition from office-working to home-working possible, it has also fundamentally changed the nature of work.

During the Industrial Revolution people started to go to factories to work. Over time that evolved to include offices. It became the norm for us to 'go to work' in some form or another. Even the idea of flexible working arrangements were considered challenging for some companies – especially those who still believed in the Theory X management system. Developed by management professor Douglas McGregor in the 1950s, Theory X is the typical operational ideology that suggests that the only way business can get people to do what management wants them to do is through strong supervision with robust rewards and punishment. Theory Y suggests that if you trust people and treat them well, they are more likely to gain job satisfaction and tap into their intrinsic motivation without the need for excessive reward or punishment.

One of the most thoroughly proven findings in social science is that bonuses and incentive packages don't improve performance, and yet businesses continue to rely on them without success.[14] Annual reviews are also a terrible way to evaluate employees and do nothing for morale or performance improvement. Gallup 2020 data suggests that 86 per cent of employees don't think their annual review is accurate. According to author Marcus Buckingham, 'The annual performance review is akin to going to a bad dentist: before you go, you dread it; while you're there, it's painful; after it's done, nothing's fixed.' Data from management consultancy firm Gartner suggests that 81 per cent of companies are considering redesigning their performance-management systems with the addition of more frequent 'touchpoints', and yet between 63 per cent and 80 per cent of organizations say they still do the annual review – largely because they still believe Theory X has a point: that people need the stick and the carrot to do good work.[15]

Instinctively we know Theory Y is true, and many of us have experienced it in our own lives, and yet it has taken a global pandemic to drive home the reality that Theory X just doesn't work. What the global pandemic has proved, even to the most skeptical, is that most employees can be trusted, and they are just as productive (often more so) when they are not working in a factory or an office. Ironically, Covid-19 may have accelerated our collective willingness and appreciation for a different way of working. Certainly, it fueled the Great Resignation and, according to Google, more people searched for 'how to start a business' than 'how to get a job' in 2021.[16] There were nearly 5.4 million applications to form new businesses in 2021 in the US, up 1.9 million from the year before. This is, according to American economist Irwin Stelzer, 'only one of several ways in which the supply side of the labor market is changing at a pace that the major institutions on the demand side are having difficulty accommodating.'[17] A mass exodus from cities saw the demand for commercial real estate plummet and more and more people began to wonder if there was a better way than the traditional nine-to-five grind that increasingly turned into a seven-to-seven grind or longer!

Web3 is the enabler that will further accelerate the global workforce to new ways of working, because it creates so many more opportunities around how

> **WEB3 IS THE ENABLER THAT WILL FURTHER ACCELERATE THE GLOBAL WORKFORCE TO NEW WAYS OF WORKING.**

people (creative talent and operational talent) come together in the web3 stack to plug into various platforms that supply operational know-how on a project-by-project basis, probably via a DAO, to combine ideas, materials and processes for creating goods and services in the on-chain and off-chain world.

Disruption in Web3

In web3 the deconstruction of operational supply, or how business combines labor, materials and equipment to create goods and services the market wants, is already in flux. Even in web2 a company could massively slim down operations in individual departments such as finance, HR and legal, and plug into a platform that took care of most of the day-to-day work. Project management platforms allowed for people in different departments, locations or even geographies to collaborate in real time. But what has always stayed the same is the baseline structure of the company that is taking advantage of these innovations. But web3 will change that. It may not happen overnight, and it's likely that we will see some form of hybrid of web3 and the existing corporate structure before business as we know it disintegrates into collaborative, mutually incentivized commercial structures such as the DAO.

We've already talked about ConstitutionDAO, which raised $34,025,859 in a matter of weeks to buy a rare copy of the US Constitution.[18] Another group, PleasrDAO, purchased the one-of-a-kind Wu-Tang Clan album *Once Upon a Time in Shaolin*, formerly owned by Martin Shkreli, for $4 million. Both of these examples demonstrate how web3 capability can quickly steer huge sums of money towards community projects or goals.[19]

As always, this shift to DAOs facilitated by web3 protocols will be another example of the Innovator's Dilemma. From the outside a DAO might look like a company that is simply hiring in various freelance consultants to complete a project or conduct business, but with a DAO those freelancers are not just suppliers; they are also owners. And those involved won't just be those with the capital or the creative talent, but also the operational and support capability to deliver the output.

We will never live in a world without professional services such as lawyers or auditors, but their role in business is going to be vastly diminished. Smart contracts on the blockchain are going to render 300-page legal agreements obsolete. The deal is signed in the transaction itself. It's open and transparent. If one party doesn't agree to the terms then they won't exchange keys, which confirms the transaction. As such, a substantial amount of the activity of the legal department is no longer required. The same with auditing. The whole of web3 is built on transparency. When all the transactions are 'on chain', the networks are open, and the algorithms manage the audit.

Let's revisit Alice and Bob to explain how web3 is going to unravel operations for business-as-usual even further. Again, stay mindful of the capability rather than the particular platform, and consider how that capability could impact your business.

Bob continued to work his way into more senior accounting roles at a very large firm. The company uses Workday. There is an HR department but most of the grunt work of HR, such as arranging employee holidays and time off, is done via Workday. The business has also followed Michael Saylor's lead and holds Bitcoin on its balance sheet instead of just cash.

In 2020 Michael Saylor, Chairman and CEO of MicroStrategy, famously stated that he didn't hold cash on his balance sheet as a company because he thought that 'cash is trash'. Instead, he started using Bitcoin as a hedge against inflation. Within a couple of weeks, he had converted $450 million of the company's cash reserves into Bitcoin while telling shareholders that cash was no longer a safe place for its excess $500 million.[20] Saylor was the first CEO of a publicly listed company to effectively endorse Bitcoin. Today, 40 or 50 other public companies have followed suit. More and more companies are going to come to this realization, which will require the traditional role of the Chief Financial Officer to morph into something new. The day-to-day operational payments of wages and supplies can already largely be automated or certainly taken care of with minimal intervention via some web2 platform. But web3 will ensure that the focus of the CFO in web3 will shift to managing treasury around crypto. This is again another Bitcoin crossing-the-chasm moment, as it becomes a treasury solution for many respected businesses.

The alternative to Bob's reality working in a business that uses web2 platforms to streamline operations is legions of individuals plugging into or creating DAOs that interest them. So instead of your employees being your employees, they will be individuals, operational talent providers and owners in the products and services you create. This can sound challenging, but reconsider Gallup's State of the Global Workplace report – 80 per cent of the full-time global workforce is disengaged, either watching the clock or actively working against the business![21] If employees were also owners, even partially, this figure would plummet, and productivity could explode.

Alice is essentially very similar to your current employees. But, as a web3 native, she's living and working outside the traditional business framework. She thinks the DAO is the future. So, during the Covid-19 lockdown, Alice decided that she wanted to create a new album, maybe collaborate with a bunch of other musicians, and put on a couch concert. She found Aragon.org, which already makes it super-easy to create a DAO in a matter of minutes. No need for lawyers, dull meetings or lengthy forms; the agreements and rules are coded into the blockchain. Although not something Alice needs right now, OtoCo can also create a corresponding traditional company in Delaware or Wyoming, which then bridges the gap between the off-chain world and the decentralized on-chain world. This is a nod to the reality that DAOs will not suddenly replace limited companies but that the two are likely to create some type of hybrid as the technology and acceptance evolves.

Are there any parts of your business that could be carved off the limited company structure into a DAO so that you can better keep your most precious creative and operational talent and co-create new products or services for the business?

Once set up, Alice also created a Discord group and invited her musician connections to get involved. Aragon has built-in governance for managing collective decisions and managing disputes. Everyone in the DAO essentially has a vote in terms of decision-making and conflict resolution and they are voting with their wallets. Once about 50 collaborators had bought into the DAO, the group needed to decide exactly what they were going to create, who was going to perform in the couch concerts and how to monitor the venture. It was discussed openly in Discord and then everyone voted based on the number of tokens they owned – one vote per token.

This system does have its issues as evidenced by the Ethereum Name Service (ENS) DAO. When Director of Operations for ENS Brantly Millegan decided to share some controversial personal opinions on Twitter, the rest of the DAO community was not happy. What followed was a month-long debate about his suitability for the role. It was put to a vote, but because the vote was based on one vote per token and not one vote per person, Millegan, who owned a lot of tokens, was able to keep his position by a margin of 5.88 per cent. This can lead to situations in DAOs where they reach a stalemate in governance, struggle to make progress or there are no ways for disruptive members to leave the group. The hierarchical model of today's business definitely has some advantages when it comes to quick decision-making. You can actually see all the latest votes openly at https://messari.io/governor/overview.

Thankfully for Alice, there were no such dramas and any problems that arose in the DAO were simply put to the vote, and the various proposed solutions were voted on and agreed upon.

Because web3 started in capital with the emergence of Bitcoin, it's perhaps not surprising that so far the most interesting operational web3 capabilities are those that will impact the CFO. While researching what was possible, Alice came across Gnosis – a decentralized treasury management platform built on the web3 stack. One of the dangers any company faces is the trustworthiness of their CFO. Remember Andy Fastow? He was Enron's CFO, one of the key figures behind a complex web of off-balance-sheet activity to conceal Enron's massive losses. He was also able to defraud Enron out of tens of millions of dollars. With a decentralized treasury like Gnosis, this type of fraud would not be possible. As well as complete transparency, Gnosis also operates a multi-signature key system, which means that no one or even two people could defraud the treasury, all while not having to rely on a bank to hold the cash.

There are also new capabilities that sit on top of a decentralized treasury like Gnosis, such as Multis, which take care of all the usual operational roles of the finance department, such as managing cash flows, paying suppliers and employees using stablecoins – but again, on a fully transparent decentralized system where all the transactions are recorded in the blockchain. Alice opted for LlamaPay instead because the project was likely to be only running during lockdown and had a relatively short expected lifespan. LlamaPay is an example of the composability of web3 where a small developer community can create a helpful solution to automate recurring salary payments in crypto in real time without taking any financial risk from using the platform. This platform is challenging the notion of what a salary even is. So, whenever anyone in the group is actively engaged in work to deliver the output their payment is streamed to them by the second. When their work is done, they are fully compensated for their work automatically and don't need to speak to Alice or anyone else in the DAO – the agreement is coded in the blockchain and delivery releases funds automatically. The very notion of being paid every two weeks or at the end of the month is now up for serious debate in web3, when creative or operational talent can be paid efficiently up to the last second.

> **THE VERY NOTION OF BEING PAID EVERY TWO WEEKS OR AT THE END OF THE MONTH IS NOW UP FOR SERIOUS DEBATE.**

The provenance of ownership of the delivery is also stored in the blockchain. This capability will be profound for supply chains. Remember the Tesco horsemeat scandal? In 2013 it was discovered that a number of products marketed as beefburgers contained horsemeat. The scandal took nearly $375 million (£300 million) off the value of Tesco.[22] But Tesco are by no means alone. Supply-chain fraud is rife, not just in the use of cheaper ingredients like horsemeat in beefburgers; it is open to abuse all the way through the supply chain. According to KPMG, this abuse can include kickbacks, foreign corrupt practices, IP theft, improper use of production assets, counterfeit, misappropriation of scrap, raw materials, fraudulent certificates of origin, free trade zone fraud, use of conflict materials and disbursement and inventory fraud.[23]

But if point of origin authenticity and a whole host of additional information was coded into the blockchain then the goods could be tracked right through the supply chain. Everledger is another web3 platform that is helping people shine a light on their supply chain using blockchain and internet-of-things (IoT) technology – the network of physical devices connected by the internet – so they can prevent Tesco-style screw-ups. Every product or service has a story. Potentially that story can build trust and develop brand loyalty, but it is often deliberately obfuscated to stop end users from knowing the full details of how, where and by whom a product is made – think child labor in fashion-brand factories. Everledger is making that story and the product journey known so that customers can trust what they buy. This is done by unboxing the lifetime story of any product from wine to clothes to shoes to diamonds to electric car batteries and beefburgers. Not only does this give provenance on the blockchain from raw materials to end product, but Everledger suggests that this will also increase demand from like-minded buyers and greater cooperation with like-minded suppliers, and showcase a company's sustainability record – which is likely to become law as the world seeks to prevent global climate collapse. Rather than making grand marketing statements that most customers consider nothing more than greenwashing, Everledger demonstrates and authenticates full supply-chain traceability.

This authentication of supply also includes people through the web3 verification of CVs and what someone has actually done. Alice only knows a couple of the people in the DAO personally – everyone else is pseudo-anonymous. She doesn't know their ethnicity, gender or sexual preferences either. All she knows is what they have done in the past and the quality of their work. Whether someone's membership is therefore accepted by the community it is based entirely on their skill set and their ability to prove the quality of their work. Platforms such as Dragonchain already make this possible. Dragonchain offers several business-ready web3 applications for streamlining and securing various elements of operations and the supply chain.

We already know from social science that natural bias and office or business hierarchies have for centuries privileged straight white men into positions of power. There isn't even anything that sinister about this – people tend to warm to people who look like them. If a straight white man is doing the interviewing (and for a very long time they were the only people doing so) there is a very good chance that the straight white male applicant will be viewed more favorably than anyone else. It's just part of human nature, but it's still deeply unfair. In an Oxford University study, it was found that applicants from minority ethnic backgrounds have to send 60 per cent more applications to get a positive response from an employer than white British candidates.[24] Women are also frequently discriminated against, especially when they have a family because it becomes harder to get back into senior roles after maternity leave. Having children does not hinder men, but it often unfairly hinders women in their careers because of the existing way of 'doing business'. Web3 is going to change all that because we will enter a world where 'employers' (probably via a DAO) will not even know the real name of their 'employees' (members of the DAO), never mind their gender, ethnicity, sexual preferences or family situation. But they will know everything they have ever worked on, all their verified experience, full details of their proven skill set and the quality of their work. This is great news for Alice or anyone else who is creatively talented or has operational experience who has missed out on opportunities because their face didn't quite fit.

> **'EMPLOYERS' (PROBABLY VIA A DAO) WILL NOT EVEN KNOW THE REAL NAME OF THEIR 'EMPLOYEES'.**

Oracles (services supplying smart contracts with data from the off-chain outside world) are also already offering a decentralized tamper-proof way of proving that something has happened without needing a trusted third party. In a world of fake news, conspiracy theories and the polarization and hate this creates, solving this problem is really important for humanity. There are several oracle-based platforms but one of the most established is Chainlink. This decentralized oracle network securely connects smart contracts with off-chain data and services to provide tamper-proof inputs, outputs and computations that support advanced smart contracts on any blockchain. TruthDAO is a citizen journalism platform with the mission to bring real, factual, non-partisan, bias-free journalism back to the world.

It's worth reiterating that the ecosystems of web2 and web3 are still largely separate, like a Venn diagram that hasn't quite been squashed together yet. Right now, the emphasis is on allowing the two worlds to communicate and do business with each other. Over time that will become even easier as web4 develops simple user-friendly apps that will sit on top of the web3 protocols and make it far easier to use its vast capability.

In addition, be mindful of the fact that some of the entities I've called out may not survive what is already a very fast-moving evolutionary process, but the capabilities they offer will, and will almost certainly re-emerge better, faster and stronger next time.

All Operations Will Be Disrupted

So much of the web3 supply movement is focused on the creative talent, whether that's the coders, developers, product designers or artists in the world of NFTs. As the world shifts, these roles cannot scale up without the support of talented operators that reskill to focus on decentralized models.

Operational supply will be disrupted first in the digital world, where people come together to create a digitally delivered product or service. But it is only a matter of time before all industries are impacted by the changes to operational supply, even if it's a new understanding of how remote workers can contribute that brings greater flexibility and operational efficiency to the supply chain. In addition, new ways of verifying and tracking labor and ingredients from source to end product will also give those who embrace that technology a competitive advantage, as it allows them to demonstrate provenance, something that is increasingly important for consumers.

Summary of Key Points

» Adam Smith and Alfred Marshall were instrumental in the emergence of operations as we understand it today. Division of labor together with increased scale, facilitated by mechanization, reduced marginal costs and increased profits.

» The focus on productivity evolved from two directions: to improve employee welfare and develop a greater drive for efficiency.

» Everything about what we now consider business-as-usual can be traced back to the Industrial Revolution. But that era is long gone.

» Where machinery and new forms of energy replaced millions of workers during and after the Industrial Revolution, digital technology and the internet started to replace millions more in the Information Age.

» What makes web3 so transformational is that it will bring the industrial era to an end, or at least massively reduce its relevance in the global economy. Web3 effectively creates brand-new rails on which all future businesses will operate.

» Operational supply will be disrupted first in the digital world, where people come together to create a digitally delivered product or service. But it is only a matter of time before all industries are impacted by the changes to operational supply.

Chapter 8

Marketing, Distribution and Commerce

Web1 and web2 brought significant demand-side disruption through far greater access to more customers. As well as upending the supply-side of business, web3 is about to bring even more demand-side disruption, but the power dynamics between company and customer will take an even more dramatic twist. The very idea of a customer is going to merge with the creator and/or participant. As mentioned in Chapter 5, stakeholders as we currently understand them will merge, and that includes the customer.

It's no longer the case that only companies create products and services that are then sold to individuals or other companies. In the world of web3, customers are also creators, suppliers, participants, advocates and beneficiaries from their own and other innovations that are redistributing the profits of traditional companies.

> **THE VERY IDEA OF A CUSTOMER IS GOING TO MERGE WITH THE CREATOR AND/OR PARTICIPANT.**

We can see this shift more clearly if we look at the progression of commerce through history. People have been buying and selling goods since the beginning of time, but it wasn't until the seventeenth century that permanent shops with regular opening hours started to replace local markets. Before long, every town had a local general store. These 'mom and pop' stores were usually small, family-run, independent businesses that catered almost exclusively to the local community. They would, therefore, sell whatever was needed by that community, from food to toys to fabrics, tools and more. The number of customers to these early businesses was limited by geography and the sales conditions of the day. For example, it wasn't yet possible to buy frozen goods, so everything was fresh, and each shop provided what the customers in the community needed on a daily basis. As towns became bigger the general store wasn't enough to meet the needs of the growing population, so specialist stores joined the general store to create high streets, and customers would visit a variety of high-street shops to get what they needed. If the demand was there, then some enterprising individual would create a shop to sell it.

As towns grew larger and some became cities, customers were plentiful in a particular geographical location. By the mid-1800s to early 1900s the over-supply of customers in one location led to the creation of department stores. The idea was simple – if you put everything that customers could possibly want and make the experience luxurious and enjoyable then customers will stay longer and buy more. Of course, all this coincided with the shift from agriculture being the dominant employer to manufacturing and industry. It's the reason towns and cities exploded in the first place, as people left the land to find more lucrative work in mills and factories. This in turn swelled the supply of customers and put more money in their pockets. The Industrial Revolution brought new jobs and new standards of living, which in turn brought broader tastes. In the US, department stores opened, such as Macy's (1858) and Bloomingdale's (1861) in New York, and Sears (1892) in Chicago. In the UK, John Lewis opened in 1864 in London and department stores such as Debenhams, Harvey Nichols and Harrods massively increased the choice on offer for customers. The stores didn't just sell goods; they were an experience where customers could watch cookery demonstrations, see lectures on new products or attend entertainment events. Although customers benefited from greater choice, it was the businesses themselves that held all the power and drove demand.

The introduction of credit in the 1920s also changed commerce because it put even more money in people's pockets. Early cards were limited to businesses, but the game changed again with the launch of Diners Club in 1950. Now consumers had ubiquitous access to credit, and they used it. It's probably not a coincidence that shopping malls emerged in the 1950s, when it also became affordable for a lot more people to drive cars.

Advertising also really took off around the same time, no doubt to cash in on the increase in available cash via credit. Plus, the cost of production of goods and services had been plummeting in many sectors since the Industrial Revolution. We also had shipping containers transporting goods and services all over the world by the mid-twentieth century. Up until this point, demand for products and services had outstripped supply. But now, for the first time, supply – or our ability to make products – outstripped the demand for those products. Advertising and branding became necessary in order to differentiate products from their competitors, attract customers and increase sales.

Growth in sales of the family car also meant that customers were no longer just confined to a high street or department store; they would travel out of their local area to visit purpose-built shopping malls. Often these malls would be anchored by one large department store with lots of additional shops clustered around it, and people were happy to drive out of their local area to frequent these malls. It was also envisioned as a cultural and social center where people could come together and not only do their shopping, but also be entertained or eat out. By 1960 there were more than 4,500 malls across the US, accounting for 14 per cent of all retail sales. By 1975 malls were accounting for 33 per cent of all retail in the US.[1]

This evolution in retail operates like a protocol as well, like an app on top of new protocols. Although the shopping mall created a steady stream of customers, it also increased competition for the retailers – hence the emergence of big-box retailers such as Walmart and Kmart in the 1960s. At the same time a new model of the two-income family began to emerge (probably to help pay for the family credit). Women didn't have time to browse shopping malls. They wanted to get in, get what they needed and get out. So, the idea of a one-stop-shop became appealing again, especially as these big-box retailers were pushing prices down. Instead of beautiful displays, Walmart discovered that if they stacked their items high and packed them tightly together, they could meet the demand for cheaper products, but the volume of sales still made it profitable – often extremely profitable. The big-box stores were attractive to customers who were looking for a convenient, friction-free, no-frills service, and they found what they needed at far lower prices, made possible by post-war law changes that allowed discount pricing.

What followed was variations on the theme: lots of big-box retailers alongside each other in retail parks, refurbishing malls to make them look more like high streets, adding entertainment complexes and restaurants or food courts.

And then the internet came along, and commerce became e-commerce.

Disruption in Web1

All the way through the history of commerce, the owner of the shops or company behind the sales held the power. They would decide what to sell and for how much, and control when things could be bought. The companies with the deepest pockets went on to create brands and could corner markets and dictate demand.

Web1 started to shift that balance of power. Although web1 still benefited companies by making it easier to access new markets outside their natural geographical location, web1 also empowered customers with more information, greater choice and the ability to accurately compare offers and find the best deal – often for the first time.

But as more and more people got online and became familiar with buying online, competition for eyeballs intensified as supply further outstripped demand. Advertising pre-web1 had been down to the big brands with the most money advertising on mass-media platforms such as TV, billboards or newspapers and magazines. There was very little targeting. It was just shotgun advertising and brand awareness to the masses in the hope that some of it translated into sales. As American merchant and advertising pioneer John Wanamaker said, 'Half the money I spend on advertising is wasted; the trouble is, I don't know which half.' There may have been direct marketing campaigns on products similar to ones the customer had bought before, or the use of catalogues, but advertisers didn't have a great deal of information on their customers. In web1, online advertising was still not that sophisticated, but it was becoming possible to collect much more information about customers.

Disruption in Web2

Web2 saw the weaponization of advertising – most consumers online had no idea how much data was being collected about them and their online behavior – yet at the same time it provided ubiquitous access to all the world's information and cutting-edge technology. It was possible to profile customers based on their social media interaction, what they liked or commented on or even what they slowed the scroll to look at. All this data created a picture of the person and what products they might therefore be interested in. No one thought much about it until their Facebook feed started to look more like an online sales catalogue than a way to stay in touch with friends and family (Facebook's original purpose).

> "WEB2 SAW THE WEAPONIZATION OF ADVERTISING."

Following the Cambridge Analytica scandal in 2018, and subsequent revelations, it became clear that the data that was being held on us, by Facebook and other big platforms such as Google, could be used against us by bad actors. This data was not just being used by advertisers to sell more products or services; it was potentially being used by political parties to change what we believed in, what we thought was true and who we voted for. It was during web2 that customers finally figured out the extent of the data capture that was happening online. Centralized platforms such as Google and Facebook knew a staggering amount of information on their users. Yuval Noah Harari, author of *Sapiens* and *Homo Deus*, highlighted just how insightful this data is when he said, 'I didn't realize I was gay until I was 21 but Google probably knew at about 12.'[2]

These platforms know more about us than we know about ourselves, and that concentration of power is nothing short of dangerous. But it has also been exceptionally lucrative. That information is sold to anyone who wants it, to create highly targeted advertising. It has also been used to spread misinformation and lies, to change recipients' thoughts and feelings and therefore their behavior, in ways that were simply not possible just a few years earlier. Christopher Wiley, one of the Cambridge Analytica whistle-blowers, would describe what was being done unwittingly to consumers as 'psychological warfare' –

using analytics to tap into a person's mood or sentiment and influence their 'hearts and minds' towards a particular outcome or candidate.[3]

Even the traditional advertising that we had all become so used to started to become overwhelming. If you've ever had the experience of searching for drain-cleaner on your phone, only to be bombarded with adverts for drain-cleaner on every device you own, then you will understand the upset that many customers started to feel in web2 and are still feeling today as web3 gathers momentum. It often feels as though we are being stalked online, and in many ways we are. Consumers may have more choice, but the backlash has been significant, with calls for greater privacy online. Turns out consumers don't like being stalked and bombarded with adverts 24/7, even if they may be relevant.

Apple has already heeded that call for increased online privacy with an operating system update in 2021 that decimated Facebook advertising revenue, and Google has already indicated that they will follow suit on Android. That smooth, straight superhighway called online advertising that gave companies unprecedented access to almost limitless customers is already full of potholes and burnt-out cars, as more and more consumers are opting out.

Disruption in Web3

Web3 will further empower customers to own and influence the networks they participate in. The traditional concepts of supply and demand are bending round to meet each other like a horseshoe as consumers become buyers *and* sellers, customers and creators/suppliers of goods and services, in a network of connected decentralized offerings that is going to massively disrupt a company's easy access to its customers – certainly in the traditional sense. Businesses will need to reimagine their relationship with their customers and treat them as partners, not targets.

Let's go back to Alice and Bob to explain how web3 is further disrupting demand. When Bob's dream of rock 'n' roll fame and fortune came to an end, he went back to the family accounting business. Pre-web1, the business attracted customers through a quarter-page advert in the *Yellow Pages*, some letterbox drops in the local area, some newspaper ads in the local paper and some strategic alliances with companies that would pass on their details to likely customers. Web1 didn't make much difference to the business because referrals were good, although they did build a pretty hideous website that acted as an online brochure for the services on offer. When web2 came along they upgraded their website and created a simple app where customers could book their services. They created a Facebook page and encouraged customers to share their experience of working with the company to build up social proof. They tried Facebook advertising, targeting households and local businesses based on their interests for accounting services, but it wasn't particularly successful.

> "**BUSINESSES WILL NEED TO REIMAGINE THEIR RELATIONSHIP WITH THEIR CUSTOMERS.**"

It's not just Bob, though, who has noticed that online advertising is not working very well anymore. It's costing too much and not delivering the rewards it once did. Plus, people are incredibly jaded by the incessant advertising.

Alice is certainly sick of being stalked by advertisers and herded towards products and services she doesn't want, so she's already signed up to Fetch. ai. The central technology of Fetch.ai is 'autonomous agents', or the creation of your digital twin, who will interact with the internet of things (IoT) on Alice's behalf. She doesn't need to trawl through hundreds of flight offers to Asia or work out where she could stay; she just gets her digital twin to do it for her and bring back the offers that are likely to be most interesting to her. This is very different from what happens online in web2. If Alice is looking for flights, she will probably start her journey at one of the search engines. The only exception to that would be if she was given a recommendation and went straight to an airline. But for most people they start their search for anything on a search engine. Alice therefore enters the flight details into a search engine and the search engine delivers some matches for her to consider. Search is the gateway to the internet – it would be useless without it. But Fetch.ai is turning that on its head. Because of Alice's digital twin and web3 user profile she is brought much more tailored, specific suggestions that more closely match her as a customer and her declared needs – but without the hours of scrolling. Success in this world will be determined by the goods and services that can most effectively partner with those digital twins, and because this is built on a web3 stack the data you enter into the system is both owned by Alice and under her complete control. Just like the money that is in your Bitcoin wallet, everyone can see it in the network (pseudonymously), but no one can take it or control it but the key holder. This continues the Supply-side Revolution where advertising and commerce become based on the direct supply of our preferences and tastes into various networks.

The Fetch.ai network connects people, devices and services, enabling the sharing of data and cooperation within a decentralized digital economy based on artificial intelligence. The idea is to free up people's time, bring about a fully-functional and reliable internet of things and allow machine learning algorithms to take away most of the stress from our daily lives – such as being bombarded with advertising 24/7. Think about how time-consuming and irritating it is to have to wade through all the offers to find the right energy deal, or decide which flight to buy. Alice just gives all the relevant information to her digital twin, where all the information is encrypted and secure and owned by Alice, and the artificial intelligence (AI) twin goes to work for her. The algorithm would then act on her behalf, not on the behalf of the advertiser. Many of these technologies are in their infancy and some of the entities I've drawn your attention to may not survive, but the underlying capabilities almost certainly will. Just as Pets.com and Webvan were too early, we now live in a world where those services are ubiquitous and have exceeded their original intention. Once the genie is out of the bottle on many of these capabilities, there is no turning back. The same is almost inevitable with our digital twin – especially if we can crack the secure AI challenge.

Imagine a world where everyone has a digital twin? How useful will advertising be then? How will companies access their customers then? What might that do to your current sales and marketing strategy?

This is a completely new problem for companies to grapple with. During web1 and web2 it was still possible to access a steady stream of customers through one of the many large, centralized platforms such as Amazon, Google and Facebook. In fact, before web3, if you wanted to access your potential customers you pretty much had to go through one of those gateways and you would pay for the privilege, with all those profits flowing back to the centralized business who owned the platform.

But that is changing, and not just because of innovations like Fetch.ai.

In many ways the battle for search has been the battle for the internet. Even in the early days of web1 people could see that search was the door through which you had to pass to make the internet useful. Google certainly realized this early on and invested heavily in Chrome. Today about 60 per cent of the web uses Chrome. Together with their ownership of the Android operating system on mobile phones, Google has an impressive reach and vast data banks, but they are still running a centralized model the same as Facebook, Apple, eBay, etc.

There have always been challengers to Chrome's dominance, one of which – Firefox – is an open-source search engine built by Mozilla. One of the leads behind Firefox went on to design the Brave browser, and today over 50 million people use it worldwide. Brave puts Alice in control, not a corporation. It is a private browser that is designed from the ground up to prevent lots of third-party technologies from snooping on everything Alice looks at online so the company behind the browser can then sell that data to advertisers. It is allegedly six times faster than Chrome and it blocks ads, so you are not stalked by drain-cleaner manufacturers. Brave is also built on web3 principles, launching the Basic Attention Token (BAT), which rewards customers for their attention. With existing web2 browsers, Alice was effectively paying with her valuable attention and personal data to browse the web by viewing ads. She had to spend that valuable attention downloading invasive ad technology that transmitted her precious data to advertisers without her consent, and it didn't offer her any benefit. But with Brave, her time is valued, her data is kept private and her attention is rewarded with BAT. Brave is therefore paying Alice for looking at certain things rather than that activity being weaponized and used against her. So far Brave and BAT are still only earning very small amounts of value for their users, but it's an idea whose time has come.

The concept of the marketplace itself is also starting to decentralize; instead of relying on Amazon or eBay to provide all the building blocks of a retailer, there are platforms emerging that are driven by a decentralized community. Alice owns a couple of NFTs, and she is aware that there are already new marketplaces opening up for her to access customers looking to buy NFTs. LooksRare is a community-first NFT marketplace that actively rewards traders, collectors and creators for participating. If Alice sold her

NFT on OpenSea, a commission on her sale and every sale goes back to the company that runs the platform, much like Amazon or eBay. But LooksRare invites buyers and sellers to be part of the community where they earn LOOKS tokens when they buy or sell NFTs, and all the trading fees go back to LOOKS token owners, not shareholders.

At this point, you may again be thinking, 'That's mildly interesting, but it doesn't concern me; my business creates physical products.' But it does concern you. Nike has always been an aspirational brand where people would save up and buy an exclusive pair of trainers. In 2021 Nike bought RTFKT, a digital design studio producing trainers and other collectables that can be worn across different online environments. At the time CEO and president John Donahoe said, 'This acquisition is another step that accelerates Nike's digital transformation and allows us to serve athletes and creators at the intersection of sport, creativity, gaming and culture.'[4] In April 2022 Nike revealed their debut digital trainers, Nike CryptoKicks, inspired by the Swoosh! brand's Dunk silhouette. CryptoKicks are customizable with eight skins made by RTFKT's community of artists and collaborators.[5] Adidas sold $23 million worth of NFTs in less than a day and instantly created a resale market on OpenSea, similar to what might happen on eBay following the release of new limited-edition shoes.[6]

The L'Oréal Group was founded in 1909 and today they create a vast range of beauty products, but they are wise enough to see the writing on the wall of web3. L'Oréal has created 17 NFT product lines and registered a number of digital trademarks for its most well-known beauty brands, indicating that it intends to enter the virtual cosmetics market. L'Oréal already owns a virtual shop in Decentraland. There is even talk of access to non-downloadable simulated fragrances in the metaverse. The trademark submissions indicate L'Oréal's intention of allowing its buyers to shop, sell and barter virtual beauty products in the virtual environment.[7]

There is a massive transfer of wealth occurring out of physical products into digital products and that will almost certainly continue. While we will always need to buy a wardrobe to hold our clothes and we will still buy beauty products to slow the ageing process and we will never be able to eat a digital apple, once the rampant speculation in this space settles down digital products will become second nature to us. Every company, regardless of what it produces now, will have to get wise to the digital possibilities. They will have to find ways to include a digital offering in their product mix.

All Demand Will Be Disrupted Even Further

Clearly, there are certain products and services where the demand is going to be disrupted more quickly than others. Companies that are still rooted in the production of physical goods and offering physical services may take longer to embrace the possibilities that the on-chain crypto space holds for them and how they can therefore expand markets and access more customers. But Nike and L'Oréal are both companies rooted in the production of physical products that customers will continue to buy in the physical world. It's just that they will make more offerings available in the digital world too. This is imperative to understand because a larger percentage of our disposable income will go on virtual goods as consumers spend more time in the virtual world. Everything in the digital space is going to be upended, but it certainly won't stop there.

And there is also little doubt that companies will have to rethink the way they access their potential customers as web3 gathers momentum. All businesses regardless of what they offer will need to collaborate and reward customers in an ongoing partnership where the customer, not the company, owns their data, and the company seeks to add so much value that the customer agrees to allow them access to their data for a micropayment that goes into their crypto-wallet. This is already possible with Monetha – a next-generation web3 loyalty program where users are rewarded for access to their data, not their loyalty to a particular company. Web3 capabilities such as cybermiles offer a word-of-mouth referral program on the blockchain. Incentive rewards are paid in a limited-release, blockchain-based token unlocking the network ownership effect for users as a double economic incentive. Or there's UTU – a web3 anonymous rating and review platform that prevents review manipulation and

> **ALL BUSINESSES REGARDLESS OF WHAT THEY OFFER WILL NEED TO COLLABORATE AND REWARD CUSTOMERS.**

compensates users for accurate reviews. These web3 capabilities completely flip the supply of customers from the company to the customers themselves by giving customers control over their data and what they interact with in the first place. Customers will own their data, which will be securely held on the blockchain, and they, not Google or Facebook, will decide who has access to that data and will be paid to access it. This mosaic of possibilities is set to replace the superhighway of advertising that was so successful for companies but annoying for customers in web1 and web2. Today Google, Facebook and Amazon command hundreds of billions of dollars in advertising revenue as the internet's gatekeepers. In a world of web3, user to user curation, collaboration and community mean those hundreds of billions of dollars will flow to the users themselves. This will feel like an effective referral system that seamlessly integrates with your personal AI.

What all businesses must grasp is that the supply of customers, and therefore sales and marketing, is being upended. For commodity goods such as toothpaste, AI will make the buying decision for the customer without exposure to brand-awareness advertising and the toothpaste will arrive at your house on a just-in-time basis depending on use

> **WEB3 AND AI WILL MEAN THAT WHAT WE NEED JUST ARRIVES.**

per household. There is no human customer in that scenario. For a long time, we have gone to the shops or browsed online to get what we need, but web3 and AI will mean that what we need just arrives based on our digital twin and what we have securely indicated is important to us. For the non-commodity products and services, every business will need to reimagine their relationship with their customer and engage with them through multiple communities where those customers are part owners (old shareholders), part contributors (old employee) and part consumers.

In addition, what is marketed and sold will not come out of corporate R&D or design functions but small independent design lead teams across all categories who might come together in a DAO. And companies as we know them in 2022 will be able to invest in and support these highly innovative design teams. And there is going to be a lot more peer-to-peer curation of commerce. Instead of going to one big retailer or one online mega-store, consumers are going to be incentivized to find more bespoke offerings that suit their needs better.

Summary of Key Points

»   Web3 is about to bring even more demand-side disruption, but the power dynamics between company and customer are about to take an even more dramatic twist.

»   In the world of web3, customers are also creators, suppliers, participants, advocates and beneficiaries.

»   Businesses will need to treat customers as partners, not targets.

»   All businesses will need to collaborate and reward customers in an ongoing partnership where the customer owns their data and can allow the company access to it for a micropayment.

»   A larger percentage of our disposable income will go on virtual goods as consumers spend more time in the virtual world.

»   Web3 and AI will mean that what we need just arrives based on our digital twin and what we have securely indicated is important to us.

»   For the non-commodity products and services, every business will need to engage with customers who are part owners (old shareholders), part contributors (old employee) and part consumers.

»   What is marketed and sold will not come out of corporate R&D or design functions but small design lead teams across all categories who might come together in a DAO.

»   There is going to be a lot more peer-to-peer curation of commerce.

Chapter 9

Web3 Innovation Plot Twist

There are several critical take-aways from Part II that anyone in the C-suite of a traditional business can still get ahead of if they embrace them now. There are many examples of traditional businesses that were first to grasp web1 or cloud in web2 and were able to accelerate out in front of their competition. The same applies with web3.

First, whether we are ready for it or not, web3 has already created critical mass for an alternative economy. Business leaders can either ignore it, fight it or figure out how to integrate with it. The next five years will reward those who can, hopefully with the help of Part II, appreciate that the Supply-side Revolution is already happening, and choose to embrace it now in some type of hybrid manner. Business-as-usual (or even, sadly, business casual) is not going to disappear overnight. Instead, there will be a transition that will require the off-chain and on-chain worlds to work together, certainly for five to ten years. But without the strategic decision to embrace and explore web3 capabilities right now, then business-as-usual simply will not survive over the longer term.

Essentially, what is happening is rapid decentralization of both the demand and the supply side of business. It is this decentralization that will drive the alternative economy. And if business leaders ignore it, they will be blindsided by it as it cannibalizes the economy they believe they are still operating in. As I was writing this book, it hit me that a lot of the eighteenth-

and nineteenth-century economists such as Adam Smith, John Stuart Mill, Alfred Marshall and Friedrich von Hayek we still rely on today were writing their theories in a world that was moving from decentralized to centralized via the Industrial Revolution. What followed was a steady march towards peak centralization – somewhere in the early twenty-first century. The economists during this period, such as John Maynard Keynes and Milton Friedman, were still all focused on an economy based on centralized power. But we are at a new crossroads. Web3 is rendering these theories obsolete because the economic landscape is changing. Besides, many modern economists, such as Elinor Ostrom, Gary Becker, Jeremy Rifkin, Thomas Piketty, Joseph Stigler and even Mark Carney, have consistently called into question the validity of these economic theories. The world needs something new, and web3 is creating that something new via this alternative economy.

> **DECENTRALIZATION WILL DRIVE THE ALTERNATIVE ECONOMY**

The timeframe for embracing web3 is now, and that is true irrespective of what type of business you operate. There is little doubt that web3 will disrupt online digital businesses first, but if you are not managing or leading a digital business that doesn't mean you can ignore web3. It just means you have a little more time to prepare.

It is also worth bearing in mind the exponential growth of technological capability and adoption. By the time web1 gave way to web2 there were around 360 million users worldwide. By October 2008, when the Satoshi white paper was published that spawned the start of web3, there were over 1,504 million users worldwide. As of March 2021, there are 5,168 million global users.[1] Granted, most of those are still using web1 and web2 capability, but once web4 comes along that will also change. One of the reasons so many companies failed in the transition from web1 to web2 was a lack of density. There simply weren't enough people online to warrant their business optimism. But 65.6 per cent of the global population is now online. Density is no longer an issue. So, when web4 comes along, where simple applications are built on top of the myriad of web3 protocols, then web3 adoption will explode via the web4 apps. Just as Napster was a pain to use and Spotify is a pleasure, so all the capabilities we explored in Part II will become much easier to use – which will radically increase adoption across that 65.6 per cent and counting.

A great deal of this adoption is down to whether or not a product or innovation is able to cross the chasm in the product lifecycle. As discussed in Chapter 3, the chasm that needs to be crossed from early adopters to the mass market, specifically the early majority and the late majority, tends to be crossed when 34 per cent of the market is onboard. If we look at internet adoption in the US between 1995 and 2013, we can see that web1 crossed the chasm around 1996. By the time web2 was in full swing, even in the mid-2000s 72 per cent of the US population was using the internet. By the time web3 emerged, even as a concept, the US population online was around 80 per cent.

I believe that the innovation plot twist that will accelerate adoption in web3 will be the seamless cooperation for the creator movement, perhaps via the DAO, also facilitated by smart contracts. When people realize that it's easier to create or join a DAO than applying for a job or registering a company, web3 will explode. Creative or operational talent will start to think en masse, 'I really enjoy working with this community on this idea and I can earn my living doing this at the same time,' so they won't jump on Indeed or LinkedIn to look for a new job but jump on Discord or join a DAO without the need for an employment contract or even an interview, and get paid instantly for work done. At that point the war for talent that has plagued business for decades is going to look like a school-yard tussle. Work begins to feel very similar to play. People of all skill sets and all skill levels will be rewarded for their early and engaged participation in the future networks. The new 'work' may feel more like being on a WhatsApp or Telegram group, creating value as a community, sharing expertise and insight and being paid for it. Add that to the ease and transformation in the supply of capital and operational talent and process, and the alternative economy will boom. This ease of access, which will fully come into its own in web4 via apps will be as transformational to web3 as HTML was to web1 and the iPhone was to web2.

Another key distinction that I hope has come through loud and clear in Part II is that the traditional stakeholders of business are merging. It's

> **THE TRADITIONAL STAKEHOLDERS OF BUSINESS ARE MERGING. IT'S MESSY.**

messy. Stakeholders may be customers, 'employees' in some new form, as well as suppliers and possibly financiers. It's also going to be messy because there isn't the operational talent to make it really work seamlessly yet. The various web3 platforms will need to work with and interact with off-chain business during the transition. But, in time, it will all come together in this new kind of interconnected network that feeds into this alternative economy, completely changing business-as-usual in every industry.

Summary of Key Points

» Web3 has already created critical mass for an alternative economy. Business leaders can either ignore it, fight it or figure out how to integrate with it.

» Business-as-usual is not going to disappear overnight, but without the strategic decision to embrace and explore web3 capabilities right now, it simply will not survive over the longer term.

» Decentralization of both the demand and the supply side of business will drive this alternative economy. And if business leaders ignore it, they will be blindsided by it.

» Web3 will disrupt online digital businesses first, but if you are not managing or leading a digital business, that doesn't mean you can ignore web3. It just means you have a little more time to prepare.

» When people realize it's easier to create or join a DAO than apply for a job or register a company, web3 will truly take off.

PART 3
TOMORROW'S WORLD

Chapter 10

Tomorrow's Business

Although we've already looked at how the various departments or functions of a business will be impacted by web3, it's also worth looking at the business of business itself and how that is also set to be disrupted by web3.

The business of business and how companies are valued is crucial to our modern economy; it defines stock markets, portfolio values, pensions and government intervention. In this chapter we are going to explore how the business of business will change as the fundamental approaches to valuation start to evolve. It is also worth pointing out that for decades the world has judged the success of businesses, assets and industries based almost entirely on share price of the escalating value of those assets. This has worked reasonably well during unprecedented periods of asset inflation, but global economies are shifting underfoot and a more inclusive and robust way of measuring value that takes usage, adoption and benefit delivered into consideration is urgently needed, and web3 will certainly usher that in.

At the time of writing (2022) the vast majority of business is still operating a highly centralized system (see Figure 10.1).

It is centralized because the decision-making control and power rests at the top, usually across a few key leaders in the C-suite acting on behalf of the shareholders (and in most cases the employees). These primary decision-makers are often physically located in the same place to facilitate cooperation and communication. This has been the dominant organizational structure for a couple of centuries, and it's worked pretty well. These types of centralized businesses may not be particularly responsive or dynamic within their markets, mainly because

FIGURE 10.1: MODERN BUSINESS - HIGHLY CENTRALIZED

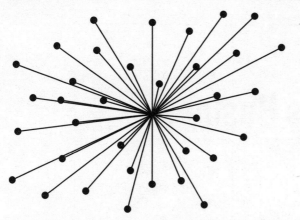

a small cohort of individuals make all the decisions, but there have been significant advantages to this approach. With a central hub, it has been easier to create consistency in how the business is managed and operated. Company policies are easier to enact, implement and oversee because of that consistency. It is also easier to coordinate and communicate with others. Indeed, a great deal of the debate around the efficacy of working remotely during the Covid-19 pandemic was primarily focused on how best to communicate when the team was not all physically in the same place.

Once in operation, the goal of most businesses is profitable growth – with the objective in the early days to either take the business public via an initial public offering (IPO), sell to private equity or build the business to generate positive cash flows. Today, almost all businesses focus on growth as the critical business metric, and it's instrumental in the valuation of a business.

In 1957 Igor Ansoff came up with the Ansoff Matrix as an explanation of the four ways that any business can grow (see Figure 10.2).

Merger and Acquisition in Decline

Ansoff's matrix is still relevant today. The only difference between now and when Ansoff suggested his growth model is the explosion of merger and acquisition (M&A). M&A effectively buys one, two, three or all of Ansoff's four avenues for growth in one strategic maneuver.

FIGURE 10.2: ANSOFF'S MATRIX

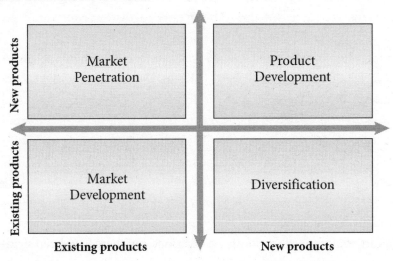

Source: slidesalad.com

M&A is a massive industry, supporting legions of banks and professional services firms across the world. If a larger company is showing slow growth, lacks market-leading innovation or is facing other competitive threats, then merging or buying another business that solves that problem is a popular option. Unsurprisingly, the largest companies in the world still rely heavily on M&A to continue their astronomical growth and sustain their high valuations. Venture capital and private equity firms also rely on their returns from M&A (or IPOs) to generate the returns in their ten-year funds.

M&A is big business. In 2021 M&A activity globally exceeded 62,000 deals – up 24 per cent from 2020, breaking prior records by some margin. The cumulative deal value of those publicly disclosed reached an all-time high of $5.1 trillion, including 130 megadeals with a deal value greater than $5 billion. Private equity and technology companies saw the highest M&A volume and values in 2021. According to PWC, this frenzied activity was 'fueled by intense demand for technology, and for digital and data-driven assets, and the pent-up deal-making demand from 2020 that was unleashed'.[1]

Decades of low interest rates have also fueled this M&A activity. But a global pandemic, cost-of-living crisis and skyrocketing energy costs are creating strong headwinds. Higher interest rates are almost inevitable to coun-ter rising inflation. Increased taxes and greater regulation could also create structural or financial hurdles that delay deals in 2022 and beyond.

But the biggest existential risk to M&A, investment banking and the business of business is actually web3. The increased activity of M&A has certainly been driven by Stage 6 of the Innovator's Dilemma, where estab-lished firms are desperately using M&A to try to catch up with technology that is getting away from them – the irony being that almost all the tech acquisitions were of disruptive web2 companies that had mastered cloud native set-ups (for enterprise) or network effects (for consumer businesses). But these M&As will not protect or even help the acquiring business with the web3 tsunami on the horizon.

Fundamentally, the reason M&A is possible at all between any two busi-nesses is because of the centralized business model where a few key leaders in the C-suite act on behalf of the shareholders. There is a Board of Directors, and if one company wants to buy another company then one of those legions of M&A experts makes an approach to the company of interest via the exec-utive team or Board of Directors. When Elon Musk wanted to buy Twitter, he needed to make an enticing offer to convince shareholders – over 60 per cent more than the market price of the shares – then he needed to get the Board of Directors to agree, and then the board basically dragged any of the last remaining unwilling shareholders to the sale. But what happens in a web3 decentralized business model?

Most large companies have already employed some form of decentraliza-tion and satellite operations in different territories, but the decentralized entity still reports back to the mothership HQ (see Figure 10.3).

The decentralization that web3 is making possible for the first time is something else completely. Ownership is pseudo-anonymous and recorded in smart contracts in the blockchain; owners are decentralized and unknown to each other. It would be impossible, for example, for Ethereum to buy Bitcoin; not just because they 'run on different tracks' but because there is no way to approach anyone or suggest a merger or acquisition – there would always be a large number of wallets (owners) or miners (creators) that resist. So, what does that do to the M&A industry?

FIGURE 10.3: DECENTRALIZED BUSINESS CONNECTED TO HQ

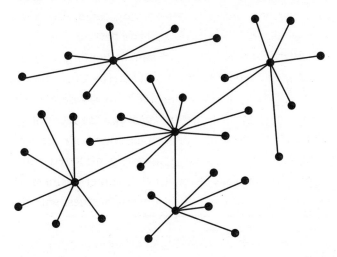

Clearly M&A will continue in a web3 world, especially in companies that are not technology based. However, as our economy becomes even more digitally native it will make modern M&A less prominent than it is today. In 1990 just 5 per cent of the S&P 500 were technology companies. At the height of the dot-com boom it reached 31.6 per cent and by March 2022 it had risen again to 28.1 per cent (see Figure 10.4).

If we look at the trajectory of internet usage over time compared to crypto use, which is foundational to web3, it is fairly safe to assume a relentless march upwards (see Figure 10.5).

As web3 gathers momentum in the information economy over the next ten years, we'll easily see a doubling of equivalent value in our digital native economy. So much value is flowing into tech and information companies, and almost certainly into businesses built on web3 – and web3 turns M&A and IPOs upside down!

> **WHAT HAPPENS TO FACEBOOK WHEN IT CAN'T BUY WHATSAPP OR INSTAGRAM?**

What happens to Facebook when it can't buy WhatsApp or Instagram? What happens to Google when it can't buy DoubleClick or YouTube. Or what will the mighty Apple do when it can no longer acqui-hire the teams critical to its innovation? Stage 6 of the Innovator's

FIGURE 10.4: RISE IN TECH COMPANIES AS A PROPORTION OF S&P 500

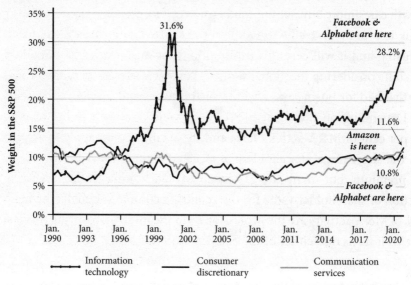

Source: Pierre Debru, WisdomTree, Bloomberg. January 1990 to September 2020. Using current GICS definitions for sectors.

FIGURE 10.5: INTERNET USAGE OVER HISTORY VERSUS CRYPTO USAGE

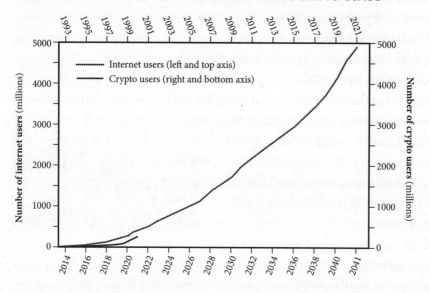

Source: International Telecommunication Union, Our World in Data, Crypta.com, Statista, Bloomberg and Wells Fargo Investment Institute

Dilemma will no longer be an option where cashed-up incumbents with declining growth can simply buy out the competition or *buy* growth.

This is a pretty extreme outcome for the M&A and investment banking industry, and it will certainly limit options for business in the pursuit of growth, but considering the global statistics on M&A success rates, it's probably not that bad for business as a whole, or the goods and services consumers access. Depending on the academic research viewed, anywhere between 50 and 80 per cent of M&A activity fails, and these failure rates apply to acquirers.[2] In the short-term, shareholders of targeted companies typically receive a large premium, but many things can go wrong, leading to the long-term destruction of shareholder value for the acquiring company. Usually the main winners of M&A activity are the professionals in the middle brokering the deal and not, as it turns out, either of the businesses in the deal.

Venture Capital

The other big sector connected to the business of business that will be impacted by web3 is venture capital (VC). Like M&A activities, VC activity in the first half of 2021 shattered all previous records as more than $288 billion was invested worldwide – up a whopping $110 billion on the previous high of the second half of 2020.[3] And like M&A the backdrop to this growth has been technology companies.

VC activity, like mainstream publishers, is focused on finding the one or two big winners or 'unicorns' that will pay for the also-rans and deliver stellar return on investment. It is essentially all about power law.

Power law is an exponential growth pattern that exists in business and nature. Essentially, the bigger a company gets the faster it grows. This is, of course, connected to network effects, and leads to a distribution that is different from the familiar bell curves.

In a power-law distribution, the largest business is typically bigger, more valuable or more powerful than the rest of the industry combined. The second largest is then larger than the rest combined, and so on. Right now, because business is still highly centralized, a few businesses can end up being dominant in their category or industry because the size of the winner gives them even more power through various advantages such as economies of scale, brand recognition and network effects.

What changes the power law in web3 is that as it becomes easier and easier for talent to come together to create a new technology service, the intensity of competition increases dramatically. The underlying protocols of web3 can also rapidly propagate, working from the open-source code of their predecessors, making changes and growing their communities and a new chain of network effects. For the users of these products and services, the combination of customer, stakeholder and producers leads to more widely distributed yet very high-quality products and services. There is less opportunity for massive companies to scale to $100 billion-plus dominant positions.

Block space scarcity and network effects

For modern web2 tech businesses, the network effect has been instrumental in driving value and use. The more participants in the protocol, the more valuable the network became, and the more useful the network became, which attracted even more participants in a self-perpetuating virtuous cycle that poured profit back to the parent company. As mentioned in Chapter 2, Metcalfe's law, which explains the network effect, states that the value of a network is proportional to the square of the number of connected users of the system.[4] In other words, every time you add a new participant to the network, they square the effectiveness of the whole network. The most valuable technology businesses are network effect businesses. They become more powerful and more dominant the bigger they get (power law).

In web2, Facebook was the dominant social graph network effect. But over time, we've seen that network effect growth start to decline. Various scandals about data usage didn't help, and new demographics didn't want to use the same platform as their parents! New social networks pop up that eat away at the network effect. Often the new networks were satisfying an unmet need or a particular feature, a lot like the hard drive example from Part I. For instance, one of the irritations of users on platforms like Facebook and Instagram is the lack of authenticity. No one is sharing their real lives, but rather their show-reel lives – filter-polished, preening and narcissistic. One platform that is making waves as I write this book is BeReal. Presented as an anti-social social network, it is being downloaded by teenagers the world over. The app will send a random notification to each user, and they have two minutes to take a photo of what they are doing at that moment and post it. The app has no filters so there is no opportunity to present anything other than their real life as it is happening.[5] With each new platform gaining traction via network effects, the incumbents such as Facebook and Instagram are continuously weakened by the new networks for a variety of reasons.

The same thing is happening in crypto but for different reasons. Web3 is an extreme network effect economy but with a twist, and that twist is block space scarcity. In web3 the network effect that created massive value for web2 businesses is now a double-edged sword. On the upside, as the network effect grows and more and more developers pile in to use the network, it becomes more useful and more valuable, and more people flood in to the new use cases. But the downside is that, as more people use it, more pressure is placed on the amount of information that can actually be processed by each block, a little like a computer running out of storage, this creates block space scarcity, which becomes an existential threat to the entire network. For example, remember Bored Ape Yacht Club – 10,000 NFTs of portraits of Bored Apes that have become a web3 phenomenon? Ten thousand owners together with other interested parties have created a sizeable community around the Bored Ape Yacht Club. And everything was going brilliantly until they launched a metaverse called the Otherside. Yuga Labs, the owners of BAYC, decided to sell off plots of virtual land at a flat price of 305 ApeCoin (their token), worth about $5,500 per plot. Of course, the highly engaged BAYC community piled into the sale. Unfortunately for them they all piled in at the same time, which overwhelmed the Ethereum blockchain and resulted in massive transaction fees. In several cases the fees charged were higher than the costs of the virtual land. Some people spent $500 to start the minting process but then never got anything.[6] Suffice it to say, the BAYC community was not happy. This is down to the scarcity of the block space and the fact that everyone rushed in to secure the virtual land at the same time, thus users experienced the downside of network effects and it damaged the network.

If people can no longer use the network, or it becomes too slow or too expensive because of the pressure on the block space, then new solutions will spring up to provide something better. And because all of web3 is open source, and decentralized, a new network can often just copy an existing one and make some tweaks on the rules that solve the most pressing problem for the user.

For example, in 2017 Bitcoin forked following a massive disagreement about how Bitcoin should work. Remember, Bitcoin is a decentralized network so there is no Board of Directors to figure out how to solve a problem or decide what business to buy via M&A. Instead, the Bitcoin mining community make decisions about Bitcoin, and in this case there was a significant disagreement between some of the community that held a lot of the mining power; in other words they had the most machines to vote with. The argument was that Bitcoin was not functioning as Satoshi had intended it to because of block space scarcity, and this problem was going to impact the success of Bitcoin. One group argued that the block space of Bitcoin should be increased from 1 megabyte to 32 megabytes so that the cost to process the block space was significantly lower, which would make Bitcoin better at being a low-cost, high-transaction network or an effective payment transfer network. The other group disagreed, believing that the small block space was instrumental in the security and longevity of Bitcoin. So, Bitcoin forked into two additional blockchains: Bitcoin Cash and Bitcoin Satoshi's Vision. Because Bitcoin is open source this was possible, and the miners who believed in each version copied all the blockchain over with the new rules with larger block space. Everyone who had a Bitcoin wallet was then able to access these new chains and instantly hold the value of their Bitcoin in their wallets across these new networks. As of writing, Bitcoin is worth $31,500 per BTC while Bitcoin Cash is $198 and Bitcoin Satoshi Vision is $55. So these networks are worth significantly less. No one was dragged via shareholder agreement – it was a choice that each Bitcoin miner could make freely. And as a Bitcoin owner, for every one Bitcoin you also had one Bitcoin Cash and one Bitcoin Satoshi Vision. This issue never arose in web2 businesses that experienced phenomenal growth because of network effects, because there was no blockchain to just copy.

But every new protocol on web3 – and there are already over 2,000 – will reach a critical point, which leads to new block spaces being created or tweaked. The block space scarcity of Bitcoin is what led to Ethereum. The key difference between Bitcoin and Ethereum is block space scarcity and what the block space can do. The block space scarcity of Ethereum will lead to something else. And this pattern will continue indefinitely, albeit with weakening value of the subsequent networks.

What happens in web3 that didn't happen in web2 or earlier because there was no blockchain is that the new players emerge in direct relationship to the blockchain and blockchain scarcity. When the blockchain isn't functional enough or fast enough, or the scarcity of trying to get information in that block space becomes too expensive, a new protocol will emerge to solve that problem. And we will get a constant propagation of new protocols emerging that offer new features and functionality. And in web3 this may constantly erode the network effect growth of the previous protocols. This is going to create intense competition that can't be solved by a web1 or web2 maneuver such as M&A, or building better moats around the business or suing the competitor for some IP infringement. Web3 doesn't care about moats or barriers to entry, and there is not much in the way of IP when everything is open source on a decentralized network! Who do you even sue when the project is founded by a pseudonymous team without a company behind it?

> "NEW PLAYERS EMERGE IN DIRECT RELATIONSHIP TO THE BLOCKCHAIN AND BLOCKCHAIN SCARCITY."

And, of course, this dynamic challenges the power-law investing model, because it will be much harder for a VC or private equity firm to find those big winners; the inevitable block space scarcity means there will be fewer winner-takes-all businesses. Instead, new networks will emerge, grow, plateau and fall away all the time as the technology advances. And there's going to be 'bridging': interconnected usage of multiple protocols that are maybe even industry specific. There's going to be significantly more competition, and it's going to be very hard to get really big (Figure 10.6). With fewer M&As happening and VC collaborations no longer able to create dominant players, because dominant players probably won't exist, the business of doing business is likely to change dramatically. As business decentralizes, there will no longer be centralized 'industries' to dominate; instead, there will be many more mid-sized solutions emerging that will suit different sections of the market. It's also worth noting that the low interest rates of the last decade have fueled a lot of tech companies with high

FIGURE 10.6: BEFORE AND AFTER EFFECT ON VC POWER LAW CURVES

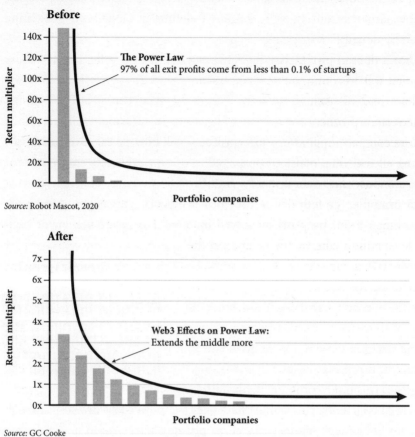

Source: Robot Mascot, 2020

Source: GC Cooke

valuations. That is also potentially coming to an end for this cycle. As a result, we effectively have a perfect storm: open-source web3 technologies, combined with a massive pool of talent who can build and develop on those technologies, higher interest rates and traditional VCs having access to less capital. Together this is going to create a shift in the power-law curve and the distribution of tech companies in the Information Age. The result: a lot more smaller winners rather than a few winner-takes-all giants, creating more opportunities for producers/creators to own a better share of the work they create.

Also worth considering is that a primary source of revenue for Big Tech is marketing or cloud spend from VC-backed companies. This will also change because of the power law. Business-as-usual currently sees $0.40 of every $1 raised by start-ups from VCs end up in the pockets of Google, Facebook and Amazon by default![7] That pattern is going to change, and it's going to create a significant dent in profitability for Big Tech. From a world of a more widely distributed web3 economy, this is significant cash flow that will eventually start pouring into the various protocols.

More competition and new networks are emerging all the time, making it possible for users to compose their own bespoke products.

> **THE BUSINESS OF DOING BUSINESS IS LIKELY TO CHANGE DRAMATICALLY.**

For example, the founder of FTX (one of the largest crypto exchanges), Sam Bankman-Fried, proposed how you could build your own version of Twitter. By leveraging a common back end on the blockchain, many different user interfaces (UI) and moderation capabilities could be built as a market with the user choosing the one most relevant to them. You would have the freedom to choose the app or UI that best suits you, and would be able to interact with people on different versions of the 'Twitter equivalent' by pulling messages from the same underlying blockchain. You could be on Twitter. I could be on Facebook, and someone else could be on TikTok but we could all be communicating with each other because all the platforms would be built on the same underlying blockchain. Just with different UIs and different user experiences on top. No longer will one person/company control speech, because it would all be on-chain. It would be trivial to integrate tips/payments/monetization for content creators creating a new type of peer-to-peer micro publishing model.

The possibilities are endless. That said, why would you? As Jeromy Johnson, an engineer at Protocol Labs (a web3 R&D organization), points out, 'There's a lot of things that people try to use blockchain for that you don't actually need a blockchain for. People try to build social networks on blockchains, and they put every tweet, or whatever they call it, and every "like" on the blockchain, and it's like, what are you doing? That's so dumb!' Johnson helped code the InterPlanetary File System (IPFS), a peer-to-peer alternative to the hypertext transfer protocol, which prevents content from disappearing from the web just because a certain URL expires or changes and is a leading example of decentralized tech that isn't blockchain. Remember, web3 is not just blockchain, it's also decentralized storage capability.[8] For web3 to work long-term we need to be much smarter about what scenarios need to be on energy-intensive blockchain and what can live on alternative decentralized storage – still web3, still secure, but not blockchain.

The Token Economy Instead of IPO

As business decentralizes through web3, questioning the status quo on valuations and IPOs, it will give way to the token economy. The token in the project is almost always the token you also use to access the network service, so the whole idea of value will shift! When you raise initial capital for the project you need to find the early investors who believe in the project enough to take the bet on the early tokens eventually having a value.

In a traditional company, a share is the representation of the ownership of the company. But the product or service you're creating and selling still needs to be made and sold using money. Ownership and utility are therefore two different things. But in web3, ownership and utility are the same thing. They are unified via a token. So, for example, Bitcoin is representative of ownership of Bitcoin on the blockchain and utility. If I have Bitcoin in my crypto-wallet, I own it and I can use it in the Bitcoin network, paying miners to register value transfers that I am making in the same currency as I am also holding. In some ways this is no different to money. I have money in my wallet, and I can use it, but I don't own a share of the central bank. With Bitcoin I do – I own part of the Bitcoin network, and as Bitcoin is used and accepted in more places for more purposes the value of the Bitcoin I hold will increase. Until Bitcoin came along money was controlled by governments, and central banks were

> **IN WEB3, OWNERSHIP AND UTILITY ARE THE SAME THING.**

usually the only institutions authorized to issue currency. Bitcoin changed that, and part of the game-changing innovation it led to in web3 is the fusion of ownership and utility into a currency or token.

This idea is often referred to as tokenomics – the science of the token economy, which covers token creation, management and exchange.

Tokenomics basically takes what central banks use as monetary policy and applies it to blockchain networks.

It is the protocols that create the networks, which give rise to the need for tokens or some unit of exchange that would then allow other people to use the network. For example, Bitcoin is a protocol, but if it didn't also create the unit of currency called Bitcoin in the network, and miners didn't validate the Bitcoin in the blockchain, then how would people use the Bitcoin network? In the same way, when the Ethereum protocol was created, a token in Ether (ETH) also needed to be created to allow people to access and use the Ethereum network. This concept goes even further: as Ethereum 2.0 moves from a network run by miners (proof-of-work) to a network run by validators (proof-of-stake), anyone who has Ethereum can become a validator and earn the usage fees without needing to run a mining network.

There are already maybe 2,000 web3 protocols that require users to purchase tokens in that network in order to use it. We've talked about some of these protocols in Part II, each having their own token or currency. Without tokens, the protocols could create the capability, but no one would be able to use them. But it's not just utility; the token also denotes partial ownership of the network!

This is like Google deciding to issue a token that you need to use to do a search on Google. But the token also makes you a part owner of Google, so as Google becomes more valuable, the token you use on the network goes up in value, so you need to use less of the token to pay for your search and the real-world costs to run the network reduces. You are essentially pre-buying the tokens to use in a network so that if the popularity of that network increases, you also benefit from that increase in value.

In web3, any business will be able to create its own token and tokenomics, whether it's a token to use the network of a protocol or an NFT for access to the product or service. The token will ultimately give your community ownership and utility in the new network.

There are different ways to create the tokens. Like Bitcoin, the network can incentivize and reward validators or miners with newly minted coins or tokens. A business could also sell a portion of the token supply to prospective users in an initial coin offering (ICO). We talked about this as an option in

Chapter 3 when we looked at the ICO bubble of 2017. Tokens are also distributed to users via certain actions or behaviors. Again, we looked at some of these options in Part II, including Axie Infinity – which rewards people with their token, Axie Infinity Shard (AXS), to play the game. The more people play, the more valuable the network is and the more valuable the token is.

Part of the problem of the ICO bubble of 2017 (and it's still an issue today) is token speculation. People have rushed into the ownership of tokens in the hope that they increase in value, but if they don't also use the tokens then the network doesn't increase in value and the token becomes junk. This is a completely new phenomenon. In the stock market you can speculate on penny stocks or decide to buy shares in the latest hot tip – perhaps an offshore wind farm – but there is very little upside or downside for you if you use that windfarm or not. Certainly not unless you can encourage thousands of other people to invest in it. But with tokens the utility of the token is what drives the value.

As such, most networks incentivize people to own, hold and *use* the tokens rather than the traditional 'buy and hold' strategy of investors such as Warren Buffett. This in itself could be revolutionary as it increases the flow of capital around the economic system rather than having the top 1 per cent stashing away trillions. In addition, proof-of-stake (POS) systems, which rely on validators to stake their own tokens, helps to ensure honesty and fairness. Each token devises the rules of how the token is created or 'minted' as well as how they are injected into and taken out of the network. In many ways these rules are the individual monetary policy of that token, devised at the start by the entity that created the protocol and the network, rather than a central bank. And those who don't play by the rules risk forfeiting their tokens.

> **WEB3 ENABLES PROJECTS TO CREATE SELF-SUSTAINING MICRO-ECONOMIES.**

Of course, even if someone creates a protocol and builds a network or platform, the decentralized nature of web3 means they no longer own it, at least not alone. It's still quite hard to predict exactly what will happen with tokens and tokenomics, so most networks are making sure that ecosystem adaptability is possible in the future via owner consensus. Imagine the central bank asking you whether you would like to increase interest rates!

Web3 enables projects to create self-sustaining micro-economies, and blockchain technology is already creating a diverse range of uses for tokens, offering significant opportunity for business in the web3 world.[9]

Complex Business Decisions Ahead

The businesses of tomorrow are still going to be very successful and they will still make vast amounts of money, but they will not be companies as we understand that term today; they will be distributed collaborations. There will be a different shape to the power law, with more winners in the middle of the curve. There will be many more successful collaborations, and the spoils will be distributed across the network, not just among shareholders. It's likely that you will start investing directly in talent (individual talent or groups of talent) through a DAO. And this is a highly complex yet enormous opportunity. Platforms will almost certainly evolve that will offer search capability on what projects to be involved with or what talent to invest in.

At the dawn of the Information Age, web2 saw the peak in centralized power in the hands of a few. Web3 will be a speedy diffusion of that power across a decentralized, distributed network (see Figure 10.7).

FIGURE 10.7: THE WEB3 DECENTRALIZED AND DISTRIBUTED ECONOMY

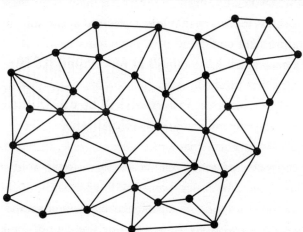

Many of the entities will issue and use tokens. That said, it's unlikely that it will be relevant for every company or collaboration to issue their own tokens. It will only be relevant to the entities that are creating protocols that other entities want to use. In which case, issuing a token will be necessary. Conservatively, maybe 20 to 30 per cent of businesses will need to issue a token, but 100 per cent of businesses will need to have a strategy for how much of the tokens they need to own of the networks they need to operate on top of.

Instead of making a cloud-computing decision about which cloud you should be operating on, you're going to have to decide which protocols you're going to be operating on as a business. And those decisions are not just tech decisions or financial decisions – they are both. It's going to get a lot more complicated.

> **MAYBE 20 TO 30 PER CENT OF BUSINESSES WILL NEED TO ISSUE A TOKEN.**

In this new world of distributed web3 services, a business will have to operate using many different tokens across the most relevant networks to provide your product or service. In reality, this will be very much like business-as-usual for companies that perhaps trade in different currencies. They make provision to be able to pay suppliers in their own currency to minimize exchange-rate risk. It will be the same in web3, but instead of holding US dollars or Japanese yen, the business will hold a number of tokens for the various networks they use. And before you panic about how many tokens you will need to own, you will only need the token for the networks you are using.

But this will require business leaders to take speculation risk on the portfolio of tokens they're holding. You could end up embracing a new project, a new protocol that you believe you'll need a lot of in your business's future, so you hold a lot of tokens in that protocol. And then that protocol goes up a hundred times in value because other companies realized they need it too. And what you end up with is a significant asset on your balance sheet. Or you could end up embracing a new protocol that sinks without trace, in which case you will need to move to a new protocol. But because of the open-source nature of web3, the switch is likely to be easier than switching banks!

Do you have a strategy for knowing which utility tokens your company should use? Which product protocols? If you're part of building one of these original protocols, how do you ensure the longevity of the protocol? How do you ensure it continues without being able to do M&A, when the new M&A might become the ability to invest and use the new emerging protocols and web3 and web4 solutions? How do you make it easy for users of earlier protocols to transfer seamlessly to yours? There is risk to companies in making the wrong choice, but that risk is diminished because of the distributed nature of tomorrow's business. The distribution, probably brought together by a DAO, may use multiple protocols across various functions or goals of the business, so even if one protocol is replaced in one area of the business it won't bring the whole operation down. Plus, it will always be in the best interests of the new protocols that emerge to ensure they make it easy for users to transition to the upgraded protocol.

Tomorrow's business leaders will have to speculate on the value of the networks. And, if you're a company that depends heavily on Ethereum, for example, you have to speculate on how you're going to pay to use the Ethereum network, and how much of that you can pass along to your customers. Remember the Bored Ape Yacht Club metaverse fiasco? In hindsight BAYC should probably have pre-minted the plots ahead of the sale to keep the costs down, and then provided a transfer service rather than a minting service. These are the new economics of all these different projects and web3 capabilities.

At the heart of the decisions regarding which protocols you use is the smart contract. Ultimately you are making a decision on which smart contract systems your business needs to be interacting with to operate efficiently. For centuries, contract law has been the cornerstone of all sorts of business agreements. Every loan, every supplier agreement, every employment contract is based on contract law. Terms and conditions of products and services are also written in contract law. The web3 revolution is largely down to the smart contract. Where Bitcoin is a highly secure currency, the Bitcoin protocol was not very useful for anything else. The smart contract was made possible by the greater flexibility of the Ethereum protocol, and its reach and use are endless. It is smart contracts that will create interoperable, integrated, secure agreements on the blockchain for greater efficiency across the network. Smart contracts make it possible to restructure just about any business on web3. All the businesses we interact with today could use smart contracts to unbundle and reconstitute into a new form on the web3 stack.

Through this world of interconnected datasets and systems you will need to have a strategy to manage many of these networks and manage a portfolio of utility tokens to participate in the relevant networks. To participate in this new ecosystem, you need to have an open approach to your data and even your codebase, as the most open, interconnected systems will be the most successful. This is the opposite operating model to most businesses today and that will present some of the biggest challenges.

One final aspect that is going to increase the complexity, but also the opportunity, is how business can contribute back to the information ecosystem relevant to their industry. Every business is going to need a strategy for how the data they use to run their business is used to increase industry-wide efficiency. This can be highly contentious to even consider, because most businesses are so deeply entrenched in protecting IP and ensuring that trade secrets don't leak from a business, but web3 is going to bring change in this regard too – whether business leaders are ready for it or not.

In an open-source decentralized platform information will be shared freely, albeit pseudo-anonymously, in a free-flowing 'wisdom-of-the-crowd' ecosystem. The wisdom of the crowd is the proven theory that, when faced with tough challenges, opening up the debate to diverse groups of people will always give a better solution than merely relying on a small group – even if that small group contains experts. But in web3, the winners will be the businesses that put their information back into the distributed economy to create better, more efficient production processes for all or better ways of serving their customers. It is this type of innovation that may well disrupt manufacturing industries. The incumbents will resist this, no doubt, but it won't matter because the cumulative knowledge that will freely circulate through the system to support

> **IN AN OPEN-SOURCE DECENTRALIZED PLATFORM INFORMATION WILL BE SHARED FREELY.**

everyone else will allow new entrants to leapfrog over the old. Established businesses will either get up to speed with web3 and recognize the benefits to all from a distributed economy, of information as well as talent, or they will get left behind.

Web3 is not a tweak on web2. It is a fundamentally new way of doing just about everything in business. Competitive advantage will not be down to size or moats or artificially constructed barriers to entry; it will be down to open-source access to open, transparent information that will make all business better. Those that flow information in and out will be more successful than those that build the moats and try to keep it behind the castle walls. This is very different from how business is done today.

It may be quite complex to navigate, certainly to start with, but ultimately it will result in more openness, greater productivity and efficiency, and much more competition. It's hard to imagine how we would operate today without email, Slack, Google or cloud computing. We are empowered by these information tools. In ten years, we will be empowered by a new set of interconnected web3 protocols that we can't imagine living without.

Summary of Key Points

» Today almost all businesses focus on growth as the critical business metric, and it's instrumental in the valuation of a business.

» Merger and acquisition is currently used widely to achieve growth, but web3 poses an existential risk to M&A, investment banking and the business of business.

» Ownership is pseudo-anonymous and recorded in smart contracts in the blockchain; owners are decentralized and are unknown to each other, making it impossible for one entity to approach another with an offer.

» Venture Capital will also be reshaped by web3. Open-source web3 technologies are going to create a shift in the power-law curve and the distribution of tech companies in the Information Age, resulting in a lot of smaller winners rather than a few winner-takes-all giants.

» In web3 any business will be able to create its own token and tokenomics, whether it's a token to use the network of a protocol or an NFT for access to the product or service. The token will ultimately give your community ownership and utility in the new network.

» Web3 enables projects to create self-sustaining micro-economies, and blockchain technology is already creating a diverse range of uses for tokens.

» Tomorrow's business leaders will have to speculate on the value of the networks.

Chapter 11

Tomorrow's 'Prosumer'

Throughout the book I've talked about how web3's decentralized, distributed, open-source nature is already merging stakeholder groups together. In this chapter we look at the impact of that merger on the individual who is already becoming a producer/consumer, or 'prosumer'.

The word 'prosumer' was originally coined in 1980 by American futurist Alvin Toffler, to mean 'individuals who consume and produce value, either for self-consumption or consumption by others, and can receive implicit or explicit incentives from organizations involved in the exchange'. It's also used in technology as a description of a product that is aimed somewhere between consumers and professionals. More recently the term has come to refer to an individual using commons-based peer production. This is the context I'm referring to, because web3 is that commons-based peer production system where people are creating, are part of the production process and are also an end user of the output.

Individuals will own their data; they will own what they create. This transition means that we move from an internet economy worth $10 trillion where 80 per cent of the value is owned by corporations to a $100 trillion web3/web4 economy where 80 per cent of value is owned by the individual. But only if we get data sovereignty right.

Data Sovereignty and Spiral Dynamics

The keystone of tomorrow's prosumer architecture is data sovereignty. None of what I will describe in this chapter will come to fruition without it. But before you dismiss it as something you don't therefore have to worry about, at least one protocol for enabling data sovereignty has already been created. It's called Solid and, perhaps rather fittingly, it has been created by Tim Berners-Lee – the creator of the World Wide Web, and HTML, which was web1's innovation plot twist protocol that massively accelerated the use and acceptance of web1.

In order to understand where we are right now, we have to look back on our shared history again. What is interesting is that our relationship to sovereignty, autonomy and ultimately control has evolved over time in line with our value systems.

One of my all-time favorite theories is Spiral Dynamics, which was originally posited in 1978 by psychology professor Clare Graves. What Graves did was identify some profoundly important patterns that help us understand ourselves and others better, and how those patterns influence human evolution. Essentially, he illuminated a values hierarchy. As professor at Union College in New York, Graves noticed that his students' responses to various essay assignments could always be grouped into four 'worldviews' or value systems that determined how the students addressed the task. Looking at a wider subject group, he was able to identify eight levels or value systems, each emerging to transcend and include the previous ones (see Figure 11.1). The theory was genius, but Graves's attempts to name it was woeful – from 'Levels of Human Existence' to 'Emergent Cyclical, Phenomenological, Existential Double-Helix Levels of Existence Conception of Adult Human Behavior' and 'Emergent Cyclical Double-Helix Model of the Adult Bio-Psycho-Social Behavior'!

Today the theory is known as Spiral Dynamics – a much more user-friendly term coined by Don Beck and Chris Cowan, who went on to work with Graves and build on his theory.

Each value is assigned a color and has certain characteristics that influence behavior. Essentially, we each engage in behavior we believe will deliver the reward we value at each level. We can see this in our own life. What we valued as a 15-year-old is unlikely to be what we valued as a 25-year-old or

FIGURE 11.1: SPIRAL DYNAMICS AND SOVEREIGNTY

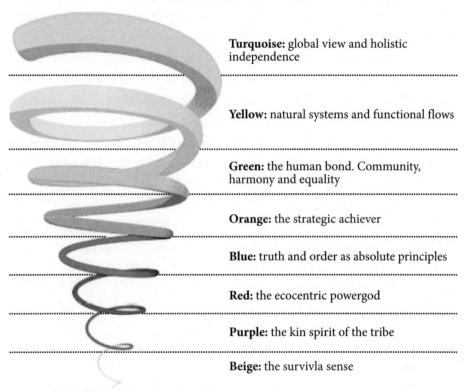

Turquoise: global view and holistic independence

Yellow: natural systems and functional flows

Green: the human bond. Community, harmony and equality

Orange: the strategic achiever

Blue: truth and order as absolute principles

Red: the ecocentric powergod

Purple: the kin spirit of the tribe

Beige: the survivla sense

Source: Said E. Dowlabani and Dr Don E Beck, 2013

40-year-old. Human beings mature. Viewed through the lens of values we can predict the likely behavior of an individual, a team, a division, a business, an industry, a nation, a region or the entire population of the planet. And that's why it's so illuminating, because it allows us to recognize the patterns that are causing so much disruption in business now and into the future.

Data sovereignty is going to be critical in getting web3 right, but the very idea of sovereignty has itself evolved. The irony is that, in the beginning, human beings had a lot of sovereignty – they roamed around the savannas doing what they wanted but survival was tough. Now survival is easier, but we don't have much sovereignty – certainly not when it comes to our data.

Each value system delivers significant benefits to the individual or collective operating at that level, but there is always a dark side, where the value system starts to break down, and it is this breakdown that triggers the evolution to the next level. The upside of beige is survival, sovereignty and freedom; the downside is that life is extremely tough and fraught with constant danger.

It is much easier to survive in a group, so individuals tend to cluster together in groups. In the purple value system, individuals willingly give up some individual sovereignty for greater protection and safety in the tribe. This is the value system where tribalism, mob rule, gangs and kleptocracy emerge. There are still plenty of examples of tribalism in the world where those involved are more loyal to the gangs than their own family. The downside of purple is often lack of action, there is too much emphasis on protection over action and so eventually a red leader will step forward to take the reins.

The red value system is the level of autocracy, power-dominated hierarchies, feudalism, dictatorship, fascism and despotism. At the red value level, sovereignty isn't so much willingly given up in exchange for some greater perceived benefit, but rather taken from individuals by another powerful individual. History is littered with examples of how this power-grab by a single despot rarely ends well and the society or culture evolves into a blue value system where rules are agreed and adhered to.

At the blue values level, principles of right over might emerge and we see coalitions, co-leadership and bureaucracies form. It's less about some individual despot taking control and more about a collective agreement to obey some higher power or set of rules for the collective good. Individual sovereignty is not crushed like it is at the red level, but willingly ceded to a higher power that probably knows best. Blue is the value system of religion and government. Rules can be helpful, but they can also stifle progress – so eventually the orange value system emerges.

Sovereignty is once again wrestled back from the collective to individual input via our vote in democracy or our progression at work via meritocracy. Capitalism is an orange phenomenon. This time, sovereignty is willingly swapped for wealth and success. The GFC of 2007 is the outcome of too many people operating at the orange value system. When all that's valued is wealth and success it's easy to justify almost any behavior. And the backlash against the greed and hubris so common in orange is what triggers the emergence of green.

In the green value system there is a push for collective consensus, shared sovereignty and social democracy. But again, when too many people want to be heard, nothing gets done, no decisions are made and progress stalls again. There is then a big jump to the yellow value system. The potential that web3 and web4 bring pulls us forward from the red, blue and orange systems to a green and yellow system.

What makes yellow and turquoise so special is that individuals and collectives operating from these value levels can recognize that all the other value levels have genuine merit. Those operating from beige to green (first tier) believe that they are right, that their behavior and actions are fully justified and everyone else is wrong. Yellow is the first level of the second tier and knows this is not true. Each value system delivers real value and can still be incredibly useful in the right place. A red leader, for example, can still be incredibly efficient when opening a new territory, or a green leader can be great at bringing people with them.

Web3 and web4 are largely green and yellow phenomena. The yellow value system is characterized by innovation with the potential to take us to turquoise – giving everyone ubiquitous access to new ways to collaborate and cooperate for mutual benefit. Green, yellow and turquoise recognize the collective merit and potential of harnessing the intellectual input of everyone over the input of just a few. Web3 creates the protocols and data sovereignty, while web4 creates the easy-to-use apps that sit on top of those protocols. Together they will facilitate individual sovereignty inside a trusted collaboration. It is, or certainly could be, the best of both worlds. Where we are free to be ourselves, work the way we want, innovate the way we want and collaborate the way we want within a secure, connected way that doesn't rely on trusted third parties.

But right now, we are stuck in a world, certainly in business, that is dominated by red and orange value system thinking. The leading edge of the global population may be green, but inside business it's still very much red and orange. These businesses are highly centralized and, in our rush to embrace new technology and access new capabilities or enjoy new benefits, we have completely given away our data sovereignty to a handful of companies that have used that data to make astronomical profits. As the web2 mantra points out – if it's free, you are the product.

To be fair, most of us didn't give away our data sovereignty willingly; we often didn't knowingly consent, and we certainly didn't appreciate the ramifications. Sure, the gory details may have been tucked away on the terms and conditions we agreed to before accessing the platform, but these are notoriously difficult for the average person to read and understand.

We are now at a tipping point for two reasons. As we have seen (mostly in the EU), when business doesn't do something meaningful about data privacy and data sovereignty themselves, then governments will step in and force them to through legislation. Plus, because of the Information Age, we are facing very different dynamics that could facilitate or limit our collective evolution.

Physical Augmentation to Intellectual Augmentation

So far, our evolution as a species has been largely down to the augmentation of our physical body. We have figured out fire and how to cook food, and scientific advancement has transformed our life expectancy. Globally, life expectancy has increased from under 50 years to over 80 years. After two centuries of progress, all of us – regardless of where we live – can expect to live more than twice as long as our ancestors, and often much longer.[1] We have figured out how to use our bodies in sport, how to engage in work and how to transport our bodies from place to place. Our entire evolution as a species has been focused largely on the physical body and what it can do.

Better education systems have also made a difference to our individual and collective intellect. Exposure to new information and knowledge has certainly made us more intelligent, despite what ten minutes on social media might indicate! For example, the 'Flynn effect' describes the phenomenon that over time average IQ scores have been increasing. The change in IQ scores has been approximately three IQ points per decade. One major implication of this trend is that an average individual alive today would have an IQ of 130 by the standards of 1910, placing them higher than 98 per cent of the population at that time. Equivalently, an individual alive in 1910 would have an IQ of 70 by today's standards.[2]

As a species we are smarter, but the biology of our cognitive equipment (i.e. our brain) hasn't changed in thousands of years. Or as professor of organizational behavior Nigel Nicholson once said, 'You can take the person out of the Stone Age, but you can't take the Stone Age out of the person.'[3]

Add that fact to the knowledge doubling curve and we, as a species, have a serious cognitive problem. Nine years before web-anything and the explosion of information that the internet created, futurist and inventor R. Buckminster Fuller proposed 'the knowledge doubling curve'. Fuller noticed that the more knowledge we accumulated, the faster we created even more knowledge. Up until 1900, for example, human knowledge doubled every 100 years or so. By 1945 the complete knowledge of mankind doubled every 25 years. By 1982 knowledge was doubling every 12 to 13 months.[4] IBM predicted that knowledge would double every 11 hours by 2010,[5] although there doesn't appear to be any update on whether that's actually happened or not. Suffice it to say, we now have access to more knowledge and data – the vast majority of which is accessible immediately via the internet – than we could even possibly digest or understand. By some estimates it would take us 28.3 million years, or hundreds of thousands of lifetimes, to read everything that is currently on the internet,[6] never mind the tsunami of information that is not.

The bottom line is: between the fight for our attention across endless possibilities and the cognitive limitations we face because our brains have not really evolved to deal with the new reality of the Information Age, we need help if we are to progress.

> **OUR BRAINS HAVE NOT REALLY EVOLVED TO DEAL WITH THE NEW REALITY OF THE INFORMATION AGE.**

That help already exists in the form of artificial intelligence (AI), but until the data sovereignty issue is solved and people feel 100 per cent sure that their data is their own and can't be used, hacked or manipulated by others, AI will never deliver the humanity-changing benefits it is poised to deliver.

Quite simply, the centralization of power and the rampant harvesting of our data for profit has left us all feeling uncomfortable about who holds data, never mind the capabilities of AI. We just don't trust that it won't then be used against us rather than using it ourselves to augment our own lives.

This is why protocols such as Solid are so critical to the acceleration of web3. It was developed because Tim Berners-Lee saw the necessity for full-scale data sovereignty where you as the customer/owner (and only you) have full and complete control over all your data, and you and you alone decide who has access to it. And you, not Facebook or Google, will be compensated for that access.

It is incredibly telling that the one person who first saw the vision of what the internet could be has also recognized the issues and invented the solution to data sovereignty. Berners-Lee has been outspoken about the dark reality of the internet. For example, he has said that the web is not working for women and girls as they are too often subjected to sexual harassment, threatening messages and discrimination. There are dangerous trends in online abuse that are forcing women out of jobs, causing girls to skip school, damaging relationships and silencing female opinions.[7] Solid could change all that and so much more.

Instead of waiting for business to do the right thing, or for governments to make them do the right thing, data sovereignty removes those barriers and liberates the possibilities of AI in a safe, secure and completely protected ecosystem that only the owner could assess and use.

One of the biggest impacts of web3 is that it will change the nature of trust and our relationship to trust; it will evolve away from institutional trust to distributed trust. With the right data sovereignty and trusted web3 capability to return our data to us, protect it and allow us to have full control over it, web4 will mean that our ability to verify information at a much more rapid scale using AI will increase trust in a trustless system and be done in a completely distributed, independent way.

Imagine the potential …

Alongside the augmentation of our physical body with tools and processes, we would be able to securely augment our minds and our time with AI. Imagine a digital twin that knew everything you knew, had all your medical records, your financial history, your banking details, your values and beliefs and your likes, dislikes and preferences. In time it would know more about you than you know about yourself, allowing for accurate predictions that could help you in your daily life and liberate your use of time. Imagine if all your systems – your computer system, phone, all your data records, buying history and your home – were interconnected and linked via an array of internet-of-things (IoT) capabilities. Your digital twin could check your

Apple watch and measure your blood pressure, constantly measuring your health in the background. It could run diagnostics on online symptom checkers and book appointments where necessary. If anxiety was detected or a drop in mood, one of your favorite songs would be played by Spotify from your Happy Playlist. But these innovations wouldn't just help you. You would own your medical records, which would be connected to your DNA profile and life events, which would be pooled in a pseudo-anonymous way to facilitate personalized medicine and healthcare. It's imperative that we are all able to control this type of information individually, as it has the power to let us live a longer, healthier life.

Your digital twin would check your calendar and book an Uber to arrive in time to take you to your meeting without any need to get involved. You still hold custody of your thoughts – those thoughts are encrypted, you hold the key – yet at the same time there is an ecosystem benefiting economically from improving what can be done to make your digital twin even more productive. In a world of distributed trust, where verification is more important than trust, a personal and impartial AI will play a critical role in ensuring that projects are what they claim to be down to the code in the smart contract. Depending on what you do for a living, your digital twin could take on part of your workload. The possible innovation plot twist for web4 may even further merge the ideas of stakeholders so that the supply of labor ends up being heavily driven by the digital twins that we curate. So, applications that replicate our decision-making process end up doing large parts of our work for us. Say you were a journalist or author; your digital twin would know so much about you, how you think and how you write that it could create first-draft documents for you to finish – liberating you to do more of what you want with your life.

This is not a new idea. In 1848 John Stuart Mill, one of the founders of classical economics, published *Principles of Political Economy*, where he predicted that once the work of economic growth was done, a 'stationary' economy would emerge in which we could focus on human improvement: 'There would be as much scope as ever for all kinds of mental culture, and moral and social progress ... for improving the art of living and much more likelihood of it being improved, when minds cease to be engrossed by the art of getting on.'[8] In other words, when we were no longer obsessed and consumed by making a living, we would be liberated to design a happy, meaningful and rounded life. Economist John Maynard Keynes wrote an essay in 1930 along the same lines called 'Economic Possibilities for Our Grandchildren'. In it he discussed the idea of 'technological unemployment', where unemployment due to innovation and advance would become so prevalent that it would outrun our ability to find alternative forms of employment.[9]

This is already happening. We talked about the large-scale loss of manufacturing jobs in Chapter 7, but what if this was a good thing, not something to be feared? Right now, billions of people the world over are consumed with work and making ends meet. Too many are locked in terrible situations, working in terrible conditions or under zero-hours contracts with no end in sight. But what if all our base financial needs were taken care of via some form of data sovereignty solution, which could liberate us all to have more say and freedom in how we spend our lives? What if that liberation triggered an innovation or cultural renaissance where people were inspired to be more creative, more useful, more productive, happier and healthier? There is little doubt that the creative industries will flourish in web3, providing so many more opportunities to engage in various projects. But the definition of 'creative' will expand significantly. For example, web3 is going to create 'tastemakers', similar to influencers in web2, where picking the next trend will deliver financial benefit. Taste itself will become a form of financial speculation. There are going to be so many more ways for us to make money and fund our lives, and that will be true regardless of socio-economic background. Our value will be in the supply of our capabilities, but also in participation – we will be rewarded for participation in the networks we connect to.

Surely, there is nothing more exciting than being able to curate a version of ourselves that is truly owned by us, an extension of who we are that can help us with all the mundane and boring stuff of life so we can spend more time pursuing things that connect with our purpose and skill sets.

Thousands of years ago, almost all of us were farming, spending most of the working week manually working hard and for long hours to produce enough for our community to eat. Perhaps in another thousand years, our digital twin will be doing most of the heavy lifting and we will be free to create the kinds of mental culture and moral and social progress that Mills talked about in 1848.

Improved Reason for Being

If all this came to pass, we would be liberated to achieve *ikigai* (see Figure 11.2).

    Ikigai is a Japanese concept referring to something that gives a person a sense of purpose, a reason for living. According to a study by Michiko Kumano, feeling *ikigai* as described in Japanese culture usually means the feeling of accomplishment and fulfillment that follows when people pursue

FIGURE 11.2: *IKIGAI* – THE JAPANESE CONCEPT MEANING 'THE REASON FOR BEING'

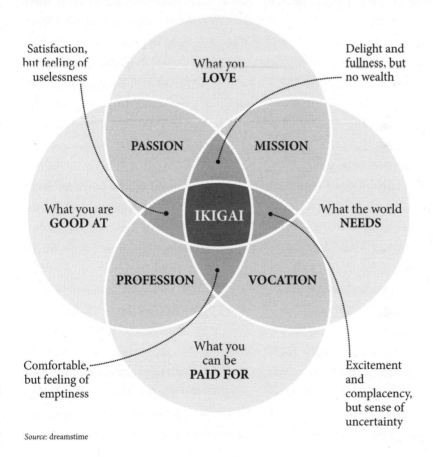

Satisfaction, but feeling of uselessness

Delight and fullness, but no wealth

What you **LOVE**

PASSION   **MISSION**

What you are **GOOD AT**   **IKIGAI**   What the world **NEEDS**

PROFESSION   **VOCATION**

What you can be **PAID FOR**

Comfortable, but feeling of emptiness

Excitement and complacency, but sense of uncertainty

Source: dreamstime

their passions. Activities that generate the feeling of *ikigai* are not forced on an individual; they are perceived as being spontaneous and undertaken willingly, and thus are personal and depend on a person's inner drives and motivations.

Interestingly, *ikigai* also corresponds to self-determination theory (SDT), developed by psychologists Richard Ryan and Edward Deci. SDT outlines what we need in order to feel intrinsically motivated, access 'flow' states and feel happy – competence, autonomy and relatedness. According to Ryan and Deci, people need to be able to demonstrate competence in their daily activities; they need to have some level of control and autonomy over their work and lives; and they need to feel connected to others they care about.[10]

This is all much more possible via open but secure data sharing, AI and the digital twin, but it's *only possible* if we solve the issue of digital sovereignty. There is no way people will trust it otherwise. The majority of users would never agree to feed troves of data into AI systems that are designed to replicate them individually if that data was held by a corporation where algorithms were constantly trying to hack their decision-making and generate value from copying their digital identity. The risks around this data being hacked, even as a web3 protocol, should not be underestimated. But the more distributed the system is (with public and private keys held in a user-friendly way by the owner/end user), the more it would make centralized attacks extremely expensive.

All the capabilities I've described above when asking you to imagine the future already exist; it's just that the data that currently makes it work lives inside highly centralized, controlled businesses that deliberately block access from the outside. These companies want to maintain control over the app, the data and the environment, so interconnectivity is simply not possible. It's technologically possible but not ideologically possible. Yet evolution only moves forward. Consumer expectations are built upon their last experience. Google to Spotify changed what it meant to consume content and information. As consumers we wouldn't settle for anything less – we are on the constant stairway to consumer expectation – this 'expectation inflation' rises over time. And with those expectations will come increased pressure to alter this ideological approach, which will run alongside the growing pressure towards restoring data sovereignty to the owner of the data and giving them full and sole control.

The reality right now is that not syncing your systems and having inter-connectivity is a privacy advantage. But once the digital sovereignty issue is solved and the technology to solve it already exists then the user will yield so many more additional advantages from syncing and connecting their systems that no one will not do it. And with the interconnectivity across decentralized distributed networks, everything gets better.

Even decentralized interconnected networks have been attempted before. For example, Fon sought to create an open interconnected Wi-Fi network that could rival a mobile phone infrastructure. Based on the principle of sharing your internet connection at home, you could access anyone's Wi-Fi if they were also part of the Fon network. You may recognize this technology as BT's OpenZone – BT saw this as a major threat and adopted the protocol, and it's still available today. Of course, that capability has since been eclipsed by the superior speed and reliability of 4G and 5G networks, but it was revolutionary at the time.

Helium, on the other hand, is attempting to do this from a web3 perspective, focusing on the internet of things – opening up the possibility that any device anywhere in the world could be connected to the 'web3 grid'. But right now, the Helium use cases are based on non-sensitive information. In some regards, Helium launching without the digital sovereignty issues solved is like Uber launching before the iPhone – it's just a little too early to gain significant traction via network effects.

In the future, the way we work will be down to our ability to cobble the various protocols and apps together in our own unique network. And because of the change in the power law that we explored in the last chapter, there will be so many AI applications in the market that don't have access to our data but are finding solutions on our behalf. This in turn will mean that the people who are most successful in their jobs and the happiest in life will be the people who can put all those parts together to become producer-consumers. Everything from what music we decide to listen to, to what we search for online to what game we decide to play to what we watch will deliver us tokens via these crazy interconnected networks. Hence the term 'prosumer'.

Incentives have always been at the heart of driving human behaviors. Theory X says those incentives must be money, in the shape of a salary or bonus, or the desire to avoid a punishment. But Theory Y has already proved that there is much more to human motivation than money. We do things for all sorts of private reasons, because the outcome is important to us and our value system. Think of dating someone, or an enjoyable walk on a sunny afternoon. If, through that interconnected network, we can get at least part of our financial needs met simply by doing what we would be doing anyway, then we are always going to be liberated to be more creative and potentially happier with the time that gets freed up as a result.

Those who compile their lives around the best web3-driven solutions will thrive. Their time will no longer just be limited to the time they as a human being have; they will have a digital twin working on their behalf, 24/7. In addition, their time will not be split into work or life; work–life balance will become a thing of the past. This will allow for greater earning potential *and* more time to pursue a life of purpose where they work in a traditional sense, maybe just three days a week, and choose to spend the other two contributing to society in ways that are meaningful to them. Perhaps they join a DAO with a stated purpose to find solutions to climate change or poverty. So much is possible for us as individuals once the data sovereignty issue is solved.

Clearly this has massive implications for business leaders, who need to find and keep talent in order to deliver their product or service. But there are hybrid ways to ensure that everyone wins.

If I were only able to give one piece of advice to business owners about web3, it would be about how essential it is for their survival that they find a way to push the ownership of data back to their customers. This will feel highly counter-intuitive because knowledge is power, but it is the inevitable evolution, not just because customers are demanding more privacy and nation states are pushing for greater legislation to protect privacy, but because web3 will make it possible for the first time. And the implications of this advance will be truly profound.

> **THERE ARE HYBRID WAYS TO ENSURE THAT EVERYONE WINS.**

Summary of Key Points

» Individuals will own their data; they will own what they create. This transition means that we move from an internet economy worth $10 trillion where 80 per cent of the value is owned by corporations to a $100 trillion web3/web4 economy where 80 per cent of value is owned by the individual. But only if we get data sovereignty right.

» At least one protocol for enabling data sovereignty, Solid, has already been created.

» So far, our evolution as a species has been largely down to the augmentation of our physical body.

» Because our brains have not really evolved to deal with the new reality of the Information Age, if we are to progress, we need help.

» Until the data sovereignty issue is solved, and people feel 100 per cent sure that their data is their own and can't be used, hacked or manipulated by others, AI will never deliver the humanity-changing benefits it is poised to deliver.

» Billions of people the world over are consumed by work and making ends meet. But what if all our base financial needs were taken care of via some form of data sovereignty solution, which could liberate us all to have more say and freedom in how we live our lives?

» In the future, the way we work will be down to our ability to cobble the various protocols and apps together in our own unique network. And, because of the change in the power law, there will be so many AI applications in the market that don't have access to our data but are finding solutions on our behalf.

Chapter 12
Tomorrow's Society

Everything is a product of evolution or incremental changes over time, and the societies we live in are no different.

We are going to experience two major changes. The first change is already underway through the adoption and use of smart contracts over legal contracts. The second change will be around the role and size of government. Once again, in order to understand what web3 will do to tomorrow's societies, we have to look at the past and appreciate how and why those incremental changes occurred and how web3 capability will reformat the landscape.

It is also worth pointing out that this chapter could easily be its own book. The challenge is that many of the issues that could and should be discussed are highly political and that politicization is a danger to understanding the capabilities, so I've deliberately avoided them. There is little doubt that right now web3 is the domain of the already wealthy and the highly educated, but it's unlikely to stay that way, especially as web4 makes access easier for all.

Whether web3 therefore delivers on its significant social promise may come down to education. In the same way that web3 will never truly flourish without true data sovereignty, it may struggle to expand beyond its current demographic boundaries without a rethink of our education system. But that rethink is already on the agenda, so it's certainly possible. Young people don't need to be stuffed with facts they will never use or could find out on Google in a few seconds. They need critical-thinking skills, problem-solving skills and a willingness to experiment, especially with new tech. Familiarity and comfort with tech will be essential, and this is already in abundance in the younger generations. Couple that familiarity and comfort with technical skill plus innovative and creative thinking and there is no reason why web3 can't be the universal boon for society that it should be.

Rule of Law

When our hunter-gatherer ancestors lived in caves, societies were limited to family groups eking out an existence and trying to survive. Once human beings realized that they could plant and tend crops to secure more consistent survival, the idea of ownership emerged, along with the notion of property rights. During the Agricultural Age, if someone went to the trouble and expense of planting a field and tending to that crop as it grew, then they held at least some form of property right over the crop. It certainly wasn't fair if someone else could come along at harvest time and just help themselves.

For thousands of years these types of disputes and disagreements were solved with conflict and bloodshed. Again, this progression from anarchy (the beige value system) onwards matches the values spiral shown in Figure 11.1: Spiral Dynamics and Sovereignty. In the purple value system, the tribal leader sorted out conflict and disagreements within the tribe. In the red value system, the autocratic leader called the shots – his word was law. By the time the blue value system emerged, the citizenry was beginning to wonder if there was a better way! When enough of a population reaches the blue value system, they question the status quo. In this case the early questioning came about, perhaps unsurprisingly, in Ancient Greece. The rule of law has its origins with the philosopher Aristotle. In his work *Politics*, he raised the question of whether it was better to be ruled by the best leader or the best laws. Although he found benefits to both, his conclusion was that the people should be ruled by the best laws – probably wise considering the brutality of at least some of the leaders in Ancient Greece.

Of course, over time the laws changed but the concept of the rule of law was largely accepted as the best option. No single person or collective is responsible for the creation of the rule of law, but in the United Kingdom, jurist and theorist A. V. Dicey was instrumental in bringing it into the public arena. In his book *Introduction to the Study of the Law of the Constitution* (1885) he contended that the rule of law was made up of three key principles:

1. That an individual has the freedom to act in any way he so wishes without punishment, provided it is not in breach of any law. This gives supremacy to the rule of law over any other arbitrary act of power that is not backed in law.
2. That no one is above the law, meaning that every subject, regardless of stature, can be held accountable to the law and punished in the courts of the land.
3. That the rule of law is based on the collective rights of all individuals. Essentially, this means that the courts will enforce individual rights on a collective basis to all subjects within its jurisdiction.[1]

Today, many countries around the world agree to be governed by the rule of law where these basic rules apply. In the US, for example, in theory this means that no one is above the law, not even the President. In practice, as we have seen in recent years, it's not quite as simple as that. The idea is valid, and the rule of law should provide modern societies with stability and a clear system for resolving conflicts between citizens within a community of any size, but the reality is quite different. Again, this follows the onward path of the values spiral. In the blue value system, the idea of right over might is what's valued. Those operating at the blue value system don't believe it is right, fair or beneficial to society when one person has absolute control. Too much can go wrong. History is littered with evidence that too much *does* go wrong. At the blue values level, doing the right thing is important. But by the time orange emerges, usually because too many rules have stifled progress, the shift in values towards pragmatism and the push towards progress, productivity and success mean that the rules get bent, broken or ignored.

This is essentially the world we live in now. There may be a rule of law that is equally applicable to all, but in practice there is one rule for one group of people and another rule for everyone else. The differentiating factor is often money. Perhaps, ironically, those with money are often held to a different, less robust standard than those without.

Contract law and smart contracts

Rule of law is a principle. There also needs to be a set of laws that the rule of law will apply to. The one that is most relevant to web3 and the changes that are coming is contract law.

Again, most contract law is heavily influenced by the Ancient Greeks (this time Plato), as well as Roman thinking. The Romans had their fair share of heinous all-powerful leaders too, so law was of particular interest to them.

In *The Laws*, Plato recognized the same basic categories for canceling agreements that still exist today. When talking about contracts, Plato states, 'If a man fails to fulfil an agreed contract – unless he had contracted to do something forbidden by law or decree, or gave his consent under some iniquitous pressure, or was involuntarily prevented from fulfilling his contract because of some unlooked-for accident – an action for such an unfulfilled agreement should be brought in the tribal courts, if the parties have not previously been able to reconcile their differences before arbitrators (their neighbors, that is).'

Roman law went even further by identifying discrete categories of contractual transactions, each with their own requirements, which needed to be fulfilled in order for promises to be enforced. Roman law represented an early division between specific kinds of contract, depending on the transaction's nature.[2]

During the Middle Ages in the UK, local court systems managed disputes, with each party having to attend court and swear an oath called a wager of law. It was formalized and developed considerably as part of the economic, political and intellectual renaissance of Western Europe in the fifteenth and sixteenth centuries. The informal agreements of old were unsuitable for the commercial and industrial societies that were emerging.

Today, everything we do that involves the delivery of value or the exchange of ownership is formalized in contract law. Needless to say, that explosion in contract law has also seen an explosion in the industry around the drafting and enforcement of agreements via the courts. Society is largely based on contract law of one form or another, and we have come to rely on trusted third parties to act in our best interest. And that doesn't always happen.

Web3 offers a different way through smart contracts coded into the blockchain. In tomorrow's society, smart contracts will replace legal contracts. There will be no need for trusted third parties or legions of lawyers, endless negotiation or for court cases to settle disputes. Everything is built into the smart contract at the time of creation, connected to the respective parties' wallets. These wallets are becoming more sophisticated, acting as treasury systems (as covered in Chapter 7) where, if required, multiple parties can be part of the agreement, signing with their keys. Once delivery has been made the asset is released. If it is not delivered, the asset is not released. All this is done in the smart contract code and doesn't require calling up the supplier to complain or getting a lawyer to draft a letter. It is all done automatically based on the agreement specified and ratified at the point of verification by the smart contract. It is also, by design, immutable and irreversible.

What we end up with is a peer-to-peer decentralized way of agreeing who owns, or who commits to, what. When ownership has been transferred, what have all parties agreed to do? What's the contract between the individual or business and society? What's the cost? Instead, without lawyers, web3 facilitates the creation of an unhackable, secure, automated record system that is automatically actioned and constantly updated, and all these agreements can reference other agreements, because of the composability of web3.

The Social Contract and Government

There has always been a balance between law, control and society. During the Renaissance and the Age of Enlightenment, it wasn't just contract law that was being discussed and redrawn. The idea of the social contract also gathered pace. Theories of a social contract became popular in the sixteenth, seventeenth and eighteenth centuries among philosophers such as Thomas Hobbes, John Locke and Jean-Jacques Rousseau as a means of explaining the origin of government and the obligations of the citizenry in that society.

The social contract is an implicit agreement among the members of a society to surrender some of their freedoms in exchange for the protection of their remaining rights and the maintenance of social order. Again, the idea has its roots in antiquity, but its heyday was the mid-seventeenth to early nineteenth centuries, when it was put forward as the leading reason for political legitimacy – the idea being that we the people relinquish some of our control and freedom to the government in exchange for protection and social order for the collective benefit.

Thomas Hobbes famously said that in a 'state of nature' (i.e. human beings left to their own devices) we would live a 'solitary, poor, nasty, brutish and short' life. In the absence of political order and the rule of law, everyone would be free to do whatever they wanted, which would lead to an endless 'war of all against all'. To avoid this outcome, the citizenry therefore agreed with each other to establish a civil society through a social contract in which everyone gains security in return for subjecting themselves to governmental oversight. Alternatively, Locke and Rousseau argued that we gain civil rights in return for accepting the obligation to respect and defend the rights of others, giving up some freedoms ourselves in order to do so.[3]

The central argument of social contract theory is that law and political order are not natural, but human creations. It is a means to an end, the end being civil society where a lot of people can live peacefully with each other without bloodshed or conflict.

And for the most part, the system has worked reasonably well. If the appointed government does not hold up its side of the bargain, the people can vote them out of office. But that system is also under pressure. For a start, the government itself has become a behemoth. Its effectiveness in its various roles and responsibilities is open for debate – regardless of political party. The political process will always, even in democracies, result in large swathes of the electorate feeling unheard. There is always about half of the voting public that doesn't get the result it wants, and there are also millions who have given up on the political process so completely that they no longer vote at all. Considering the sharp decline in the quality of political leadership across the planet over the last decade, this is perhaps unsurprising.

If you also include the billions in 'dark money' used to buy or curry political favor by wealthy individuals and companies via lobbying, then it's easy to see why people are so profoundly disenfranchised with the political system. Can we really say that modern government enacts policies to protect its citizenry and facilitate a civil society, or is it now more accurate to say that government enacts policies to protect business and wealthy individuals at the expense of the citizenry? Various political scandals over the years certainly point to the latter.

Web3 could provide a much-needed upgrade to governments by facilitating a significantly lighter government. It would be naive to suggest it could ever replace government, and that would probably be unwise, but the best of government as we know it today could be included as we transcend into something better.

The emergence of lighter government

The role of government varies from country to country, but it almost always includes these four important areas:

» The preservation of order.
» Managing economic conditions.
» Redistribution of income and resources.
» Provision of public or utility good.

Let's just look at each one through the lens of web3.

PRESERVATION OF ORDER

Most governments manage the preservation of order pretty well. We have the rule of law, and the police and armed forces enforce that law in various jurisdictions. Everyone knows what will happen if they break the rules: a fine or the loss of their liberty. But it has not always been so sedate. The preservation of order has led to significant bloodshed over many centuries. It has resulted in two world wars and countless other conflicts. As a species, we have developed devastating ways to kill others whom we believe are impinging on our 'way of life', and governments have used those tools when needed. By and large, we now live in peaceful societies, but the same tragedies are still being played out all over the world – most recently in Ukraine.

Preservation of order often comes down to a belief of ownership or that some imagined right has been impeded. What would happen, though, if ownership was no longer contained in old parchments or legal written contracts but via smart contracts on the blockchain? War and conflict would reduce significantly, because we would be able to protect property rights and individual freedoms with algorithms and electricity instead of guns and bombs.

> **WAR AND CONFLICT WOULD REDUCE SIGNIFICANTLY.**

Web3 can do nothing about man's propensity for violence, but so much of that violence, certainly in the past, has been down to disagreements around who owns what or which despotic leaders want to take another country's land or resources. It will take time for us to realize that we don't need so many guns and bombs, but theoretically, when all ownership is recorded in the block-chain, these disputes would reduce and the size of government funding and resources earmarked for the preservation of order could be used elsewhere. Preservation of order as a function of government could be reduced.

MANAGING ECONOMIC CONDITIONS

Right now, the government has a strong role in managing our economic reality through the levers of interest rates via the central bank, as well as the collection of taxes. But, in the world of cryptocurrency, there is no central bank.

It's time for a change anyway. Centralized banking has become hyper-politicized and many economies, including the US and the UK, are wrestling with historical levels of debt in a shrinking economy. As a result, the system, with its various economic levers, simply doesn't work like it once did to rebalance the economy. For example, inflation rates across the world are fast approaching double digits. The typical response to high inflation is to increase interest rates, but with many governments holding colossal levels of debt, raising interest rates would cause even more issues with government finances. As people panic about the cost-of-living crisis they stop spending, which in turn causes a recession or even a depression.

The levers to manage economic conditions no longer work because governments have borrowed well beyond their means and it's virtually impossible to roll that back to manageable levels in the current system. It is pretty clear that the central banking model of IOUs and quantitative easing has been pushed to its absolute limits.

> **THE LEVERS TO MANAGE ECONOMIC CONDITIONS NO LONGER WORK.**

Governments are also fearful and skeptical of crypto for obvious reasons – they can't control it. But cryptocurrency only works *because* it's decentralized. If governments seek to write central banking principles into a centralized algorithm, the outcome could be disastrous. Imagine: if the government controlled crypto, it could not just tell its citizenry to save more or spend more, it could effectively instruct the algorithm to save or spend money on your behalf. Not good.

Web3 gives us the tools, protocols and in-time applications where we can manage our own economic conditions without as much government intervention.

REDISTRIBUTION OF INCOME AND RESOURCES

The only way the current tax system works effectively is if everyone pays their taxes. When everyone pays their share and contributes to the greater collective good, whether they use that good or need that good right now, then tax income can facilitate services and redistribute incomes and resources more evenly through all of society. But the taxation system in most countries is no longer fit for purpose. It's often mind-numbingly complex and outdated. And those with access to greater means also have access to greater opportunities to pay even less tax. The distribution of tax money is also extremely inefficient as it's structured as a 'given' and not treated as a scarce resource that needs to be managed effectively. Private enterprise may be more effective and efficient at distribution if a web3 model is applied where public goods are treated more as a collective common that is managed with the right set of incentives.

If we have a leaner government, that means reduced tax rates that simplify over time. Tax itself could also become a form of smart contract where it's integrated into the web3 ecosystem in exchange for the services only a government or local community is able to provide.

And perhaps, more importantly, once the data sovereignty issue is solved then the need for some form of government-funded universal basic income (UBI) may no longer be needed. At the start of 2017, Finland became the first country in the world to trial the use of UBI where a random group of 2,000 unemployed people were paid the equivalent of $630 per month. Only, the payment came with no obligations or stipulations – if the individual got a job in the trial period, they would still receive the money.[4] Initial findings from the first of a two-year program showed positive effects on health and stress, but no improvement in work status.[5] Although there was a slight increase in entrepreneurial activity. People like Elon Musk and Mark Zuckerberg have both stated that they believe such an approach is valid and holds the key to tackling widespread inequality.[6] Additional trials are already being run in Canada, Spain, the Netherlands and Scotland.[7]

In some circles UBI is viewed as inevitable, and interestingly the strategy has support from both the right and left of politics. The right sees UBI as a way of making a leaner, less bureaucratic welfare state, and the left sees it as a way to combat poverty and inequality. But the reality of UBI is not political or even ideological. It is practical. We have already seen the decimation of well-paid manufacturing jobs across the world. Those jobs are not just disappearing to countries with cheaper employment – they are just disappearing altogether, as automation improves. This was true before the Covid-19 pandemic, and it is even more urgent in the post-Covid recovery.

Those against the idea say there is no government on the planet that can afford to dole out a regular payment to every citizen. But a robust welfare state always improves the overall benefits to society. Besides, the alternative may be worse. Covid had a profound impact on informal workers (estimated to be around 1.3 billion people) as well as migrants, with almost 100 million displaced in India alone. If a large part of an entire generation loses its livelihood, with no social safety net to catch it, the social costs will be unbearably high. Economic instability will follow the flare-up of social tensions. According to the World Economic Forum, for UBI to work the taxation system needs to be fair and effective, and it isn't.

Countries will have to work together, exchanging data across borders, to stop people and corporations from evading taxes. Simply put, we must continue to strive for more advanced systems for redistribution to create a happier and more productive society. With good conscience, we should look to avoid profits that come so clearly at the cost of our environment or people. Right now, too many multinationals have been able to leverage the global tax system to provide their services and generate enormous amounts of cash that is not entered back into the system productively, whether that's through share buy-backs or just cash sitting in the Cayman Islands. This is capital sitting on the sidelines missing an opportunity to create more economic growth and prosperity. Apple, Amazon, Google and Walmart, to name just a few, generate mind-boggling profits and pay limited amounts in taxes, after taking advantage of all the wrinkles in tax systems. If the top thousand corporations in the world were fairly taxed, it would allow for a modest UBI to be tightly and reasonably dispensed in countries across the world.[8]

But what if that didn't even need to happen?

When data sovereignty is returned to the owners of the data – and that is inevitable – then it is likely that an interconnected network of micro-payments will flow to individuals based on their use of or engagement with various applications and platforms. Instead of Google and Facebook making billions in advertising revenues, companies will pay the customer for the right to approach them about offers that the customer identifies may be of interest to them.

PROVISION OF PUBLIC OR UTILITY GOOD

Provision of public or utility good for most governments includes, but is certainly not limited to, the provision of accreditation and the administration of various entities such as businesses and professional qualifications. Again, smart contracts would record the progress of qualifications and skills so that on the completion of deliverables, the accreditation, pre-built into the smart contract, would be enacted. There would be no need to apply for certification. The smart contract would deliver it automatically based on the fulfillment of the agreements in the smart contract.

> **IMAGINE A LOCAL COUNCIL CREATING A DAO TO BUILD A NEW ROAD.**

Some of the hardest things the government helps with is pooling capital together for long-term infrastructure projects or the welfare and health systems. As evidenced by the ConstitutionDAO, the DAO set up to try to buy a rare copy of the US Constitution, web3 will allow people to come together really quickly to fund and collaborate on local and national projects they care about. Imagine a local council creating a DAO to build a new road. The local people may be more than happy to contribute to that fund if it saves them money on garage bills and tax. Plus the DAO ensures that no one can run off with that pool of money created for the road.

The outcome will be that we are left with a leaner government. We will always need the government, and there are no web3 solutions right now for national security, foreign diplomacy or the protection of our natural rights. Whatever system we end up with, there will also be some people who try to game the system, so a strong and effective government will still be needed to umpire the game. But it may be a fraction of the size it is now. Smaller government means less cost, fewer politicians (which has to be a good thing) and more focus placed on the people who can actually solve our growing list of existential problems – us!

Creative, dynamic and constructive local government

One of the most exciting possibilities of a lighter national or federal government is a more empowered and dynamic local government driven by web3 inclusion and connectivity.

As economist Elinor Ostrom points out, 'There is no reason to believe that bureaucrats and politicians, no matter how well meaning, are better at solving problems than the people on the spot, who have the strongest incentive to get the solution right.' When local government is reimagined, the bureaucrats, politicians and people on the spot in the local community are all incentivized to find and implement the best solutions.

Web3 offers considerable opportunity for greater transparency, security and collaboration. The removal of the need for third parties and the open-source nature of web3 means that tomorrow's towns, cities and local communities are going to be able to use blockchains to create more trusted, transparent and verifiable versions of existing processes.

Web3 could transform voter security so that everyone, regardless of their hopes, fears or politics, could trust the outcome. The blockchain is efficient in a way that paper is not, and publicly verifiable in a way that centralized computing systems are not. As such, blockchains will, eventually, revolutionize voting. They are already experimenting with this in Miami, with a voting scheme based on citizen NFTs – with votes limited to one per person using proof-of-humanity verification on the blockchain.

Or what about transparency in spending? One of the bugbears of citizens is the worry that local councils are not spending their citizen contributions wisely or are being too wasteful. Web3 would make it possible for local governments to make a whitelisted, internal-use-only stablecoin for tracking internal government payments. Every tax payment from an individual or business could be tied to a publicly visible on-chain record minting that number of coins. There are already ways to keep the amount of the tax payment hidden for privacy reasons, while still giving the citizens confidence in the transparency and accuracy of the process. Transfers between departments could be made on-chain for total transparency, and the coins would be redeemed only by individual contractors or employees claiming their payments and salaries.

Another of the major issues with local and national government is the monotonous regularity with which projects commissioned by the government take longer to deliver than promised, and always cost considerably more. Take the UK Government's abysmal attempt to create a track-and-trace system during Covid. It cost $37 billion over two years and never worked.[9] Imagine a world where that was no longer possible. Where contracts between national or local government and suppliers were recorded in the blockchain via smart contract. Where money would be released to the contractor as deliverables were met in accordance with the costs they submitted during the bid process. There would be no way for projects to come in millions over-budget. The agreement would be recorded in the blockchain and honored.

The power of the blockchain is that anything on it can be publicly verified very easily. There are already lots of ready-made, freely available tools to help people do that. Any application built on a blockchain can immediately plug into, and interface with, other applications in the entire global blockchain ecosystem. Plus, the decentralized, distributed nature of web3 also allows for high-volume, real-time feedback on hundreds or even thousands of different issues within the community. With an invested and engaged citizenry not only willing to offer up new ideas but to be part of the implementation of the solution, either via funding or offering up their time or talent into a DAO, then there is no end to the good that could be created in these new web3 communities.

Blockchains could also be used by local governments to implement new and experimental forms of ownership for land or other scarce assets, as well as forms of democratic governance.[10]

When exploring radical new territory, there are always more options, and most are limited only by our imagination. But there are already several places around the world that are experimenting with a localized medium of exchange or community token.

Web3 presents an exciting solution to many problems by offering a different way to own part of the communities that we live in. Imagine if your town, city or community created a divisible and fungible city token that residents could hold as many units of as they wanted or felt comfortable with, and whose value goes up as the community prospers. As a local, their birth certified on the blockchain, they could be eligible for some free tokens or ongoing payment via tokens as a UBI to help compensate for the loss of housing opportunities in the area. As the tokens go up in value as the community is made even better and more sought-after, everyone benefits, not just homeowners and businesspeople, but all residents of the community too.

Tokens could also create new sources of revenue for local government while creating economic alignment with residents. The token becomes more valuable as the community becomes more attractive, and there is an in-built incentive for the people in the community to hold the tokens.

So much of what gets done in government, local or national, is influenced by those with the deepest pockets, corporate lobby or those with the ear of power. Systems such as quadratic funding (QF) – the democratic funding of

TOKENS COULD ALSO CREATE NEW SOURCES OF REVENUE FOR LOCAL GOVERNMENT.

public goods where everyone gets an equal vote – could spell the end of that influence. For example, a local council might engage in a QF round, where the community contributes to the projects they feel should be funded and supported; a matching partner offers funds to match the community's contributions, but not on a 1:1 basis. Instead, the match is more aligned to the sentiment of the community as opposed to the sheer dollar value amount raised by any grantee. The number of contributors matters more than the amount funded, thus making the projects enacted much more democratic and less prone to wealthy influence.[11]

Many of the initiatives and possibilities discussed in this section are already happening around the world, although mainly in the US. The possibilities are endless for us as citizens and business leaders.

The new collective power (the commons)

Tomorrow's society will be more equitable, built on the web3 collective commons where people are working together for the greater good. Instead of looking to the government to solve society's problems (which rarely works anyway), we collaborate on the commons to solve them ourselves, in our local communities, in countries and across the world. The world is facing a depressing array of wicked problems right now and not only are we not solving them, we can't even seem to agree which are real problems!

Climate change certainly fits that description. There are still millions of people around the world who don't believe climate change is real or who choose to ignore the existential threat it poses. In environmental circles web3 is often viewed as part of that threat, largely because of high energy use in blockchains and therefore the technology's carbon footprint. According to a Cambridge University and International Energy Agency study in 2019, over the course of a year Bitcoin alone consumed about the same amount of energy as Switzerland.[12] They have even created a Bitcoin Electricity Consumption Index, which is updated every 24 hours.[13]

> **TOMORROW'S SOCIETY WILL BE MORE EQUITABLE, BUILT ON THE WEB3 COLLECTIVE COMMONS.**

According to the Bitcoin Mining Council studies, 58.5 per cent of the energy used to mine BTC in the last quarter of 2021 was created through renewable energy.[14] And while this is a positive step in the right direction, more does need to be done. At the same time, however, we need to be having a much more nuanced and informed discussion about these issues.

It is an easy argument to make, and a popular one for journalists and activists alike. But it's not a simple debate with web3 on one side and environmentalists on the other. I would consider myself an environmentalist, but I am also a passionate advocate for what web3 can do for the world, including its role in combating climate change.

The central point in this argument is proof-of-work. Bitcoin uses proof-of-work to verify which new transitions should be added to the digital ledger known as the blockchain. It's the way the network verifies that the transaction is valid and that someone isn't trying to do something they shouldn't, such as spend the same money twice. Proof-of-work is based on an advanced form of mathematics called 'cryptography'. Powerful computers are then used to solve very difficult, unique mathematical equations, which verify that the transaction is authentic. Proof-of-work is very secure but the computer power necessary to solve these equations, and therefore verify the transaction on the blockchain, uses a lot of electricity. In many ways Bitcoin's value and that of other cryptocurrencies, certainly the ones using proof-of-work, are represented by the value of electricity, which does provide a fundamental valuation, creating a foundational support for the network effects as well as making the network extremely secure. Interestingly, in 1921 Henry Ford proposed the idea of an energy currency. The 4 December edition of the *New York Tribune* led with the story 'Ford Would Replace Gold with Energy Currency and Stop Wars' (see Figure 12.1).

FIGURE 12.1: FORD'S PREDICTION OF AN ENERGY CURRENCY

What he went on to describe – a currency backed by energy measured in kilowatt-hours (kWh), issued only to a certain definite amount and for a specific purpose – is basically Bitcoin.[15] His plan was to kickstart the idea at the hydroelectric plant at Muscle Shoals Dam in Alabama, a place I have visited many times in my youth as it was a short trip from where my family are originally from.

Of course, it didn't happen, but Bitcoin and many of the other cryptocurrencies could certainly be considered energy currency. The challenge we have now, which was not yet known in Ford's day, is just how polluting much of that energy is, and how its long-term use on an industrial scale, especially using fossil fuels, would have a catastrophic impact on the planet.

But all energy is not equal. And usage is not equal. The fact remains that the places in the world who could benefit from renewable energy are often a long, long way from the energy grid. It's all very well having wind farms in the Highlands of Scotland, but there is a massive amount of infrastructure involved in transporting that energy, storing it and therefore making it useful.

One thought-provoking concept floated by CoinShares' Chief Strategy Officer Meltem Demirors is that Bitcoin (as well as other energy intensive protocols) is actually a battery, because it 'makes energy mutable, portable, storable and transferable by turning it into money'.[16] Essentially the idea is a recognition of the infrastructure and transportation issue that hampers energy creation and use – that many of the geographical locations in the world that are highly suitable for renewable energy would incur massive costs to connect that power to the grid. For example, it may be energy efficient to put acres of solar farms in the middle of the Australian outback, but the cost of connecting the resulting renewable energy to grid so that it becomes useful to the bulk of Australian residents that are located on the coasts would be prohibitive. Even the process of getting energy onto the grid using existing infrastructure loses about a third of the energy from the original source.[17] But those locations could use the energy to mine Bitcoin, therefore transforming abundant renewable energy that is not currently used by anyone into money that could be used by local communities, individual landowners or governments. Instead of scratching out a living trying to raise animals across thousands of acres of Northern Territory scrub, landowners or farmers could install solar farms that run proof-of-work verification, earning Bitcoin or other tokens. Surely that is better for the environment, uses less water and doesn't require animals to suffer through extended drought?

As I said, energy is not equal. As a result, solar and wind energy may be a really good fit for proof-of-work protocols.

In addition, there are protocols that are seeking to address this energy-use issue. Proof-of-stake systems still verify on the blockchain, but they use much less energy. Ethereum moved to proof-of-stake in September 2022, a move it estimates will cut its energy usage by 99.95 per cent. Instead of mining, proof-of-stake validation increasingly comes from users buying in (owning a stake) to approve transactions. They are effectively saying that this information or transaction is accurate and valid, and I stake my own money as proof. For example, someone might stake 1 ETH and, once the decentralized network validates that it's correct, the person who stakes the 1 ETH will get their 1 ETH back again, along with maybe 0.01 ETH as confirmation and validation.

Proof-of-stake doesn't require so much computational power to validate the block, but it is less secure than proof-of-work, although it is definitely sufficient for some transactions. Besides, once the network is big enough, perhaps initially built on proof-of-work, the risk is more to the validator as more and more nodes in the network can detect inaccuracy, which would mean they lose their stake.

Proof-of-stake platforms are faster and more efficient. Solana, a newer blockchain that uses proof-of-stake and 'proof of history', a mechanism that relies on time stamps, can process 65,000 transactions per second (compared with Ethereum's proof-of-work rate of about 15 per second and Bitcoin's seven. That's about as much energy as two Google searches. Some companies are adopting a hybrid approach to blockchain, which offers the benefits without the constraints. According to Ethereum's co-founder Vitalik Buterin, 'There are a lot of really interesting new architectures, which put certain things on the blockchain but not others. A social network, for instance, could record your followers and who you follow on the blockchain, but not your posts, giving you the option to delete them.'[18] It's really not necessary to put every utterance or picture of every meal on the blockchain!

According to data security experts, these hybrid models can also help companies comply 'with the right to erasure' where personal data should be kept private from the blockchain in an "off-chain" data store, with only its evidence (cryptographic hash) exposed to the chain. That way, personal data can be deleted in keeping with General Data Protection Regulation (GDPR) without affecting the chain.[19]

In the world of the web3 economic systems, there is clearly a benefit and symbiotic relationship between a fundamental proof-of-work currency and a more flexible, less energy intensive proof-of-stake solution. Proof-of-work, like Bitcoin, is slower and very specific. As such, it is much more secure. Proof-of-stake will see the emergence of lots of more flexible, potentially vertical specific blockchains that could be significantly more efficient but potentially less secure. Both indirectly depend on the stability of Bitcoin. And then you have situations where you don't even need a blockchain. You could just use centralized storage like IPFS, which is order of magnitudes more cost effective, requiring virtually no energy.

We need all three and we need to be smart about what goes on what platform: proof-of-stake for smart contracts and many other applications; proof-of-work for the global store of wealth and settlement of high-value transactions, especially if proof-of-work can be moved to 100-per-cent renewable energy; decentralized off-chain storage for everything else.

It is also worth remembering that web3 will change business-as-usual, and any environmental impact will also be offset against the reduction in current practices that are not environmentally friendly either. Plus, according to the Cambridge Electricity Consumption Index, Bitcoin uses 126.67 TWh per year, cement production uses 384 TWh, and iron and steel use 1233 TWh.[20] But if we can get smart about renewable energy that is connected to the grid, and renewable energy that is remote (so just used for web3) then we wouldn't be using so much cement, iron and steel to create the infrastructure.

It's almost impossible to quantify, but even if fewer people use cars and trains to go to a place of work and instead plug into a decentralized interconnected network, there are additional environmental benefits to be reaped – not to mention quality-of-life benefits. As we covered in the disruption of talent supply, we are already in a world where more of us are working remotely, even on web2 architecture. That will accelerate as more options emerge on the web3 stack. As someone who has been subjected to enormous amounts of unnecessary air travel, this in itself will be one of the greatest positive impacts on the environment.

Plus, if web3 provides new ways to verify the supply chain, companies would have nowhere to hide and would no longer be able to greenwash their environmental credentials. The only way we will solve the climate crisis is if the polluters are named, shamed and financially impacted for non-action. Web3 can make that possible.

As I've said before in this book, web3 is not a new flavor of the internet; it is an entirely new offering that will fundamentally expand the scale and scope of human–machine interactions. It will empower us to interact with any individual, system or machine in the world, without having to pass through fee-charging, data-hogging middlemen, and this shift will facilitate a whole new wave of previously unimaginable businesses and business models: from global co-operatives to DAOs to self-sovereign data marketplaces.[21] At least, all these things are possible and more if the issue of data sovereignty can be solved authentically. The possibilities of web3 are truly astonishing, but human–machine interaction, especially if we factor in AI and machine learning, will only come to fruition with full data sovereignty. If done properly, on top of secure data sovereignty protocols, human beings, businesses, lighter government and machines will share more data, securely and with more privacy for the greater individual and collective good.

> **IF WEB3 PROVIDES NEW WAYS TO VERIFY THE SUPPLY CHAIN, COMPANIES WOULD HAVE NOWHERE TO HIDE.**

These capabilities have the potential to make tomorrow's societies better in every way. As Marc Andreessen, co-founder of VC firm Andreessen Horowitz and Netscape, says, 'Software is eating the world.' His prediction that software would disrupt traditional industries is nothing to what web3 and web4 will do, but the disruption will reach far beyond industries into societies and entire global economies.

We have already seen how quickly vast sums of money can be pooled for causes that people feel passionately about. In the case of the ConstitutionDAO, that $34,025,859 was raised to buy a rare copy of the US Constitution in a matter of weeks.[22] Billions of people around the world are passionate about the environment and about solving the crisis. Imagine the intellect, drive and money that could be unleashed on this problem if those billions of people could get involved through a DAO instead of just creating a placard and picketing climate conferences!

Summary of Key Points

» Today, everything we do that involves the delivery of value or the exchange of ownership is formalized in contract law. Web3 offers a different way through smart contracts coded into the blockchain.

» Web3 facilitates the creation of a virtually unhackable, secure record system that is automatically actioned and constantly updated.

» Web3 could provide a much-needed upgrade to governments by facilitating a significantly lighter government.

» One of the most exciting possibilities of a lighter national or federal government is a more empowered and dynamic local government driven by web3.

» The removal of the need for third parties and the open-source nature of web3 means that tomorrow's towns, cities and local communities are going to be able to use blockchains to create more trusted, transparent and verifiable versions of existing processes.

» Tomorrow's society will be built on web3 collective commons, where instead of looking to the government to solve society's problems we collaborate to solve them ourselves, in our local communities, in our countries and across the world.

Conclusion

We have covered a lot of ground.

Throughout history we have often referred to monumental events in similar terms: the Great War (First World War), the Great Depression, the Great Resignation … web3 has triggered the Great Unbundling and the end of business-as-usual.

Where web1 and web2 disrupted the demand-side and how we accessed things, web3 and beyond will disrupt the supply-side, or how we are coming together to create things. Web3 brings a completely new architecture that heralds the next era of the internet where the need for centralized trust is vastly diminished, and the Information Age is rebuilt on a trustless model, with fewer profit-seeking gatekeepers hogging the wealth. Instead, we end up with a far more productive society where the rewards are more equitably distributed. We may own less but benefit from more, connect to more, contribute to more and share more.

With each era we see a repeated pattern of Protocol–App Inversion. In web1 we saw the emergence of new game-changing protocols such as File Transfer Protocol (FTP), Internet Protocol (IP), Usenet and a Simple Mail Transfer Protocol (SMTP) for email. Many of these protocols were truly brilliant and we still use them today, but they were developed by techies and engineers for other techies and engineers. As such they were not always easy to use or access. In order to cross the chasm in the product lifecycle, they need to reach out beyond the innovators and early adopters to the mass market. Web2 therefore saw an inversion to building user-friendly apps to make those protocols not only simple to use, but fun and addictive as well.

In each era there is also an innovation plot twist protocol or piece of technology that massively accelerates the uptake and expansion of that era. In web1 it was HTML. In web2 it was the iPhone as well as Android. The smartphone allowed new businesses to emerge, such as Uber and Deliveroo – which would not have been possible without mobile internet. And while Apple didn't invent the smartphone, they made it intuitive, simple to use and stunningly beautiful. Customers were hooked.

In web3 we see the flip back to protocol development. This time we are witnessing the emergence of new types of 'cooperation protocols', starting with Bitcoin but going far beyond, and these protocols are already upending the supply-side of business. This Supply-side Revolution is going to disrupt the supply of talent, capital and operations as well as further disrupt demand. Where web1 and web2 completely changed how businesses sold their products and services, web3 is putting the power in the hands of producers, creators, coders and collaborators who will come together in new ways to completely change how those products and services are created and offered to customers in the first place!

It's still unclear what the innovation plot twist will turn out to be for web3, but my guess is that smart contracts, the DAO (which provides the new way for people to come together to collaborate and create things) and NFTs will demand that every business rethinks its product mix.

Business has always delivered greater prosperity to the world. That will not change. It's just that the dominant vehicle will not be a company as we understand it today, and the spoils will not just go to the C-suite and shareholders; they will be distributed more equitably through what we currently understand as stakeholder groups – only web3 merges those stakeholder groups where an 'employee' will also be a 'shareholder' and a supplier and possibly even a financier. It is the emergence of true stakeholder capitalism.

This is good news. Modern business and the global economy are long overdue an upgrade. Not least because they are built on a world that no longer exists, namely the Industrial Revolution and centralized power. Web3 will bring that upgrade for the Information Age and facilitate greater cooperation, decentralized redistribution of wealth and the ability to really solve some of the world's most pressing problems.

Because of the proven theories discussed in this book, such as Innovator's Dilemma and Spiral Dynamics, you will now hopefully not only understand web3, but be able to predict the disruption of web4, which is just around the corner. Web4 will be a consolidation once again, where the winning protocols of web3 will be simplified and made much more user-friendly. Although all the architecture already exists, it's still not that easy to use the innovations of web3, particularly if you are not that comfortable with tech. Web4, however, is going to make accessing these game-changing technologies as easy as opening Spotify and requesting your favorite song!

As Max Mersch and Richard Muirhead from Fabric Ventures so eloquently put it, 'Web3 enables a future where distributed users and machines are able to interact with data, value and other counterparties via a substrate of peer-to-peer networks without the need for third parties. The result: a composable human-centric and privacy-preserving computing fabric for the next wave of the web.'[1]

But again, none of this will happen without full data sovereignty. Data sovereignty, where we own our own data and decide who has access to what parts in a fully secure, encrypted ecosystem, is critical if the humanity-benefiting advantages of web3 are to be realized. Without that trust in self-ownership over a centralized

> **DATA SOVEREIGNTY IS CRITICAL IF THE HUMANITY-BENEFITING ADVANTAGES OF WEB3 ARE TO BE REALIZED.**

power we will never allow AI to work its magic. AI capability could increase exponentially because of web3. And this will be even more transformative for society and humanity than the Industrial Revolution – only this time we will not be coming out of the fields to work in factories and cities; we will be coming out of offices to work wherever we want, in much more creative roles, with more flexibility and autonomy to strike a work–life balance that suits the various stages of our lives. But only if AI is built on web3 principles.

AI developed any other way is unlikely to deliver its game-changing capabilities for humanity. But this is not the only thing that can go wrong …

What Could Go Wrong?

The biggest threat to web3 is the usual mistakes we make as a species.

There is little doubt that the Supply-side Revolution of web3 has the potential to bring enormous productivity gains, improved efficiencies and opportunities to many of us. As a result, fear and greed emerge in abundance.

Human beings tend to be afraid of what they don't understand. This has been true since the beginning of time, and it will still be true at the end of time. In the late fifteenth and early sixteenth centuries, Leonardo da Vinci created plans for several flying machines, including a flapping ornithopter and a machine with a helical rotor. He based his designs on his study of birds and bats. But the world was not ready for human flight. Religion was the rule of law and only God could fly. Cultural zeitgeist and outdated belief structures will always apply a speed limit on progress. It would take another 400 years before science had unraveled enough of the mysteries of the universe to accept human flight as a possibility. In December 1903, the Wright brothers claimed the first human-powered flight. Just 66 years later, Neil Armstrong landed on the moon, declaring, 'That's one small step for man, one giant leap for mankind.' Web3 is another giant leap for mankind – if we don't mess it up.

For some people, the fear of the unknown will simply mean that they avoid or ignore web3 for as long as possible. For others, especially the entrenched players currently profiting handsomely from the highly centralized status quo, web3 poses an existential threat to their power advantage, revenue models and influence. As such, they are often extremely invested in making sure that the status quo is preserved.

It is very easy to tilt the debate and muddy the waters of understanding in a subject as complex as web3. The problem we face right now is that web3 is on a human-made knife edge where a combination of bad outcomes, facilitated largely by fear or greed, are throwing up the specter of really bad legislation that could stifle web3 for decades.

Bad outcomes

Bad outcomes happen for a number of reasons. It may just be that the bad outcome is the result of a bad idea. These scenarios play right into the hands of those who are seeking to sow fear and stifle progress so they can continue to profit from the status quo.

TerraUSD (UST) is a classic example of this issue. Anything is possible in web3 but Terra probably won't survive its meltdown in May 2022. Someone may come up with a new use for some of the underlying code but there is unlikely to be a phoenix rising from the ashes moment for Terra. The concept behind Terra is not great. An algorithmic stablecoin has never worked before;[2] it's too easy to manipulate by the actions of a single party. Terra required a back-up system that we haven't really seen work before, in that it was using its reserves to pay people who invested in Terra 20 per cent APR. There is a saying in life that applies to just about everything – if something sounds too good to be true, it usually is. It's amazing how good an idea can sound when there is talk of a 20 per cent return plus.

There is nothing that new about what happened to Terra. In every new era of innovation, bad ideas emerge. It's part of the innovation cycle. What makes bad ideas so damaging in web3 is that they can grow into big problems before they fail. And often that is because the investors and speculators, hungry to get into web3, are not informed enough to question the validity of the idea. Instead, greed keeps them focused on the promised returns.

Within days of the Terra collapse, the uninformed media online and off was swamped with articles on the death spiral of crypto. Fear drove all crypto-currencies to lose value. This is, however, no different from the vagaries of the stock market. Speculation and rumor are often enough to decimate share prices regardless of how strong the fundamentals of the business are.

Fear and greed also create a rich and lucrative opportunity for bad actors. This combination also inevitably leads to bad outcomes, which further fuel the naysayers, the ill-informed and those desperate to preserve existing profitable business models that will be impacted by web3.

Human beings are human beings. There will always be an element of humanity who try to hack, cheat, steal or otherwise game the system. The initial coin offering (ICO) bubble of 2017 that burst spectacularly in 2018 is a good example of this. Some of the tokens, such as Bitconnect, were just a scam.

Bitconnect was nothing but an old-school Ponzi scheme where new money was used to pay previous investors or reimburse those who wanted their money back. Founded in 2016 in the run-up to the ICO bubble, it promised insanely high returns (1 per cent compound interest per day), arguing that it was all now possible because of blockchain technology. Fear of missing out (FOMO) and greed created a potent cocktail that saw the Bitconnect coin

(BCC), worth $0.17 at ICO, reach an all-time-high of $463 before falling away to nothing. Today the term 'Bitconnected' is a meme used by crypto investors to describe losing money on questionable projects.[3]

There are countless other examples such as Mt. Gox and Quadriga. In 2014 one of the world's largest online cryptocurrency exchanges, Mt. Gox, unexpectedly shut down after getting hacked and losing 850,000 Bitcoin – valued at the time at nearly $400 million. Meanwhile, in Canada, a new online cryptocurrency exchange called Quadriga emerged. Thirty-year-old founder Gerald Cotten announced at the time, 'People like the fact we're located in Canada and know where their money is going.' Five years later, people didn't know where their money ($135 million) or Cotten was![4] Rumor was that he faked his own death in India.[5]

Where there is money to be made, there will always be people who become incredibly ingenious at getting their hands on it. And yet those outcomes only confirm what we know about humanity and do not necessarily say anything about the underlying technology. If anything, it further demonstrates the need for some trusted algorithmic system that circumvents human weakness.

Many of the techniques used to fleece overly keen speculators have been around forever – pump and dump is a technique often used in the stock market even though it's illegal. As in libel laws, however, it's incredibly hard to prove. Essentially, one group of investors who hold a lot of shares in a certain company but want to sell them will start talking up that share on social and mainstream media. If the company has reach and influence, it can easily lead to an increase in buying activity. This 'pumping' falsely inflates the share price, and the company then dumps the shares, now worth considerably more than they were when they decided to sell. The same thing happens in crypto. Even if it's not a deliberate strategy, one tweet from someone like Elon Musk can massively inflate or deflate a stock or cryptocurrency. This is ridiculous, but it's a product of human nature – FOMO and greed. Even in the traditional markets, Archegos, a well-established hedge fund, was taken out by the WallStreetBets meme. The hedge fund had taken a large short position on GameStop and when WallStreetBets saw this they were able to rally their meme army to buy the stock. No one knows who is behind WSB, but at the end of the day it shows the power of the community to come together and get behind a meme. These are the new rules to play by.[6]

Often in the web3 space losses are pounced on as evidence that the architecture of the blockchain or decentralized storage is not working or is not as secure as it's made out to be. Again, this is rarely the truth. There have been hacks; Mt. Gox was hacked and one of the first DOAs was hacked. The project known as The DAO was launched in 2016 on the Ethereum blockchain as a revolutionary project that would act as an investor-directed venture capital firm. It raised $150 million of ether (ETH) in three weeks, making it the largest crowdfunding campaign in history at the time. But computer scientists were concerned that a bug in The DAO's wallet smart contracts would allow them to be drained. Before it could be fixed someone exploited the vulnerability in its code base and $60 million worth of ETH was stolen.[7]

As the technology and architecture evolves, there are always going to be cases like this because of weaknesses in code, but as it matures these weaknesses will be eradicated. As I mentioned in the Prologue, the Terra collapse of May 2022 will eventually make the whole ecosystem stronger as the protocols that are just not run strongly enough are weeded out of the system.

There was a huge furor after some Bored Ape Yacht Club NFTs were hacked. But this time it was not down to a weakness in code, at least not the NFT code. This time the hack was to the BAYC Instagram account, where scammers posted a fraudulent link for a fake airdrop to all the followers. The link led to a copycat website offering free land in the BAYC's upcoming metaverse, the Otherside. Again, if something is too good to be true, it probably is – but FOMO and greed ensured that some people did click on the link, which contained a classic phishing attack but targeted at web3 token transfer. This meant that, once the link was clicked, the attacker could connect the user's MetaMask crypto-wallet with the scammer's wallet, and they drained the assets. It was basically a phishing attack and the hacker managed to steal 91 NFTs worth an estimated $2.8 million, including 54 Bored Ape Yacht Club NFTs.[8]

Naysayers see these scenarios as proof that the technology is not safe. But most of the time they have happened because a human being was fearful or too greedy and has nothing to do with the security of the system.

That said, there is also a darker side of web3. It would be naive to suggest there is not. The encryption, pseudo-anonymity, removal of trusted third parties, secure digital ownership and store of value, while revolutionary, has also drawn the attention of criminals. If you are unlucky enough to be the victim of ransomware, the demanded payment will always be to a crypto-wallet. Web3 tactics are used widely for nefarious activity and have helped to drive the criminals further underground. The paradox is that blockchains are open, therefore anyone can interpret the code, but encryption makes identification of an individual person very difficult.

But again, these bad outcomes are due to human nature and not technology. As the ecosystem gets stronger, it will hopefully be harder and harder for fraud to occur.

Collectively, these and many more bad outcomes are then used to justify *really* bad legislation.

Bad legislation

There is little doubt that some legislation has been a boon for business and innovation, even in web3. As pointed out by tech, politics and law writer Gilad Edelman, the fintech sector owes much of its existence to the 2010 Dodd–Frank Act, passed in the aftermath of the financial crisis. In it there is 'a section requiring US banks to let customers access their account data in a format that can be read by computer applications. You can thank that provision for the ability to sync up your data with personal finance apps like Betterment and Mint.'[9] Edelman also mentions the Open App Markets Act – a bill that has bipartisan momentum in Congress and would force Apple to permit downloading apps not offered in its App Store.

Sometimes legislation can be really helpful, but sometimes it's just daft. Surely one of the daftest pieces of legislation ever enacted in the UK was the 'red flag law' to regulate the use of mechanical vehicles on the roads. The Locomotive Act of 1865, also known as the Red Flag Act, stated that 'at least three persons shall be employed to drive or conduct such locomotive', one of whom needed to walk in front of the moving vehicle on foot waving a red flag to warn horse riders and pedestrians of the approaching vehicle (see Figure C.1).

That was law for 31 years in the UK! A similar red flag law was passed in 1894 in the US, although it was abolished just two years later when the UK did the same.[10] Clearly this was an attempt to hark back to the past and find bizarre

FIGURE C.1: RED FLAG ACT

ways to keep people employed and dampen down the fear of this newfangled contraption – the car. But it was ridiculous.

The other issue with legislation is that it is too slow, and frankly the people making the laws don't fully understand the landscape. This is especially true in technology. Who can ever forget some of the confusion on display by US senators when Facebook CEO Mark Zuckerberg testified before the United States Congress in the wake of the Cambridge Analytica scandal? Forty-four US senators, average age 62, demonstrated quite conclusively that they did not understand Facebook or any part of the online world.[11] South Carolina Senator Lindsey Graham asked, 'Is Twitter the same as what you do?' Utah Senator Orrin Hatch asked, 'How do you sustain a business model in which users don't pay for your services?' And Hawaii Senator Brian Schatz asked, 'If I'm emailing within WhatsApp … does that inform your advertisers?' If these lawmakers don't even know the basics of web1 protocols such as advertising revenues and that no one emails anything in WhatsApp, how can they possibly understand the complexity of blockchain or web3 well enough to propose or enact anything but the modern-day equivalent to the red flag law?

One such legislative suggestion is the creation of a Bitcoin backdoor. Because Bitcoin is the foundational blockchain on which all the others are built, the idea, put forward by US Senator Bill Foster, who also co-chairs the

Congressional Blockchain Caucus, is that a trusted third party, such as the courts, should have access to a crypto backdoor. His argument, shared by many, is that this is the only way to grapple with crypto-ransomware attacks and other criminal behavior. The court would therefore be able to use its access to a 'very heavily guarded key', a 'cryptographic backdoor in essence', allowing it to reverse transactions on the blockchain.[12]

This is a staggeringly bad idea. The whole point of web3 is that it is a decentralized, trustless system. A backdoor of any type will be found and exploited. It's human nature. Even if it was incredibly secure and only used in extreme circumstances, its existence would trigger hackers and fraudsters to look for it and they wouldn't stop until they found it.

Such legislation could be the death knell of web3. China has already banned cryptocurrencies outright, along with Algeria, Bangladesh, Egypt, Iraq, Morocco, Oman, Qatar and Tunisia. In the US the Biden administration issued an executive order in March 2022 directing the federal government to look into regulating cryptocurrencies.[13] Suffice it to say, governments all over the world are watching the space and they are nervous of the implications. The risk of any type of government-backed digital currency that is then centralized could be catastrophic. Imagine if that government then had direct access to your crypto-wallet and could set individual interest and inflation rates to initiate spending behavior that some faceless bureaucrat in government deemed necessary!

Clearly, legislation can be useful to protect the people who are the most vulnerable or have the lowest levels of understanding, but it still relies on a trusted third party for enforcement. Considering that so much political power is up for grabs to the highest bidder, it means that the legislation that is passed is often the legislation that helps those with the deepest pockets. In the US, Princeton University sought to understand how much public opinion influenced Congress and the laws they passed. Not much, it turns out. Princeton concluded that the preferences of the average American appear to have only a miniscule, near-zero, statistically non-significant impact on public policy. Considering that, once elected, US senators spend 70 per cent of their time fundraising, it's therefore pretty obvious who impacts public policy;[14] the billionaires and special-interest groups who donate to those politicians. Considering that many of these interest groups are hell-bent on stopping web3 in its tracks, it's a massive risk that legislation will therefore hold back innovation.

Europe may not have as much money in politics, and there is a more collaborative social democracy that takes privacy and data security very seriously, but even so the threats and opportunities there are significant. First the threats … there is already an attempt to ban proof-of-work because of its so-called damage to the environment, but as discussed in the last chapter, this issue is far more nuanced than all proof-of-work being bad. We just need to be informed and smarter about when and where it is used. There are also attempts by the EU to own consumer data on behalf of the citizens – again, this would be catastrophic. Only full data sovereignty, where data is owned by the individual alone, will work. As someone calling themselves @punk6529 (https://twitter.com/punk6529) puts it, Europe is in danger of building the best stop signs!

The US approach to light legislation means they have often raced ahead across many industries. This is certainly true in tech. It is significant to note that Spotify may be the only massive web2 company to emerge in Europe – all the rest have been in the legislation-light US. So, where America is making the best cars and building the best roads, the EU seems intent on building the best stop signs.

This is a tragedy because the EU is actually really well placed to capitalize on web3 and make the whole EU block web3-friendly. According to Patrick Hansen, Head of Strategy and Business Development at Unstoppable Finance and a RegTrax contributor for the EU, it is seeking to find a 'third way' between the techno-authoritarianism seen in parts of Asia and the surveillance capitalism in the US.[15]

Hansen suggests that crypto and web3 offer the 'third-way' path the EU has long been looking for. 'Not only do web3 values perfectly align with the sought-after notion of digital sovereignty, crypto would also make the EU more financially independent from the US and offer a unique economic opportunity to revive its struggling economy in the web2 era.' He also puts forward a solid argument for there being several geopolitical reasons why Europe, compared to the main global superpowers US or China, actually has the greatest potential upside from embracing, adopting and supporting web3.[16]

Web3 has the capacity to build safeguards and agreements into the system that will be enforced by the algorithm, not a third party of any kind. Get this right and it will be safer than any backdoor or even socially democratic legislation. Besides, legislators will not be able to keep up. All that will end up happening if one jurisdiction imposes draconian or daft legislation is that the web3 talent will move to a jurisdiction that is more favorable.

At time of writing, 2022, the UK is in a unique position to take advantage of that fact. For the first time in many years the UK can make their own laws, and choosing to become a web3-friendly jurisdiction could attract a lot of talent and capital. The UK might just be one of the best places for this to happen, given our location between the US and Europe, our time zone, talent, financial services heritage and new law-making status. Other smaller nations, from Switzerland to Malta, the Bahamas and Singapore, have all shown their potential to move fast and support innovation.

There is clearly a risk from inappropriate or daft legislation, but there is also a risk where old-world legislation meets a completely new business landscape. For example, limited liability companies limit personal exposure should something go wrong. Will a DAO? There are already lawsuits against protocols or individual coders that are not protected by any form of limited liability because web3 is supposed to circumvent the need.[17] In another case, actor Seth Green created a TV series called *White Horse Tavern* – the main character being Bored Ape NFT #8398. Only that NFT, along with three others, were stolen in the Instagram BAYC phishing attack mentioned earlier. This left Green in a legal gray area. Although the owners of the NFTs have the rights to license and distribute them, the agreement did not extend to stolen NFTs. But if he clicked on the link, it would have probably been costly and very time-consuming to prove theft, leaving his TV show in limbo. Green eventually bought it back, which was effectively like paying a ransom.[18]

Change always creates resistance, but at the same time some change is inevitable. As a species we can only handle so much change at a time; when it goes too fast, we don't connect with it, or it creates hype and we jump in because of FOMO. S-curves and hype cycles demonstrate this behavior over and over again.

Some change emerges and then falls away. But the Supply-side Revolution of web3 has already begun to cross the chasm. The supply of capital has already successfully crossed. It is therefore inevitable that web3 is here to stay. The path to maturity will not be smooth, but it is assured.

Web1 started as a way to deliberately set information free and facilitate global communication in the event of a nuclear war. Ironically, it was a way to solve the Byzantine generals problem. Web1 promised decentralization but it didn't deliver. It was supposed to empower us all to create websites and share information, but most of us just viewed other people's. Web2 companies realized that and centralized it on top of its open protocols to create Big Tech.

We face the same challenge all over again with the various web3 protocols. Only this time we have centralization masquerading as decentralization. In January 2022, Moxie Marlinspike, creator of open-source encrypted messaging app Signal, made a very incisive point. He argued that people crave ease-of-use and convenience, as such centralized services always end up imposing themselves on top of decentralized technologies. In the same way that people didn't want to build their own websites in web1 and run their own servers, web3 is still cumbersome and difficult to access. As a result, almost all web3 apps currently in existence rely on one of two companies, Infura and Alchemy, to make current web3 capability usable. People also need to have a digital wallet, which means that, in reality, nearly every web3 product currently relies on a middleman to say what's happening on the blockchain. Even worse, Infura and MetaMask, one of the most popular crypto-wallets, are owned by the same company – ConsenSys.

Is this decentralization in name only?

Writer Gilad Edelman states, 'If cryptocurrency was originally about decentralizing money, web3 is about decentralizing ... everything. Its mission is almost achingly idealistic: to free humanity not only from Big Tech domination, but also from exploitative capitalism itself – and to do it purely through code.'[19] But if centralized services always end up imposing themselves on top of decentralized technologies, it's unclear where that leaves web3's mission. In response to Marlinspike's critique, Vitalik Buterin, the creator of Ethereum, agreed that the criticism was valid for the current web3 ecosystem, but that Marlinspike was 'missing where the blockchain ecosystem is going'. Buterin maintained that the decentralized web is catching up quickly. Work is being done to create libraries of code that will make it easier for other developers to start working on web3 projects. He added, 'I think the properly authenticated decentralized blockchain world is coming and is much closer to being here than many people think.'[20] I am much more inclined to agree with this approach and, as a product leader focusing on web3 and web4, this is how I intend to build ecosystems.

There is little doubt that blockchain makes the mission of decentralization fundamentally different from previous attempts. It looked like web2 might deliver the promise of decentralization because new platforms and technologies allowed ordinary users to create and upload content that could reach millions, but instead we became the product, and the data was hoovered up by big business in highly protected, centralized systems. Network effects, the power of big data and good old-fashioned corporate greed delivered the antithesis of decentralization. According to English computer scientist Gavin Wood, who helped program Ethereum, web2's downfall was trust. We needed to trust big platforms like Facebook and Google to do the right thing. We probably should have been alerted to the possibility for something to go wrong in that equation by Google's famous early motto, 'Don't be evil.' I say this at the same time as acknowledging that there are many good things Google has brought to market.

Instead of hoping that these platforms decide not to be evil, web3 is about building systems that don't rely on trusting people, corporations or governments to make moral choices. Just get the cryptography to make evil impossible. And blockchain is the technology that makes evil impossible. Instead of web2's 'don't be evil', web3 means we 'can't be evil'.

Recommendations

Remember the Professor Nicholson quote: 'You can take the person out of the Stone Age, but you can't take the Stone Age out of the person.'[21]

We can't not be human beings, so we need to be sensible. Whether a citizen or a business leader, we need to take steps to protect our keys and if something sounds too good to be true, it probably is. When it comes to web3, certainly for the next few years, be an open-minded healthy skeptic.

If you are a business leader, take what you have learned in this book and consider your web3 strategy. Do you have one? If you don't, get one. Find people in your business who are already interested in the area and recruit them to a web3 taskforce. Experiment professionally and personally. There is something pretty magical about doing your first transaction on the blockchain. Maybe start getting involved in building a crypto portfolio, learning about areas of interest.

If you are at the start of your career, or looking for where you can add more value, then focus on building skills in the 'supply side' that most impacts your passions and interests so you can live a meaningful life on your terms.

Summary of Key Points

» Throughout history we have often referred to monumental events in similar terms: the Great War (First World War), the Great Depression, the Great Resignation ... web3 has triggered the Great Unbundling and the end of business-as-usual.

» Web3 brings a completely new architecture that heralds a new era of the internet where the need for centralized trust is vastly diminished.

» Because of the proven theories in the book, you will now hopefully not only understand web3, but be able to predict the disruption of web4 and beyond.

» The biggest threat to web3 are the usual mistakes we make as a species.

» There is little doubt that the Supply-side Revolution of web3 has the potential to bring enormous productivity gains, improved efficiencies and opportunities to many of us. As a result, fear and greed emerge in abundance.

» The problem we face right now is that web3 is on a human-made knife edge where a combination of bad outcomes, facilitated largely by fear or greed, are throwing up the specter of really bad legislation that could stifle web3 for decades.

Epilogue

Web3 is not just blockchain. It's important to remember this because there are plenty of scenarios where a permanent record on a blockchain is overkill and decentralized storage would suffice. As web3 matures and gives way to web4, our understanding of the technology will allow

WEB3 IS NOT JUST BLOCKCHAIN.

us to be more sophisticated in our application of the right tech to the right scenarios, while keeping a close eye on environmental objectives for humanity and the planet.

My predictions are that we will see:

» An explosion in applications that make it seamless for people to come together and work on producing a good or service. It is going to be easier to join a DAO and become an owner and a producer than it is to apply for a job, go to university or raise money. It will feel like chatting on WhatsApp, Telegram or Slack, but instead you will be creating value, working and earning in real time.

» Genuine solutions to data sovereignty that will accelerate innovation considerably. A solution, which already exists in the Solid Project, could be part of the innovation plot twist of web4. With data sovereignty solved, there is no end to the human/AI combinations that could revolutionize our lives. It will be fascinating to see what teams come together to create AI as a service, leveraging datasets that they do not own or even entirely understand, while providing massive value back to the user and hopefully all of humanity.

» A renewed appreciation and application of mathematics and proven algorithms that will give us new products or services. Using smart contracts to apply advanced mathematical approaches to human problems will become an interesting area to watch.

» A renewed surge of meritocracy. Those that get ahead will be the ones who can compile their own web3 ecosystem and interconnect secure AI most effectively.

» A significant growth in teams that are 'remote native'. These teams will favor the introvert, long forgotten in an extrovert world. It will no longer matter if someone has the ability to communicate well in a standard job interview or VC pitch; their expertise and know-how will speak for itself, verified on the blockchain. We will see far less discrimination and hopefully more cooperation and inclusion in a less divided world.

» The hundred or so protocols that already exist will allow for a proliferation of web4 as well as aggregation and bridging systems to sit on top of those proven, secure protocols. If I'm right, we will see a shift in the capital and talent supply from building new blockchains and other non-blockchain protocols to building apps that work on those protocols, and we will help connect them all up in a distributed mesh, which we compose for our own unique purposes and desired outcomes. Central to that evolution and innovation will be data sovereignty.

I have drawn heavily from both the Innovator's Dilemma and Spiral Dynamics in this book, not only because they are my all-time-favorite theories, but because they allow us to appreciate patterns and generate a map around disruptive innovation and where it will take humanity. As such, they both help us to recognize where we are at any given time and predict the future based on repeating patterns around innovation and value systems.

Let's revisit Spiral Dynamics one more time (see Figure E.1):

As explained earlier, each value is assigned a color and has certain characteristics that influence behavior. At each level we value certain outcomes over everything else, and those outcomes and drivers influence what we pay attention to, how we think, feel and behave. Understanding values and how they

FIGURE E.1: SPIRAL DYNAMICS AND WEB3 ENGAGEMENT

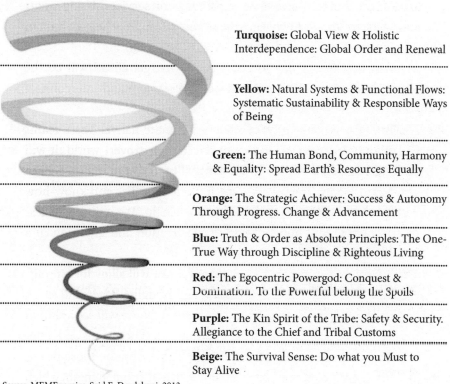

Turquoise: Global View & Holistic Interdependence: Global Order and Renewal

Yellow: Natural Systems & Functional Flows: Systematic Sustainability & Responsible Ways of Being

Green: The Human Bond, Community, Harmony & Equality: Spread Earth's Resources Equally

Orange: The Strategic Achiever: Success & Autonomy Through Progress. Change & Advancement

Blue: Truth & Order as Absolute Principles: The One-True Way through Discipline & Righteous Living

Red: The Egocentric Powergod: Conquest & Domination. To the Powerful belong the Spoils

Purple: The Kin Spirit of the Tribe: Safety & Security. Allegiance to the Chief and Tribal Customs

Beige: The Survival Sense: Do what you Must to Stay Alive

Source: MEMEnomisc, Said E. Dowlabani, 2013

differ can liberate us from division and allow us to position anything, including web3, in a way that makes sense to each value level. Web3 and web4 could revolutionize our world, but only if we understand them. That understanding is always influenced by our value system.

For those operating in the beige value system, web3 (or perhaps more specifically web4) will deliver new ways to make money and survive, at least financially. Considering the proliferation of smartphones, including in some of the world's poorest regions, this is good news. As mentioned in Chapter 5 there are already people in the Philippines, Argentina and Venezuela who are using 'play-to-earn' web3 capabilities to make or supplement their income. If this means that fewer people in the world are forced into horrendous environments in order to make a living, then surely this is good for humanity?

For those in the purple value system, web3 offers new forms of safety and security. For those in the red, web3 gives us new forms of control over our own data and what we do and engage with in our lives. There are also countless ways to gain more status and have fun, which is also important to those in the red value system. It might not be so good for the red authoritarian leaders around the world, but for their 'subjects' web3 is a game-changer. Those operating in the blue value system will be encouraged and relieved about the existence of algorithmic laws that will replace the need for trusted third parties, which have shown us time and again that they are not to be trusted. For the pragmatic, performance-focused orange value system, the opportunities to make money, often from multiple sources with web3 and beyond, are stratospheric. Web3 also offers significant efficiency improvements – all of which are important to the orange value system. There may be a few of the top 1 per cent who have hoovered up so much of the world's wealth who feel threatened by this advance, but economists have already proved that it is wage growth and equality that drives economic growth, not wage suppression and inequality. According to Richard Wolff, Professor Emeritus of Economics at the University of Massachusetts Amherst, 'The way [America] became a rich, powerful, capitalist country in the hundred years before the 1970s was by providing workers with rising wages.'[1] Even the IMF has confirmed that inequality is damaging for economic growth.[2] Considering we now live in a world where eight men have the same wealth as 50 per cent of the planet, rising inequality is a wicked problem we must solve.[3] Web3 offers a genuine solution. Instead of a raft of draconian legislation and tax hikes on the wealthy, which is almost inevitable without web3, web4 will provide everyone with access to real financial opportunities so they can personally and collectively benefit from their talent or participation in a more equitable manner.

For those in the green value system, currently the leading edge globally, web3 offers a way to collaborate that has been impossible up to now. There is a glimmer of true social democracy and the redistribution of wealth without the endless seeking of consensus. The blockchain and smart contracts will finally facilitate decentralized collaboration on a mass scale.

For those operating in the second tier or yellow and turquoise, innovation and systems are the drivers in yellow, and humanity and society are the drivers in turquoise. Web3 fits the bill for both.

Web3, and especially web4, will help everyone move up the spiral so that the new leading edge globally becomes yellow. This will be transformational for us as a species because yellow is the first value system where divisiveness starts to fall away. Instead of, 'I'm right, you're wrong,' we will have, 'You are partially right and so am I.' That creates room for dialogue, greater acceptance of difference and more inclusion. This is the world I want my children to grow up in. Web3 (and web4) will make that happen, and it is desperately needed to help heal a deeply divided world.

In essence, what we value does and should evolve as we mature as human beings and as a species. As we mature – 'we' being individuals, teams, businesses, cultures, governments and societies – our world view changes, and that change also alternates between individualistic and collective. Beige is all about individual survival; purple is collective safety; red is individual status, power and control; blue is collective rules and stability that benefits all; orange is individual success, and green is collective consensus, equality and social goals. Yellow, where we are heading, moves back into the individual focus but, because it's second tier, there is an expansive remit where innovation is viewed as a solution to society's many problems. Turquoise, which is collective again, looks at complex human systems. Remember what makes second tier so special is that when operating from those levels we recognize, often for the first time that every value system has merit. There is no 'I'm right'/You're wrong' binary position which opens us up to finding much better collective solutions.

> **THERE IS ALWAYS A PARING BACK OF ALL THAT IS MADE POSSIBLE AT EACH NEW VALUE SYSTEM.**

This endless two-step also follows a path of 'transcend and include'. Each move up the spiral allows the next wave of innovation to transcend what went before, include the good bits and innovate past the unhelpful or negative bits. There is always a paring back of all that is made possible at each new value system, so that only the useful and collectively beneficial survives. This is because there is always a dark side or dysfunction at every level that goes too far within that value system, creating new sets of problems that trigger the impetus for the emergence of something new and better. It isn't hard to see the evidence of the dark side of web1, web2 and web3. We are, I believe, already moving into the paring-back phase of web3 where only the strongest, smartest and safest protocols will survive.

I am an unapologetic web3 evangelist because web3 and web4 offer us the greatest collective opportunity to evolve as a species beyond the physical augmentation that has dominated our advance over the last few thousand years. Get this right, specifically data sovereignty and human/AI collaborations in the web3 stack, and there is no end to what we can achieve.

In 1974 Clare Graves, the creator of Spiral Dynamics, published an article entitled 'Human Nature Prepares for a Momentous Leap'.[4] The opening paragraph reads:

> *For many people the prospect of the future is dimmed by what they see as a moral breakdown of our society at both the public and private level. My research, over more than 20 years as a psychologist interested in human values, indicates that something is indeed happening to human values, but it is not so much a collapse in the fiber of man as a sign of human health and intelligence. My research indicates that man is learning that values and ways of living which were good for him at one period in his development are no longer good because of the changed condition of his existence. He is recognizing that the old values are no longer appropriate, but he has not yet understood the new.*

Standing on the shoulders of a theoretical giant, I repeat this sentiment – one that is as apt today as it was when he wrote it.

My own research and involvement in web-based innovations over the last 20 years also indicates that something is happening to humanity. The ways of living that were good for us in the past are no longer good because of the changed condition of our existence. We are recognizing that the old business models and ways of living are no longer appropriate, but too many have not yet understood the new.

Today, the momentous leap that human nature is preparing for is web3 (and web4).

ABOUT THE PUBLISHING

Despite being offered various deals over the years from traditional publishers, I decided instead to demonstrate the new technology I'm covering in the book and how this new Supply-side Revolution will work. As such, my intention is to publish this book by selling all the rights to a decentralized autonomous organization (DAO) that then issues a non-fungible token (NFT). It would be a little odd to wax lyrical about the game-changing nature of web3 while plugging into the traditional publishing industry. Publishing itself has gone through some pretty major supply-side shifts already. Certainly from the authors' perspective, publishing has been democratized through the unbundling of the industry. Instead of having to find a traditional publisher, who would manage all the various inputs and processes to create the physical and digital book as well as distribution, all those inputs and processes or component parts of publishing have become available as standalone individual offerings. This gives the author far more choice and control over the finished book. Web3 offers some really exciting *new* opportunities for authors. I have therefore tried to combine the best of both worlds. That said, at the time of writing, I'm still unsure how it will all work in practice.

So far, the journey to publish this book as a DAO was not as easy as I first imagined, as I explained in the book; we are still very much in the protocol era. Protocol development has been crucial to the advance of each era of the internet, but it is only once the apps have been developed on top of the protocols that those protocols are made easy to use. As such, figuring out how to use a DAO reminded me of trying to build a website back in the mid-Nineties, needing to learn HTML code and tinkering for hours to try to make it look good, always knowing at the same time that something big was happening!

The other complexity arose from the need to physically publish a book. Right now, web3 is very much geared towards the, on-chain, digital world, but I wrote this book not to preach to the already converted – the crypto and web3 natives; I wrote it for business leaders and individuals who need to understand what it is and how it's going to disrupt business-as-usual. It was therefore imperative that it was available as a traditional printed book available to buy on Amazon and beyond. After all, 70 per cent of books bought on Amazon are still physical objects. There is still something special about holding a book in our hands and reading from a page, not a screen. If I had pursued a pure on-chain web3 route, I would be publishing this book on a decentralized storage platform such as IPFS and you would be buying the book with crypto.

Instead, I have chosen to work with the experienced publishing talent at Whitefox, to get the best editing, typesetting, book cover design, indexing and distribution, while being able to maintain 100 per cent of the ownership rights. This ownership of copyright, which I would not have had with a traditional publisher, allowed me to then sell the rights to a DAO.

Right now, there is not an easy bridge between old-school publishing and web3 in some type of on-chain and off-chain hybrid, but it is just a matter of time. In the meantime, as the book will be sold on Amazon and by other leading booksellers, while it's going to be owned by a DAO and ultimately the NFT holders who choose to buy copies and collectables and own fractional rights to the book, the royalties will continue to be paid in dollars and will then need to be converted back to crypto and paid out to the token holders.

This is purely an experiment, with NFT buyers being part of this pioneering project and having the chance to own something unique. Only time will tell how successful this experiment will be…

ACKNOWLEDGEMENTS

I haven't been this excited about technology and its potential impact on business and society since first discovering the internet back in the mid-Nineties. After spending the last decade learning and playing with various crypto and web3 projects in my spare time, I wanted to make my own contribution to the community by writing a book targeted at educating the next one billion users. The research in this book is not targeted at the crypto natives, but instead the crypto curious. I would not have been able to write this book without the incredible contributions made across this ecosystem that continues to amaze me every day. My curiosity was first piqued in 2010 when a friend, Ludwik, told me to check out Bitcoin (I wish I had bought some then!). For some reason the abstract concept made instant sense, but at the time it was very hard to get involved – there was virtually no ecosystem; it was designed for engineers. From that point I went from being intrigued to being a massive crypto skeptic to then finally falling down the crypto rabbit hole. I have enjoyed countless hours discussing the pros and cons of crypto and web3 with friends and colleagues such as Jamie, Ernest, Will and Nick ever since. Over the years I have typically spent a couple of hours every day in the evenings or on weekends reading about web3 and how it could potentially change the world.

I've combined that acquired knowledge with my love of product and business strategy, learning from and applying some of the greats such as *Good to Great* by Jim Collins, *Seven Powers* by Hamilton Helmer, everything by Clayton M. Christensen, *The Inevitable* by Kevin Kelly, *Sapiens* by Yuval Noah Harari, as well as Benedict Evans's essays and thought leadership on all things tech. I'd also like to thank Alan Watkins for helping me to live and breathe so many advanced frameworks, in particular Spiral Dynamics, and Paul Wiefels for the countless fascinating discussions on Crossing the Chasm and business strategy.

It's also worth noting that in the world of web3 the very best cutting-edge thinking is often found in real-time Twitter threads. So much of my learning has been advanced through Twitter, especially by @CL207, @Melt_Dem, @nsquaredmacro, @lightcrypto, @cburniske, @Crypto_McKenna, @Cooopahtroopa, @RaoulGMI, @adamscochran, @CroissantEth,

@PastryEth, @TuurDemeester, @punk6529, @lopp, @SBF_FTX, @dpuellARK, @MustStopMurad, @CryptoHayes, @cdixon, @VitalikButerin, @twobitidiot.

Thanks also go to the knowledgeable and engaged participants of the Telegram and Discord groups that I'm part of. These communities are an incredible source of learning, knowledge sharing and lively debate. I also want to thank the team at Messari for the incredibly high-quality analyst research they produce. Thanks also to my collaborator, the incredible Karen McCreadie, who has helped me order my thinking, research where necessary and ensure that what I wanted to say has been said. Thank you to the team at Whitefox Publishing who have been able to put this together and to Paddy Herridge for the marketing strategy.

Thank you, James, Baz, Paul, Duncan, Caroline, Damian, Paddy, Adam and Erik for taking the time to review the manuscript and provide feedback – it was improved by your input. Thank you also to the many friends and family who have given me feedback on the project, title and cover.

And finally, I'm grateful for the feedback and patience of my wonderful wife, Carro, and to my three children. I did try to get the kids to read the manuscript as well, but as they are all under eight years old it was a big ask. My eldest did, however, say the introduction was very interesting!

References

Preface

1   Pastry (2022) 'LUNA: The Ticking Time Bomb', DiFi News May 12 Available at: https://pastry.xyz/supaposts/luna-the-ticking-time-bomb/ (Accessed: 12 August 2022).

2   *The Economist* (2022) 'The cryptocurrency sell-off has exposed those swimming naked', May 18.

3   Galloway, S., (2022) 'Trustless', No Mercy/No Malice July 17 Available at: https://www.profgalloway.com/trustless/ (Accessed 12 August 2022).

4   Stackpole, T., (2022) 'What Is Web3?' *Harvard Business Review* May 10.

Introduction

1   Wendover Productions (2015) 'Containerization: The Most Influential Invention That You've Never Heard Of', YouTube December 15.

2   Allison, I., (2018) 'Decentralization experts unpack the problems of "Web 3.0"', *International Business Times* February 2.

3   Viguerie, S. P., Calder, N. and Hindo, B., (2021) '2021 Corporate Longevity Forecast' Innosight May.

4   Brown, R., (2019) '5 of the World's Oldest Companies', Investopedia Jun 25.

5   Thurston, S., (2015) 'The Typical Lifespan of a Business, According to Science', Business News Business Administration Information April 8.

6   Mochari, I., (2016) 'Why Half of the S&P 500 Companies Will Be Replaced in the Next Decade', *Inc.* March 23.

7   Morgan, J., (2017) 'The War for Talent: It's Real and Here's Why It's Happening', *Inc.* December 22.

8   Kaplan, D. et al., (2019) 'Where Have All the Long-Tenured CEOs Gone?' Korn Ferry.

Chapter I

1   Christensen, C., (1997) *The Innovator's Dilemma: When New Technologies Cause Great Firms to Fail* Boston: Harvard Business Review Press.

2   Harrison, C., (2018) 'The HCI Innovator's Dilemma', IX Interactions December.

3   Christensen, C., (1997) *The Innovator's Dilemma: When New Technologies Cause Great Firms to Fail* Boston: Harvard Business Review Press.

4   Podushak, N., (2021) 'CompuServe – First Consumer Service', This Day in Tech History.

5   Gunther McGrath, R., (2015) '15 years later, lessons from the failed AOL-Time Warner merger', *Fortune*.

6   Michel, A. and Holpuch, A., (2012) 'Why did Facebook buy Instagram for a whopping $1bn?' *Guardian* April 9.

7   Vincent, J., (2014) 'So why did Facebook pay a staggering $19bn for WhatsApp?' *Independent* February 10.

8   Franklin, J. and Moise, I., (2022) 'JPMorgan plots "astonishing" $12bn tech spend to beat fintechs', *Financial Times* January 15.

9   Shevlin, R., (2022) 'JPMorgan Opens a Bank Branch in The Metaverse (But It's Not What You Think It's For)', *Forbes* February 16.

10 Rogers, E. M., (1962) *Diffusion of Innovation* New York: Simon & Schuster.

11 Walmart History, Corporate Walmart website: https://corporate.walmart.com/about/history; accessed 12 August 2022.

12 Vamos, J., (2022) *Four Voices: Managing love, loyalty, family wealth and succession through the generations* Sydney: PublishingCentral.

13 Roser, M., Ritchie, H. and Ortiz-Ospina, E., 'Internet', Our World in Data (2019). https://ourworldindata.org/internet; accessed 12 August 2022.

14 *The Week*, (2022) 'Most valuable companies in the world', *The Week* April 1.

Chapter 2

1   Naughton, J., 'For the first time in its history, Facebook is in decline. Has the tech giant begun to crumble?' *Guardian* (2022).

2   First Round Review (no date) 'From 0 to $1B – Slack's Founder Shares Their Epic Launch Strategy', First Round Review.

3   Wallace, T., (2017) 'How Amazon and Independent Ecommerce Brands Grew Online Sales 18,233% in 20 Years', BigCommerce.

4   Lucas, P., Ballay, J. and McManus, M., (2012) *Trillions: Thriving in the emerging information ecology* New Jersey: John Wiley & Sons.

5   Cagan, M., (2018) *Inspired: How to Create Tech Products Customers Love* New York: John Wiley & Sons.

6   Naughton, J., (2022) 'For the first time in its history, Facebook is in decline. Has the tech giant begun to crumble?' *Guardian* February 6.

7   Smith A (2022), Facebook's attempt at a global cryptocurrency finally been shut down', *The Independent* February 01.

Chapter 3

1 Stackpole, T., (2022) 'What is Web3?' *Harvard Business Review* May 10.

2 Davidson, J. D., and Rees-Mogg, W. (1997) *The Sovereign Individual: Mastering the Transition to the Information Age* London: Simon & Schuster.

3 Pearson, T. (2017) 'The Blockchain Man', Ribbonfarm October 10.

4 Pearson, T. (2017) 'The Blockchain Man', Ribbonfarm October 10.

5 Martin, R. L. (2011) *Fixing the Game* Boston: Harvard Business Review Press

6 Lopp, J., @lopp (2019) Twitter post September 20 Available at: https://twitter.com/lopp/status/1175113754406805510?s=20&t=Fc4gHBzjn2GGKGBZp5mSvQ, accessed 12 August 2022.

7 David, J., (2011) 'The Crypto-Currency: Bitcoin and its mysterious inventor', *New Yorker* October 3.

8 Pearson, T. (2017) 'The Blockchain Man', Ribbonfarm October 10.

9 Szabo, N., (2017) 'Money, blockchains, and social scalability', Unenumerated Blogspot February 09.

10 Simply Explained (2017) 'How does blockchain work', YouTube November 11 Available at https://www.youtube.com/watch?v=SSo_EIwHSd4; accessed 12 August 2022.

11 Duffin, E., (2022) Number of registered active lobbyists in the United States from 2000 to 2021, Statista June 21.

12 Mayer, J., (2016) *Dark Money: How a secretive group of billionaires is trying to buy political control in the US* London: Scribe Publications.

13 Sparks, H., (2021) 'Infamous Bitcoin pizza guy who squandered $365M haul has no regrets', *New York Post* May 24.

14 Koetsier, J., (2017) 'ICO Bubble? Startups Are Raising Hundreds of Millions of Dollars Via Initial Coin Offerings', Inc., July 14.

15 Qureshi, H., (2019) 'The ICO Bubble Explained in Three Moments', HackerNoon March 4.

16 Guillaume, D., (2022) '2021 was huge for Bitcoin as countries and companies worldwide embraced it', Bitcoin Magazine January 4.

17 Hall, J., (2022) 'Bitcoin, Bukele and a bevy of central bankers meet in El Salvador', Coin Telegraph May 17.

18 Stackpole, T., (2022) 'What is Web3?' *Harvard Business Review* May 10.

19 Simply Explained (2017) 'Smart Contracts', YouTube November 20 Available at: https://www.youtube.com/watch?v=ZE2HxTmxfrI; accessed 12 August 2022.

20 Zuboff, S., (2019) *The Age of Surveillance Capitalism: The Fight for a Human Future at the New Frontier of Power* London: Profile Books.

21 Morgan, K., (2021) 'The Great Resignation: How employers drove workers to quit', BBC Worklife July 1.

22 Deluard, V. @VincentDeluard (2022) Twitter August 5 Available at: https://twitter.com/vincentdeluardstatus/1555591557893435392?s=21&t=iFN0qUNMqp5yXbEJ_gy1og ; accessed 12 August 2022.

Chapter 4

1   Moore, B. D., (2022) 'Stock Market Facts & Statistics: 102 Jaw Dropping Stats 2022', *Liberated Stock Trader* August 12.

2   Conway, E., (2022) 'Ukraine war: As its military continues its relentless invasion – Russia is fighting an invisible parallel conflict', Sky News March 25.

3   Maples, M., (2018) 'Crypto Commons', *Medium* June 28.

4   Maples, M., (2018) 'Crypto Commons', *Medium* June 28.

5   Naughton, J., (2022) 'For the first time in its history, Facebook is in decline. Has the tech giant begun to crumble?' *Guardian* February 6.

6   Attenborough, D., (1979), *Life on Earth*, Episode 13, BBC/Warner Bros.

Chapter 5

1   Thackray, L., (2022) 'First "virtual hotel" opens in the Metaverse', *Independent* May 6.

2   Works, F., (2022) 'The great unbundling: What every business leader needs to know about Web3', *Fast Company* March 24.

3   Stackpole, T., (2022) 'What is Web3?' *Harvard Business Review* May 10.

4   Dailey, N., (2022) 'NFTs ballooned to a $41 billion market in 2021 and are catching up to the total size of the global fine art market', *Markets Insider* January 6.

5   Di Liscia, V., (2021) '"First Ever NFT" Sells for $1.4 Million', *Hyperallergic* June 10.

6   Shawdagor, J., (2022) 'Bored Ape Yacht Club (BAYC) NFT fetches $2.85M in ETH', *Bankless Times* February 1.

7   Ifeanyi, I., (2022) 'The Bored Ape Yacht Club apes into Hollywood', *Fast Company* January 18.

8   Ifeanyi, I., (2022) 'The Bored Ape Yacht Club apes into Hollywood', *Fast Company* January 18.

9   Redman, J., (2021) 'Mila Kunis' "Stoner Cats" NFT Sale Pulls in $8M – Animated Series Can Only Be Watched by NFT Holders', *Bitcoin.com News* July 29.

10 Msoh, S., (2022) 'Top talent is leaving Facebook, Amazon, Google for Web3 and crypto', Crypto-news-flash.com February 23.

Chapter 6

1   Kusimba, C., (2017) 'When – and why – did people first start using money?' *The Conversation* June 20.

2   Duffin, E., (2022) 'Number of registered active lobbyists in the United States from 2000 to 2021', *Statista* June 21.

3   Brettell, K., (2022) 'Analysis: As sanctions "weaponize" U.S. dollar, some Treasury buyers could fall back', *Reuters* March 29.

4   Merrouche, O. and Nier, E., (2010) 'What Caused the Global Financial Crisis? – Evidence on the Drivers of Financial Imbalances 1999–2007', IMF Working Paper November 1.

5   Financial Crisis Enquiry Commission (2011) The Financial Crisis Inquiry Report, US Government, May 1.

6   Neate, R., (2022) "'We've had a run-on champagne:" Biggest UK banker bonuses since financial crash', *Guardian* February 16.

7   Jones, E. T. and Altunbas, Y., (2022) 'Stock markets have been a one-way bet for many years thanks to the "Fed put" – but those days are over', *The Conversation* February 21.

8   Frank, R. H. and Bernanke, B. S., (2007) *Principles of Macroeconomics* (3rd Ed) Boston, McGraw-Hill.

9   Wikipedia List of Stock Market Crashes: https://en.wikipedia.org/wiki/List_of_stock_market_crashes_and_bear_markets; accessed 12 August 2022.

10   Minsky Moment, Wikipedia: https://en.wikipedia.org/wiki/Minsky_moment; accessed 12 August 2022.

11   Flynn, K., (2018) 'Did Kylie Jenner really screw over Snapchat?' *Mashable* February 22.

12   Samson, A., (2021) 'Tether and Bitfinex agree to pay $18.5m penalty after New York probe', *Financial Times* February 23.

13   Staff Writer, (2022) 'Explained: Algorithmic stablecoins and how they are different from other stablecoins?' CNBCTV18.com May 17.

14   ConstitutionDAO: https://juicebox.money/#/p/constitutiondao; accessed 12 August 2022.

15   Brown, A., (2021) 'What Is A DAO – And Why Is One Trying to Buy the U.S. Constitution?' *Forbes* November 16.

Chapter 7

1   Freeman, J. B., (2018) *Behemoth: A History of the Factory and the Making of the Modern World* New York: W. W. Norton & Company.

2   Smith, A., (1776) *The Wealth of Nations*.

3   Marshall, A., *Economics of Industry* (1892) and *Principles of Economics* (1890).

4   Freeman, J. B., (2018) *Behemoth: A History of the Factory and the Making of the Modern World* New York: W. W. Norton & Company.

5   Ibid.

6   Watkins, A. and Dalton, N., (2020) *The HR (R)Evolution: Change the Workplace, Change the World* Oxon: Routledge.

7   Tolman, W. H., (1901) 'A "Trust" For Social Betterment', *The World's Work* New York: Doubleday.

8   Gallup, (2021) State of the Global Workplace Report.

9   Freeman, J. B., (2018) *Behemoth: A History of the Factory and the Making of the Modern World* New York: W. W. Norton & Company.

10   Rifkin, J., (2014) *The Zero Marginal Cost Society: The Internet of Things, the Collaborative Commons, and the Eclipse of Capitalism* London: Palgrave Macmillan.

11 Rifkin, J., (2014) *The Zero Marginal Cost Society: The Internet of Things, the Collaborative Commons, and the Eclipse of Capitalism* London: Palgrave Macmillan.

12 Taylor Gatto, J., (2006) *The Underground History of American Education* Oxford: Oxford Village Press.

13 Taylor Gatto, (2009) J., *Weapons of Mass Instruction* Gabriola Island: New Society Publishers.

14 Kohn, A., (1993) *Punished by Rewards: The Trouble with Gold Stars, Incentive Plans, A's, Praise and Other Bribes* New York: Houghton Mifflin Company.

15 Buckingham, M., (2022) 'Annual Reviews Are a Terrible Way to Evaluate Employees', *Wall Street Journal* April 30.

16 Bienasz, G., (2022) 'Google's Year in Search Shows Spiking Interest in Entrepreneurship', *Inc.* December 10.

17 Stelzer, I., (2022) 'The US labour market is not fit for purpose', *The Times* May 1.

18 ConstitutionDAO: https://juicebox.money/#/p/constitutiondao; accessed 12 August 2022.

19 Brown, A., (2021) 'What Is A DAO – And Why Is One Trying to Buy the U.S. Constitution?' *Forbes* November 16.

20 Nelson, D., (2020) 'Bitcoin CEO: MicroStrategy's Michael Saylor Explains His $425M Bet on BTC', CoinDesk September 15.

21 Gallup, (2021) State of the Global Workplace Report.

22 Fletcher, N., (2013) 'Horse meat scandal wipes £300m off Tesco's market value', *Guardian* January 16.

23 KPMG 2017 Supply Chain Fraud Report.

24 Nuffield College, (2019) 'New CSI Report on Ethnic Minority Job Discrimination', University of Oxford News.

Chapter 8

1 Harmon, J. and Zim, E., (2021) 'The rise and fall of the American mall', *Insider* April 13.

2 'The Edge of Humanity', (2020) Conversation between Sam Harris and Yuval Noah Harari, *Making Sense* podcast #138.

3 Cadwalladr, C., (2017) 'The great British Brexit robbery: how our democracy was hijacked', *Guardian* May 7.

4 Hahn, J., (2021) 'Nike gets "metaverse-ready" with acquisition of virtual sneaker company RTFKT', *Dezeen* December 12.

5 Lim, J., (2022) 'Nike and RTFKT unveil virtual trainers NFT', theindustry. fashion April 25.

6 Stackpole, T., (2022) 'What is Web3?' *Harvard Business Review* May 10.

7 Cox, D., (2022) 'L'Oréal Prioritizes NFTs and the Metaverse', *CryptoNewsZ* March 1.

Chapter 9

1   Internet growth statistics, Internet World Stats: https://www.internetworldstats.com/emarketing.htm; accessed 12 August 2022.

Chapter 10

1   Levy, B., (2022) Global M&A Industry Trends: 2022 Outlook, PwC.

2   Van de Pol, M., (2020) Mergers & Acquisitions Report, PwC Corporate Governance.

3   Teare, G., (2021) 'Global Venture Funding Hits All-Time High in First Half of 2021, with $288B Invested', *Crunchbase News* July 7.

4   Naughton, J., (2022) 'For the first time in its history, Facebook is in decline. Has the tech giant begun to crumble?' *Guardian* February 6.

5   Smith, A., (2022) 'BeReal: What is the new app selling itself as the anti-social media platform?' *Independent* April 11.

6   Hern, A., (2022) 'Yuga Labs apologizes after sale of virtual land overwhelms Ethereum', *Guardian* May 2.

7   Seufert, E. B., (2018) 'Is it healthy for start-ups to spend so much money on user acquisition?' Mobile Dev Memo November 26.

8   Edelman, G., (2022) 'Paradise at the Crypto Arcade: Inside the Web3 Revolution', *Wired* May 10.

9   Hussey, M., (2019) 'What Is Tokenomics?' *Decrypt* January 16.

Chapter 11

1   Roser, M., (2020) 'It's not just about child mortality, life expectancy improved at all ages', Our World in Data September 23.

2   Nagdy, M., (2019) 'Intelligence', Our World in Data.

3   Nicholson, N., (1998) 'How Hardwired Is Human Behavior?' *Harvard Business Review* July-August.

4   Sorokin, S., (2019) 'Thriving in a World of "Knowledge Half-Life"', CIO April 5.

5   IBM (2006) 'The Toxic Terabyte: How data dumping threatens business efficiency', IBM Global Technology Services July.

6   Gibson, J., (2016) 'How long would it take to browse the entire internet?' Quora.

7   Sample, I., (2020) 'Internet "is not working for women and girls", says Berners-Lee', *Guardian* March 12.

8   Mill, J. S., (1848) *Principles of Political Economy* London: John W Parker.

9   Watkins, A. and Dalton, N., (2020) *The HR (R)Evolution: Change the Workplace, Change the World* Oxon: Routledge.

10   Pink, D., (2009) *Drive: The surprising truth about what motivates us* New York: Penguin.

Chapter 12

1 The Lawyer & Jurists (no date) History of the Rule of Law: lawyersnjurists.com.

2 History of Contract Law, Wikipedia: https://en.wikipedia.org/wiki/History_of_contract_law; accessed 12 August 2022.

3 Social Contract, Wikipedia: https://en.wikipedia.org/wiki/Social_contract; accessed 12 August 2022.

4 Henley, J., (2018) 'Money for nothing: is Finland's universal basic income trial too good to be true?' *Guardian* January 12.

5 Charlton, E., (2019) 'The results of Finland's basic income experiment are in. Is it working?' World Economic Forum February 12.

6 Reynolds, M., (2018) 'No, Finland isn't scrapping its universal basic income experiment', *Wired* April 26.

7 McFarland, K., (2017) 'Overview of Current Basic Income Related Experiments', Basicincome.com October 19.

8 Wignaraja, K. and Horvath, B., (2020) 'Universal basic income is the answer to the inequalities exposed by COVID-19', World Economic Forum April 16.

9 UK Parliament Committees, (2021) '"Unimaginable" cost of Test & Trace failed to deliver central promise of averting another lockdown', UK Government Website.

10 Crypto Cities Blogpost (2021), vitalik.ca October 31.

11 Weiss, K., (2021) 'Gitcoin Grants – Quadratic Funding for the World', gitcoin.co.

12 Baraniuk, C., (2019) 'Bitcoin's energy consumption "equals that of Switzerland"', BBC News July 3.

13 Cambridge Bitcoin Electricity Consumption Index: https://www.cbeci.org/; accessed 12 August 2022.

14 Smith, C., (2022) 'Mining BTC uses more than 50% of renewable energy', Know-Techie January 26.

15 Redman, J., (2021) 'How Henry Ford Envisaged Bitcoin 100 Years Ago – A Unique "Energy Currency" That Could Stop Wars', *Bitcoin.com News* October 11.

16 Belizaire, J., (2021) 'Bitcoin Is a Better Battery', *Medium* March 5.

17 Wirfs-Brock, J., (2015) 'Lost in Transmission: How Much Electricity Disappears Between a Power Plant and Your Plug?' insideenergy.org November 6.

18 Stackpole, T., (2022) 'What is Web3?' *Harvard Business Review* May 10.

19 Compert, C., Luinetti, M. and Portie, B., (2018) 'Blockchain and GDPR: How blockchain could address five areas associated with GDPR compliance', IBM White Paper.

20 Cambridge Bitcoin Electricity Consumption Index, Comparisons: https://ccaf.io/cbeci/index/comparisons; accessed 12 August 2022.

21 Mersch, M. and Muirhead, R., (2019) 'What Is Web 3.0 & Why It Matters', Medium November 2.

22 ConstitutionDAO: https://juicebox.money/#/p/constitutiondao; accessed 12 August 2022.

Conclusion

1   Mersch, M. and Muirhead, R., (2019) 'What Is Web 3.0 & Why It Matters', *Medium* November 2.

2   Stevens, R., (2022) On Impossible Things Before Breakfast: A post-mortem on Terra, a pre-mortem on DeFi, and a glimpse of the madness to come, NYDIG June.

3   Nicolas, (2021) 'The story of Bitconnect, world's biggest crypto scam yet', *Cointribune.com* August 27.

4   Murphy, J., (2019) 'Quadriga: The cryptocurrency exchange that lost $135m', BBC News February 17.

5   Tangermann, V., (2019) 'Did a Crypto CEO Fake His Own Death to Abscond With $190 Million?' *Futurism* May 2.

6   The Capitalist, (2021) 'Archegos Hedge Fund Implodes as Big Banks Take Cover', *CEO Journal* March 30.

7   Cryptopedia Staff (2022) 'What Was The DAO?' Cryptopedia March 16.

8   Khatri, A., (2022) 'Hacked BAYC Instagram Account Scams Users Out of Millions', *cryptodaily.co.uk* April 26.

9   Edelman, G., (2022) 'Paradise at the Crypto Arcade: Inside the Web3 Revolution', *Wired* May 10.

10   Red flag traffic laws, Wikipedia: https://en.wikipedia.org/wiki/Red_flag_traffic_laws; accessed 12 August 2022.

11   Tait, A., (2021) 'Five clueless questions United States senators asked Mark Zuckerberg', *New Statesman* April 11.

12   Sinclair, S., (2021) 'Blockchain Caucus Co-Chair Says Crypto "Backdoor" Is Key to Unmasking Bad Actors: Report', *CoinDesk* June 30.

13   Stackpole, T., (2022) 'What is Web3?' *Harvard Business Review* May 10.

14   NowThis Politics (2019) 'Jennifer Lawrence is "Unbreaking America's Political System Failures"'.

15   Zuboff, S., (2019) *The Age of Surveillance Capitalism: The Fight for a Human Future at the New Frontier of Power* London: Profile Books.

16   Hensen, P., (2021) 'Europe's Third Way is Web3: Why the EU Should Embrace Crypto', law.standford.edu.

17   Tokar, D., (2022) 'Crypto-Savings Lawsuit Puts Principles of DeFi to the Test', *Wall Street Journal* January 13.

18   Hogg, R., (2022) 'Seth Green pays $260,000 ransom for a stolen Bored Ape Ethereum NFT meant to feature in his new TV show: report', *Business Insider* June 11.

19   Edelman, G., 'Paradise at the Crypto Arcade: Inside the Web3 Revolution', *Wired* (2022).

20   Stackpole, T., (2022) 'What is Web3?' *Harvard Business Review* May 10.

21   Nicholson, N., (1998) 'How Hardwired Is Human Behavior?' *Harvard Business Review* July-August

Epilogue

1 Wolf, R (2012) 'KPFA: Richard Wolff – Capitalism Hits the Fan', YouTube.
2 Inman, P., (2014) 'IMF study finds inequality is damaging to economic growth', *Guardian* February 26.
3 Elliot, L., (2017) 'World's eight richest people have same wealth as poorest 50%', *Guardian* January 16.
4 Graves, C. W., (1974) 'Human Nature Prepares for a Momentous Leap', *The Futurist*.

Glossary

Airdrop: Not the same as an AirDrop on your iPhone, this is a free distribution of tokens or coins from an entity directly to the user's or member's crypto-wallet based on their pro rata ownership.

Altcoins (alts): A combination of the word 'alternative' and 'coin', altcoins or alts were initially used to describe any cryptocurrency that wasn't Bitcoin but are now cryptocurrencies that are relatively new to the market and have relatively low valuations.

Application programming interface (API): An interface between computers or programs that allows information or instruction to pass between them.

Avatar: A chosen digital rendering to represent a person/user in a video game, on the internet or any other virtual space such as the metaverse.

Bitcoin: The first cryptocurrency. Widely considered the most established, most secure and most valuable.

Bitcoin mining: The process of creating new Bitcoin by solving an increasingly difficult computational puzzle.

Blockchain: A distributed digital ledger that's used to record information and transactions on an immutable database, which means that information can't be tampered with or altered once it's been recorded.

Block: Blockchains are made up of blocks or individual units in which data is stored. Each block, depending on the protocol it's built on, can hold different amounts of information and is verified in different ways. These blocks are linked or chained together for added security – hence the term blockchain.

Centralized exchange: Cryptocurrency exchange where organizations coordinate trading on a large scale, similar to a stock market.

Centralized system: A hierarchical system where the power and decision-making authority is concentrated in the hands of a relatively small number of individuals at the top.

Coin: A cryptocurrency built on its own native blockchain to be used as a store of value and medium of exchange within that ecosystem.

Consensus mechanism: The systems used by cryptocurrencies to validate the authenticity and security of transactions on the blockchain. Proof-of-work or proof-of-stake are different examples of a consensus mechanism.

Cryptocurrency: A digital currency designed for transaction through a computer network that is not reliant on any central authority such as the government or a central bank.

Cryptography: Secure communication techniques that ensure only the sender and intended recipient of a message are able to view its contents.

Crypto-wallet: Mobile application that allows users to store and retrieve their digital assets.

Dapp: A decentralized application built on a decentralized blockchain network using smart contracts and web3.

Data: In a web3 context data refers to a user's personal information, such as personal details and transaction details. One of the pillars of web3 is to protect that data and return ownership and sovereignty over that data to the user.

DeFi: An abbreviation of 'decentralized finance' to indicate an open financial system that doesn't rely on centralized authorities or intermediaries like banks to conduct financial activities.

Decentralized exchange: A crypto exchange that allows direct peer-to-peer exchanges to take place online.

Decentralized autonomous organization (DAO): Member-owned communities without centralized leadership that allow people to come together in new ways to create products and services or solve problems.

Digital twin: A virtual rendering of a physical object that is designed to be as dynamic and environment-dependent as the objects they're imitating.

Whether a bridge or a human being, the digital twin is a simulation that can provide valuable information to help the real bridge become stronger or the real human being to be more productive and avoid monotonous tasks.

Discord: Community-based communications and instant-messaging platform used by gamers and crypto enthusiasts.

Distributed networks: A computer system where programming, software and data are spread out across more than one computer.

Encryption: A process by which a plain text document is combined with a shorter string of data, called a key, to produce ciphertext.

Ethereum: An open-source decentralized blockchain network that builds on the capability of blockchain while offering more flexibility than the Bitcoin protocol. Ethereum uses smart contracts, and ETH, Ethereum's currency, is the second most valuable cryptocurrency in the world, after Bitcoin.

ERC-20: An Ethereum token standard, providing a standardized smart contract structure for fungible tokens.

ERC-721: An Ethereum token standard that allows for the creation of unique tokens or NFTs. Unlike ERC-20, ERC-721 tokens have specific properties that allow each to be uniquely identified and valued independently of each other.

Fiat: A currency established as legal tender, often backed and regulated by a government, such as the US dollar.

Fork: A change to the blockchain protocol where two blocks are generated but point to the same block as the parent block. When the changes are minor it's known as a soft fork. When the changes are more fundamental, they result in a hard fork, leading to the formation of a separate chain with different rules.

Full node: A blockchain node which stores the blockchain's complete history, as well as verifies and relays transactions.

Fungible: An economic term that refers to a commodity that is precisely equal in value and therefore exchangeable with other identical versions of that same commodity. A $1 bill, for example, is fungible, because it can be exchanged for any other $1 bill – they have the same value and therefore, to all intents and purposes, are identical.

Gas: In a web3 context gas is a fee paid by the user to conduct a transaction or execute a smart contract on the Ethereum blockchain.

Genesis block: The first block of a blockchain network.

Hash: A process by which a piece of data is processed into a small piece of data (usually 32 bytes). This smaller piece of data looks completely random, and you cannot recover any meaningful information about the original data from it. However, it has the important property that the result of hashing one particular document is always the same. Additionally, it is crucially important that it is computationally infeasible to find two documents that have the same hash.

Hash rate (aka hash power): The rate at which a computer can generate guesses to a cryptographic puzzle. Hash rate can also refer to the overall power being used by the entire network on a proof-of-work blockchain.

Initial coin offering (ICO): The selling of tokens to the public to raise capital for a crypto-based project similar to an initial public offering (IPO).

Layer 1 (L-1): This is the blockchain platform itself, also referred to as the base layer, mainchain or mainnet. Bitcoin, Ethereum and Fantom are all L-1.

Layer 2 (L-2): These are the solutions that are built on L-1 blockchains. L-2s typically improve transaction speed, scalability, privacy and cost efficiency.

MetaMask: Software built for the Ethereum blockchain that functions as a crypto-wallet.

Metaverse: A virtual networked online landscape that people inhabit, as avatars, for synchronous interactions and experiences, accessing the shared virtual space through virtual reality, augmented reality, game consoles, mobile devices or conventional computers.

Minting: The term used to describe the process of registering a digital asset on the blockchain, thereby turning it into a purchasable non-fungible token (NFT). Once a NFT has been minted, it cannot be altered.

Non-fungible token (NFT): A digital asset based on Ethereum's ERC-721 token standard that can be used to represent ownership of a variety of digital assets including art, photography, music and more.

Node: Any device connected to a blockchain network. Different nodes have different levels of responsibility and may help validate transactions, store the blockchain's history, relay data and perform other functions. Because blockchains are peer-to-peer networks, nodes come together to create the network's distributed infrastructure.

Off-chain: Committing every transaction on-chain can be expensive, inefficient and in many cases unnecessary. Off-chain, therefore, means any transaction or data that exists outside the blockchain.

On-chain: A catch-all term that includes any transaction or data that is available on the blockchain and visible to all nodes on the blockchain network.

Oracle: A service supplying smart contracts with data from the outside world. Smart contracts are unable to access data that exists off-chain, so they rely on oracles to retrieve, verify and provide external information.

Peer-to-peer (P2P): A term used to describe a network of individual computers exchanging information with one another without the oversight of a central server. Management of a P2P network is distributed among its constituent computers.

Private key: An alphanumeric code that must be entered by a user in order to access their crypto-wallet or authorize an exchange of blockchain-based assets or currency.

Proof-of-stake (PoS): A consensus mechanism for validating transactions and establishing new blocks in the blockchain. Each validator's role in the process is directly proportional to the size of their stake in the cryptocurrency that's involved in the transaction.

Proof-of-work (PoW): Another consensus mechanism for validating transactions and confirming new blocks in the blockchain. A PoW mechanism requires each participant in a cryptographic process to submit proof that they have expended a certain amount of contributory computational effort.

Protocol: The foundational software layer of a program. Protocol has become a general term used to refer to both Layer-1 blockchain networks and the Layer-2 applications built on top of them.

Public key: An alphanumeric code that's connected with a particular crypto-wallet. Similar to a bank account number, a public key is the code that other users would input to send assets directly into your wallet.

Pump and dump: The dubious practice of hyping assets, whether crypto or shares that a user owns, for the purposes of raising the asset value so the owner can sell at a higher price.

'Satoshi Nakamoto': The pseudonym for the person/collective who wrote and published the famous white paper called 'A Peer-to-Peer Electronic Cash System' in 2008, which became the forerunner to Bitcoin.

Satoshis/Sats: The smallest denomination of Bitcoin, equal to 0.00000001 bitcoin.

Smart contracts: Blockchain-based computer programs that are designed to automatically go into effect as soon as the parties privy to the contract have fulfilled their respective obligations. Once a smart contract has been coded and their terms have been agreed upon, they become fully automated – no need for a trusted third party to make sure everyone does what they agreed to do. The parties either deliver and the contract executes, or they don't and it doesn't.

Stablecoin: A token with its value pegged to another asset. Stablecoins are usually backed by a currency, like the US dollar, but can also be pegged to physical assets like gold or Bitcoin.

Token: Unlike a coin, a token is a digital asset created on an existing blockchain. Tokens can be used to represent digital and physical assets, or to interact with dapps.

Tokenomics: A blending of the words 'token' and 'economics', it is an umbrella term that refers to all of the various qualities of a virtual currency that can cause its market value to fluctuate.

User experience (UX): Design discipline for optimizing how users interact with and perceive an application, interface or system. The better the UX, the more people will use it.

Web1: The first iteration of the internet, characterized by static websites that displayed information. There was virtually no user interaction or user-generated content.

Web2: The second iteration of the internet, characterized by user-generated content and improved user interfaces and UX.

Web3: The third iteration of the internet, which leverages blockchain technology, open-source applications, and the decentralization of data and information. Web3 aims to redistribute power from Big Tech and return ownership of data and content to its users.

Index